Postcolonial Mission

Postcolonial Mission
Power and Partnership in World Christianity

Editor
Desmond van der Water

Associate Editors
Isabel Apawo Phiri
Namsoon Kang
Roderick Hewitt
Sarojini Nadar

Sopher Press
Upland, California

© 2011 Sopher Press
Please direct inquiries to info@sopherpress.com.
ISBN 978-1-935946-00-7

Contents v
Dedication vii
Acknowledgements xi
List of Contributors xiii

Foreword
    Sam Kobia xv

Introduction
Sketching an Agenda for Postcolonial Partnership in Mission
    Des van der Water, Isabel Apawo Phiri, and Sarojini Nadar 1

Part One
1. "Growing Up and Increasing and Yielding Thirty...": Change and Continuity in the Council for World Mission, 1997-2007
    Steve de Gruchy 11
2. Council for World Mission: A Critical Appraisal of Postcolonial Partnership in Mission
    Des van der Water 33
3. Partnership in Mission: A Critical Appraisal of the Partnership of Women and Men
    Isabel Apawo Phiri 61
4. Building Communities of Hope: A Case Study in Postcolonial Mission
    Roderick Hewitt 79

Part Two

5. Constructing Postcolonial Mission in World Christianity: Mission as Radical Affirmation
    Namsoon Kang   105
6. The Bible *In* and *For* Postcolonial Mission
    Sarojini Nadar   131
7. From Mountain to Valley: An Ecumenical Evangelism in the Interfaith Context
    Jooseop Keum   155
8. Economic and Ecological Justice: Challenging Mission in the 21st Century
    Rogate Mshana   177
9. Contexualization, Worldviews and Plurality: A Caribbean Womanist Reflection
    Marjorie Lewis   205
10. Mission as Praxis for Peace-Building, Healing and Reconciliation
    Paul Isaak   237

Conclusion
    Unfinished Agenda for Postcolonial Mission
    Des van der Water   265

Selected Bibliography   273

In Memory of Steve de Gruchy

Steve de Gruchy died tragically on 21 February 2010 in an accident at Mooi River, KwaZulu-Natal, South Africa. At the time of his death, he had already done substantial work in the editing of this book. In recognition of his contribution both to the creation of this volume and to the Council for World Mission's journey, this book is dedicated to his life as a great theologian.

He was born on 16 November 1961 in Durban, South Africa. He completed his schooling at South African College High School (SACS) in 1979. He continued his studies at the University of Cape Town obtaining a MA in Religious Studies, a STM from Union Theological Seminary, New York, and a DTh at the University of the Western Cape in 1992. His doctoral thesis focused on the themes of justice and liberation in the work of the theologian Reinhold Niebuhr.

Steve was an ordained minister in the United Congregational Church of Southern Africa, and served as a hospital chaplain and local church minister in Cape Town until April 1994. He then became Director of the Moffat Mission, in Kuruman in the Northern Cape Province of South Africa (May 1994-June 2000). Here he was able to integrate his academic background in Christian social ethics with practical questions of social development in a post-apartheid context, and to explore the links with both the mission heritage and contemporary missiological questions. He established the Kalahari Desert School of Theology to pursue matters of theological reflection and mission amongst the laity and clergy in that context. The practical work at the Moffat Mission in Kuruman, together with his academic work in social ethics, led to Steve being appointed the first Director of the post-graduate Theology and Development Programme at the University of KwaZulu-Natal (UKZN) in July 2000. At the time of his death, Steve was the head of the School of Religion and Theology at UKZN.

With a strong commitment to the Ecumenical movement, Steve had many links with the World Council of Churches, World Alliance of

Reformed Churches and whilst at Kuruman he began a long-term working relationship with the Council for World Mission (CWM). In 2006, accompanied by his wife, Marian, and their three children, Thea, David, and Kate, Steve spent a six-month sabbatical (sponsored by CWM) in the UK, with part of his time based at the University of Cambridge and part of his time as Scholar in Residence at the CWM headquarters at Ipalo House in London. While there he researched the history and theological developments of CWM. Two major pieces were produced by Steve from this research – the first being a volume that collates and contextualizes all the major theological pieces of the CWM; the second an illuminating article which traces and reflects upon the contours of CWM's theology of mission, which appears as the first contribution in this book.

We acknowledge with deep gratitude the work and time that Steve invested in the initial editing processes of this book, and regret deeply that he will not see the fruits of his labour. Nevertheless, we dedicate this book to his memory and hope that it will be a fitting testimony to his commitment to the principles of mutuality, partnership and equity in the practices of mission in the 21st century and beyond.

Steve de Gruchy
16 November 1961 — 21 February 2010

Acknowledgements

To acknowledge that this volume is the product of a collaborative venture is to state the obvious. But the obvious does not necessarily communicate the fact that those persons and parties who collaborated on this project did so because of conviction and commitment, and not merely because of duty and determination. Each of the writers has brought to bear on their respective article a conviction and a commitment to their topic in particular, and to the underlying message of the book in general. Each individual contribution is therefore acknowledged with due appreciation and gratitude.

Right up until the time of his sudden and tragic death, Steve de Gruchy had been working with a single-minded passion, as co-editor on the volume, to bring this project to completion. Dedicating this book to him therefore comes naturally and together with other co-editors we acknowledge their special contribution to ensuring that this book sees the light of day.

The task of providing administrative support and specialist copy-editing fell to Lorraine Pritchard and Karen Buckenham, respectively. Their contribution is likewise acknowledged with thanks and appreciation.

Most of the primary source material for this book has been drawn from within the life, work and witness of the Council for World Mission (CWM) itself, with the CWM at the same time also being the subject of this study. This book locates itself therefore within a CWM tradition of recognising that critical self-reflection should always be a part of its journey of discourse and enquiry as a partnership in mission. It is to be acknowledged and appreciated therefore that CWM has seen its way to both sponsoring this research while at the same time being prepared to receive and engage with its findings.

Above, we acknowledge and give thanks to God, by whose grace and mercy we continue to journey in mission partnership until all the kingdoms of this world becomes the kingdom of our God and of God's Christ.

List of Contributors

Steve de Gruchy taught at the School of Religion and Theology, University of KwaZulu-Natal, South Africa. He was an editor of this volume until his untimely death on 21 February 2010.

Roderick Hewitt recently joined the faculty of the School of Theology and Religion at the University of KwaZulu-Natal. He served CWM as Executive Secretary for Mission Education from 1986 to 1997 and as Moderator from 2003 to 2009.

Paul Isaak is Professor of Missiology at the Ecumenical Institute, Château de Bossey, Switzerland. He taught theology in his home country at the University of Namibia before joining the Bossey faculty in 2007.

Namsoon Kang is Associate Professor of World Christianity and Religions at Brite Divinity School, Fort Worth, Texas, USA. She taught at the Faculty of Divinity, University of Cambridge, UK, and with the Methodist Theological Seminary, Korea. She is the President of WOCATI (World Conference of Associations of Theological Institutions).

Jooseop Keum is Programme Executive on Mission and Evangelism of the World Council of Churches (WCC). He is also editor of WCC's *International Review of Mission*. Previously he worked as Executive Secretary for Mission Programme with Council for World Mission from 2003 to 2007.

Samuel Kobia is Chancellor of St. John's University in Limuru, Kenya. He was General Secretary of the World Council of Churches during 2004-2009.

Marjorie Lewis is President of the United Theological College of the West Indies, where she has taught since 2004. Previously, she was Sub-Regional Officer for the Caribbean Conference of Churches, a Project Officer for Oxfam UK, and General Secretary of the Jamaica Council of Churches.

Rogate Mshana is Director for Justice, Diakonia and Responsibility for Creation, World Council of Churches.

Sarojini Nadar is Director of the Gender and Religion Programme and Associate Professor in the School of Religion and Theology at the University of KwaZulu-Natal. The university named her as Top Woman Researcher of 2009.

Isabel Apawo Phiri is Professor in African theology in the School of Religion and Theology at the University of KwaZulu-Natal.

Desmond van der Water is General Secretary for the Council for World Mission. Previously he served as mission enabler and general secretary with the United Congregational Church of Southern Africa from 1992 to 1995 and 1997 to 2001 respectively. He also taught Church History at the Federal Theological Seminary of Southern Africa from 1989 to 1992.

Postcolonial Mission in World Christianity: Power and Partnership in Contestation

A Foreword by Samuel Kobia

I fully agree with Philip Jenkins that, "the era of Western Christianity has passed within our lifetimes, and the day of Southern Christianity is dawning." There are a number of characteristics that signify this phenomenon: The decline of membership among churches in Western Europe and North America and their reduced abilities to contribute financially to the work of the ecumenical movement, while increasing their ties to confessions and denominations; the reduced influence and status of these Northern churches in society, politics, governance, advocacy, and common witness, while turning inward for security to institutions and bureaucracies; the shift of Christianity's centre from the North to the South numerically, theologically, and doctrinally and away from denominationalism, hierarchy and structure; the yearning for spirituality among people of all ages, but especially the youth, and the decreasing capacity of the churches to meet these needs; the tension between traditional denominations and the ever increasing non-denominational congregations and local churches.

While it is true that the Western-led missionary endeavours and colonial exploits were inextricably bound up together, it is equally true that there was a great deal more to Southern Christianity than the European-led mission movement. Otherwise Christianity in the global South could not have survived the demise of the colonial empires.

In the 1970s, African churches called for a moratorium on Western missions because the work of the latter stunted rather than nourished the growth of the church in Africa. At the dawn of the third millennium, the reason behind the moratorium has become ever more evident. The church in the (missionary) 'sending' countries is waning while the church in the 'receiving' countries is thriving. The church in the global South would, in all probability, be suffering the same fate as her western counterpart were its growth left in the hands of the colonial mission. The phenomenal growth of Southern Christianity is credited not to the European-driven mission, but rather to the indigenous evangelists and lay preachers. In less than a century since its inception, the Korean Church has transformed herself from a 'missionary receiving' church to a 'missionary sending' church. That was only possible when Korean Christians took charge of their missionary work.

What this narrative shows is that at the beginning of the 21st century we are challenged to take a hard look at the way we think and do mission. Partnership in mission is not a new concept altogether, but it needs to be critically re-evaluated. With this publication the Council for World Mission (CWM) provides an important ecumenical leadership in the right direction. It brings a rich dimension to the approach of mission work during our times. It represents a paradigm shift in several significant respects.

The publication challenges the paradigm of globalization, a process that gained great currency at the dawn of the 21st century, dominating economic, social and political thought. For the ecumenical challenge to this process to be meaningful, it must be theologically grounded and missiologically accentuated. Engaging the issues of the 21st century in all their social, economic and political manifestations and implications requires an acceptance of a shift of the missiological perspective that had been developed in the colonial era. For a long time, Christian mission was seen as a kind of sermon addressed to the world. This publication shows that the shift has to be based on the recognition that God is present in the world and that the people of God are called to witness to, and participate in God's reconciliation, healing, and transformation in all the aspects of life on earth-holistic mission.

Through the essays in this publication, the CWM provides a dynamic framework for the churches, in all their diversity, to engage closely with the contemporary social thought in addressing the most pressing challenges in the world today. This allows for an interweaving of ethical, ecological, ecclesiological, and missiological perspectives in the process of the paradigm shift that is engaging an increasingly multi-religious world.

At the outset of the 21st century, a key concern of the ecumenical movement is to offer an alternative vision to the culture of violence which dominates so much of the modern life in all the parts of the world. This goal has far-reaching consequences for the churches' mission to the world. How can the churches in their service express themselves in the spirit, logic and language of a culture of peace in the midst of violent communities? The mission to which the churches around the world are called challenges us to respond honestly to this question in obedience to God's mission - to transform unjust and oppressive contexts and structures.

The challenges in this contemporary world are too strong for a divided approach to the mission of the church. It calls for a new discernment of partnership in mission. *Postcolonial Mission: Power and Partnership in World Christianity* could not be more timely. It has the capacity to inspire and prepare churches in all the regions in their work of carrying out the mission of the Church in a world in dire need of justice, peace, healing and reconciliation, and to a creation groaning for liberation. It is the CWM's special gift to the ecumenical community and to individual churches. I commend it to the students of mission, to theologians and to all those willing to respond to the call of Jesus Christ, to enhance our understanding of contemporary expressions of Christian mission.

Geneva, September 2010

INTRODUCTION

Sketching an Agenda for Postcolonial Partnership in Mission

Desmond van der Water, Isabel Apawo Phiri, and Sarojini Nadar

Sketching an agenda for postcolonial partnership in mission is a mammoth task, particularly because mission has been so intricately entwined with the colonial agenda for such a long time. This book aims to add a distinctive voice to the understanding of what should be on the mission agenda in a postcolonial era. As the centre of gravity of Christianity has shifted from the global North to the global South[1] it is indeed significant that all the authors of this book are from the global South, and it is they who are proposing what should be on the agenda for mission in a postcolonial era. This is because the *context* of the people setting the agenda determines the *content* of the agenda.

There have been numerous attempts at shifting mission discourse from colonial to postcolonial interpretations.[2] The Council for World Mission (CWM) has been one such body that has attempted to reflect this shift from a model of mission as power, to mission as partnership. This book is a volume of collected essays that seeks to examine what the CWM has said and done about mission since 1977, when it first claimed

---

[1] See David B. Barrett, "AD2000, 350 million Christians in Africa," *International Review of Mission* 53, 233 (1970): 39; Andrew F. Walls, "Africa in Christian History: Retrospect and Prospect," *Journal of African Christian Thought* 1,1 (1998): 2; Kwame Bediako, "Africa and Christianity on the Threshold of the Third Millennium: The Religious Dimension," *African Affairs* (2000) 99: 303-323.

[2] See the work of the World Council of Churches, Lutheran World Federation and World Alliance of Reformed Churches in this respect.

to be postcolonial in its understanding of mission. In other words, 1977 was understood by the CWM as a historical marker – a change from doing mission in a colonial framework to doing mission in a postcolonial framework. This change was marked by an understanding that mission must occur as a partnership between the churches in the Global North and the global South. Therefore the CWM understood the mission field as being 'from everywhere to everywhere.' While the term postcolonial is helpful in marking the periodisation and the change in the CWM's thinking regarding the content and method of mission, this volume of essays seeks to critically assess the extent to which the chronological marker matches an ideological change and a change in the practice of mission.

The change, however, has not come about without tension. This book examines these tensions through a case study of the work of the CWM. It further examines the contestation between power and partnership that derive from the colonial missionary heritage and the ideological frameworks that lie behind the exercise of power within partnerships. The CWM is a good case study of power and partnership in contestation. This is because the CWM's main precursor, the London Missionary Society, had been rooted in a colonial model of mission, with the European colonial centre sending missionaries to the colonised regions of the world. The establishment of the CWM therefore represents a bold venture in postcolonial engagement of mission on the basis of partnership, in which the values of mutuality, respect and equality amongst the partners were to be paramount. This paradigm shift in relationships called for a radical departure from the power dynamics that prevailed during the colonial era.

As a case study of a postcolonial mission project, this book offers a critical appraisal of the actual CWM experience, whilst seeking to identify essential elements for an agenda in the ongoing partnership journey of postcolonial mission. One of the core strands of the postcolonial mission movement is the dynamic between the new values of partnership and the deeply ingrained attitudes of power and control. It is well established in history that kingdoms, governments, political parties, corporations, rulers and leaders seldom willingly surrender or give over power. This phenomenon is no less true within global Christianity. In the postcolonial mission era therefore, partnership and

Introduction 3

power have been in contestation, or, in the phrase popularised during the Apartheid era in South Africa, a 'site of struggle.'

In this volume, which is neither a history of, nor an apologetic for the CWM, each author explores the main trajectories of CWM's partnership journey since its inception, offering critique and drawing insights from the various areas of mission engagement through the lenses of a range of core themes in mission thinking and practice. The authors of the essays are not birds of the same ideological feather. In relationship to the CWM, they are a mixture of insiders and outsiders, a kind of hybrid with openness and common commitment to critical reflection on themes within a postcolonial journey of partnership in mission. Each author draws from their rich and diverse experiences of Christianity in both the global South and the global North. Their experiences draw on the context of world Christianity in the academy, the ecumenical movement and the churches, global mission engagement, theological education and ministerial formation. As a collection of essays critically reflecting on what the CWM has said and done about mission since its formation, this book seeks to speak not only to the CWM but also to the academy and to the global ecumenical and mission community, thereby locating itself alongside other contributions to the Edinburgh 2010 movement and alongside the burgeoning field of postcolonial mission studies in the 21st century. In what follows, we offer a brief summary of how an agenda for postcolonial mission has been constructed through the various chapters of this book. The book is divided into two parts.

Part One deals with experiences of partnership in World Mission. In this section there are four chapters. Each chapter presents the main contours of the experience of a postcolonial mission project in the shape of the CWM. In the first chapter, the late Steve de Gruchy sets the scene with an historical overview and a periodization of the mission history, leadership changes and major theological developments of the organisation. De Gruchy draws on his extensive scholarly and practical involvement with CWM over several years, including spending part of his sabbatical in 2007 as Scholar-in-Residence at the organisation's secretariat offices in the United Kingdom, researching key documentation and publications. Drawing on his sabbatical research, he identifies and reflects on key moments and critical junctures in the interplay of power with the 'changing of the guard,' as the organisation transitioned from a colonial era mission society to a postcolonial mission movement.

In the second chapter, Des van der Water sketches the broader global and missiological context which gave birth to the ideology of partnership upon which the CWM is based, and outlines both the converging and diverging contours of this new venture as a global ecumenical mission enterprise. In his capacity as General Secretary of the CWM, van der Water brings 'to the table' of this book an insider's perspective, attempting nonetheless to maintain a balance between sympathetic understanding and rigorous critique. A central question raised in van der Water's chapter is the nature and extent to which the noble ideals and objectives of partnership, articulated in the organisation's founding document, has been achieved some three decades after its establishment.

One of the growing items of an agenda for postcolonial mission is that of gender justice and the empowerment of women. The CWM has endeavoured to engage the issues of gender justice in mission through its Community of Women and Men Programme. In the third chapter, Isabel Phiri critically examines this programme and argues that the question of partnership in mission is an issue of social justice. She asserts that while the sharing of power has been problematic for partners in the North and South, this sharing of power is even more difficult within the South itself, when it comes to sharing power between men and women. Bringing her vast experience in the field of African feminist theology to bear on the work of the CWM, Phiri concludes that 'the issue of gender justice has been the hardest for the CWM to address. However, through the use of different strategies, efforts are being made to promote gender justice in all CWM churches.' Her article has served to highlight that this is one of the areas of an unfinished agenda.

In the last chapter of this section, drawing on his many years of experience as staff member and moderator of the CWM, Roderick Hewitt argues that the CWM's identity, vocation and practice finds true fulfillment in building communities of hope. According to Hewitt, if the CWM represents a postcolonial venture in mission engagement, then its authenticity must be assessed on the basis of a practice of partnership that eschews unjust relationships and instead embraces values of mutuality, respect and equality. The fact that different contexts for mission are shaped by plurality and contradiction within difficult living environments calls for greater human solidarity and common witness among churches in order that people may experience life in all its fullness. As such, Hewitt makes the point that the building of communities of hope requires risky engagement with the joys and sorrows of ordinary people, and that any genuine expression of postcolonial mission engagement places reciprocity at the heart of relationships. Hewitt outlines some of the concrete steps taken to realise this vision, such as viewing the church's mission as the responsibility of the whole people of God and not some elite lay and clergy personnel. It also lifts up the contributions of women, youth and children in shaping the church's mission agenda and the equipping of personnel who can facilitate renewal and transformation in local churches and communities. In Hewitt's assessment, the partnership of churches in mission in CWM represents a potent sign of hope building in this life-denying world.

Part Two covers a selected range of significant themes that characterises the mission and ministry work of CWM since its formation. This part is prefaced by chapter five which is a theoretical framework and a working definition for the concept of postcolonialism, written by Namsoon Kang. Kang, who hails from the global South but comes with extensive experience as Associate Professor of World Christianity and Religions in the global North, brings her substantial academic expertise and insights to bear on the subject of power relations and the ambiguities evident within the postcolonial era in general and with particular reference to the CWM experience. Against the background of the complex nature of Christian mission, Kang contends that Christian theologians and practitioners should explore the ways in which they could actively produce, promote and mobilize the passion for transformation and justice in the life of churches and people within particular socio-political contexts. The concept of postcolonial mission that she posits moves beyond the boundaries of gender, race, ethnicity, religion, citizenship or sexuality. Kang views postcolonial mission as boundary crossing and thereby capable of promoting solidarity, equality, justice and peace between, and among, people of different backgrounds and persuasions. In her assessment, Christian postcolonial mission can be a powerful movement and practice of geopolitical alliances across the globe, transcending traditional boundaries to give substance to God's 'yes' to all creation.

In chapter six, Sarojini Nadar deals with the three-fold concerns of the authority of the bible — the un-critical and the un-contextual uses of the bible in mission -- raising important questions about the role of the bible in and for mission. She brings her expertise as a feminist biblical scholar to bear on her analysis of the ways in which the CWM uses the bible in, and for, mission through: (i) a survey of the biblical texts the organization has used as its *raison d'être* for mission; (ii) describing the challenges that mission faces in the context of globalization and increasingly conservative uses of the bible for mission; and (iii) examining possibilities of using the bible not only for mission, but also in mission, through a case study of a contextual bible study on Mark 7:24-30.

In chapter seven, Jooseop Keum, Secretary to the World Council of Churches' Commission on World Mission and Evangelism, assesses the work of the CWM as it relates to the themes of ecumenism and evangelism. He asserts that evangelism is more than converting "non-believers" or people of other faiths to the religion of Christianity. Instead, he argues, evangelism is also about "the issue of holistic salvation of humanity and creation." Further, he asserts that "ecumenism is more than the visible unity of the churches." Instead it extends to inter-faith unity as well. Having defined these themes more holistically, Keum then evaluates the work of the CWM assessing the extent to which the CWM has adopted these more holistic definitions of ecumenism and evangelism in mission. He concludes that while the CWM has made significant progress in this area, much more work needs to be done.

The question of economic and ecological justice in the world, and the CWM's contribution to the quest for a more just order, is one that came into focus particularly within the last century as levels of economic disparity and inequality between the global South and North have escalated significantly. This topic is discussed by Rogate Mshana in chapter eight. Mshana is an economist who has engaged extensively in the fields of economic development and in particular on the impact of economic globalization. He reflects on principles and practices *vis-à-vis* CWM's partnership journey, raising questions about the extent to which the CWM has advanced in its objectives in mission work and witness, and the extent to which it is transformative in relation to the issues of economic and ecological justice.

Introduction

Marjorie Lewis, in chapter nine, offers a Caribbean womanist reflection on how the CWM has engaged with the issues of contextualization, worldviews and plurality. Viewing the work of the CWM through the theoretical lenses of Caribbean womanist theology called Nannyish t'eology, Lewis demonstrates the importance of contextualisation and plurality in the postcolonial mission project. Drawing upon the theme of one of CWM's General Assemblies, "Taking the Gospel Home," Lewis asks the important question, "What does it mean to take the gospel home?" when one is living in a plural context. She argues that Nannyish t'eology provides a signpost for how one can "take the gospel home."

In the thirty-plus years of its existence, the CWM, as part of its mission witness, sought to encourage and enable its member churches to be places that sow seeds of peace building, healing and reconciliation within the spirit of "sharing the experiences of Christ across all boundaries." This is instead of the colonial period's imperialistic and expansionist ideology of "to spread the knowledge of Christ among heathen and other unenlightened nations." The final chapter in this book Paul Isaak, Professor of Missiology at the Ecumenical Institute in Bossey, Switzerland, offers reflections on mission as praxis for peace-building, healing and reconciliation from an ecumenical mission point of view, and is shared as a critical appraisal of the praxis of the CWM with special reference to the postcolonial situation. . Isaak holds that Christian mission and ministry means that God breaks into our world and invites us to be involved in the creative and liberating dynamics of God's love in history. Moreover, while human efforts cannot remove sin from the world, God's creativity involves us in these dynamics, so that we engage in seeking partial, provisional and relative victories today, especially in mission and ministry as praxis of peace-building, reconciliation and healing—with special reference to HIV and AIDS, which is one of the priorities of the CWM.

Whilst all the chapters in this book offer a wide spectrum of items for an agenda for partnership in postcolonial mission, nevertheless we recognize that the agenda remains unfinished.

Part One

1

"Growing Up and Increasing and Yielding Thirty...": Change and Continuity in the Council for World Mission, 1997-2007

Steve de Gruchy[3]

> Some seed fell among thorns, and the thorns grew up and choked it, and it yielded no grain. Other seed fell into good soil and brought forth grain, growing up and increasing and yielding thirty and sixty and a hundredfold. (Jesus, in Mark 4:7, 8 NRSV)

The Council for World Mission came into existence in 1973. However, a major change in the structure and governance of the Council in 1977 saw the emergence of an exciting new development in mission, a global partnership of churches committed to mission 'from everywhere to everywhere.' This new partnership celebrated its thirtieth anniversary in 2007, providing an opportunity to stand back and reflect on the journey of the Council over these three decades to see what can be learnt about mission in our changing world. For a curious thing about the missiological energy of the CWM is that there is an inordinate focus upon the 'ur' event, the foundational moment, the 'big bang' that brought CWM together in 1977; and there is not much institutional and communal reflection on what has been learnt about this attempt to

---

[3] School of Religion and Theology, University of KwaZulu-Natal, South Africa. The research for this paper was undertaken whilst I was Scholar in Residence at the CWM offices in London, August – December 2007. The support and assistance of the Council and the staff in London is humbly acknowledged.

journey together in partnership over the past thirty years. It is as if the CWM has a doctrine of creation, but no corresponding doctrine of providence!

This essay suggests that, like the seed that fell into good soil (Mark 4), there has been a fair deal of "growing up and increasing" over the past three decades, and that this is worthy of reflection in itself. Indeed, by focusing on this 'growing up and increasing and yielding,' in the form of a case study on one particular mission society, we may gain some helpful insights about the engagement of the global church in mission today. To do this, I propose to work in four broad sections. First, to provide an overview of the history of the CWM broken into five phases or chapters so that readers may become familiar with the story; second, to explore the changing missionary theology within the CWM as represented in five key documents emerging in those thirty years; third, to explore how the theology has been rooted and grounded in the life of the Council and the member churches; and finally to identify what I take to be the fundamental characteristics of the life and work of the CWM. In undertaking this close reading of what one mission society has actually been engaged in over the past thirty years, we can provide some helpful insights into wider missiological theory and practice.

1. A Short History of the CWM in Five Chapters

To make sense of the past thirty years, it is helpful to break down the history of CWM into five periods, phases or 'chapters.'

1.1. Anticipation and Preparation (1966 – 1976). While this essay focuses on the thirty years of the CWM from 1977 to 2007, it is nevertheless important to be reminded of the period of anticipation and preparation in the decade that preceded the changes. In 1966, the London Missionary Society (founded in 1795) and the Commonwealth Missionary Society (founded in 1836 as the Colonial Missionary Society) came together to form the Congregational Council for World Mission (CCWM). A new governing structure saw the Congregational Churches and Unions in Great Britain share responsibility with the Churches and Unions of Australia, New Zealand and South Africa. This signalled for the first time a partnership between the North and the South, although it was still confined to the white settler populations of the Commonwealth. Then in 1972, the formation of the United Reformed Church in the UK - which drew the Presbyterian Church of

England and its mission body, the Foreign Missions Committee (founded in 1847), into a relationship with the dominant body in the CCWM - meant that the word *Congregational* was removed from the title, and in 1973 it became the Council for World Mission.[4]

Upon its formation, the Council had agreed to six regular, yearly reviews. The first was scheduled for Singapore in January 1975. A crucial element in the lead-up to this meeting was the 1972/3 meeting of the World Council of Churches' Commission for World Mission and Evangelism (CWME) in Bangkok entitled, *Salvation Today*. This meeting focused on issues such as contextual theology, cultural identity, and relationships between churches of the North and South. Given this context, CWM invited leaders from the 'daughter' churches to be present in Singapore, and this review conference proposed far reaching changes to the Council:

> The Consultation came to the unanimous view that as now constituted the Council represents only a very restricted understanding of the missionary task (from the west to the developing nations of Africa, Asia, The Pacific, and the Caribbean); that it perpetuates the relationship of donor and recipient; and that it fails to give adequate place to the talents of every church in the one cooperative enterprise.[5]

Three key elements find expression in the re-shaping document, *Sharing in One World Mission*, that have continued to be of significance for CWM. First, mission is understood to be a task of the whole church and not just of interested individuals. "We have come to know and love Jesus Christ through the life of the church. We believe that churches everywhere are the primary bearers of the good news to each community."[6] Second, mission is from everywhere to everywhere and

---

[4] The standard histories of the LMS are as follows: For the period from 1799 – 1899, Richard Lovett, *History of the London Missionary Society*, Vols 1 and 2 (London: Oxford University Press, 1899); 1899-1949; for the period from 1895 – 1945, Norman Goodall, *History of the LMS* (London: Oxford University Press, 1954); for the period from 1945 – 1977 see Bernard Thorogood, ed. *Gales of Change: Responding to a Shifting Missionary Context. The Story of the London Missionary Society 1945-1977* (Geneva: WCC, 1994).

[5] *Sharing in One World Mission* (CWM, 1975), Para 1.3.

[6] *Sharing in One World Mission*, Para 2.5.

not just from the North to the South. "Every church is both a receiver of help and a giver of its talents."[7] Thirdly, it was recognised that to be a partnership of churches, of necessity, involves ways in which people can learn from each other, that power, money, resources and knowledge can be shared, and that people learn to value "the different ways of discipleship in which Christ leads others."[8]

1.2. Learning to be a Council (1977 – 1986). For the first ten years of its life the Council continued to be led by General Secretaries from Britain (Bernard Thorogood and Barrie Scopes), and this gives us the parameters for the first period of the life of the Council. It is clear that while the shape and vision of CWM changed in 1977, it took a long time for these matters to become a reality in the life of the Council. Some of this was anticipated in 1977, when the Council noted:

> We therefore long to take this present opportunity for change as a moment when we who are British may welcome more fully the influence of our partner churches in the Third World. But we are aware that this willingness to learn does not come easily.[9]

These first ten years of the new CWM were characterised by a deep struggle over the question as to what kind of leadership could embody the vision of the Council. This was symbolised by the resignation of the Jamaican, Maitland Evans, after just two years of working in London as a result of growing pressure for a General Secretary from the South. At the same time, one must not underestimate the huge task involved in re-shaping an organisation with so much tradition while integrating it with Presbyterian mission work and further, continuing to care for missionaries in the field who had started their work under the old system yet found they had little say in the changes which now impacted upon their lives. As a result of these tensions missionary numbers dropped dramatically after 1977.

Yet there was also progress in this period. The Council began with 22 member churches, and with the integration of Presbyterian Churches, predominantly from Asia, this number rose to 28, giving the Council the basic composition it continues to have to this day. The first

---

[7] *Sharing in One World Mission*, Para 2.6.
[8] *Sharing in One World Mission*, Paras 2.7, 2.8 and 2.9
[9] *Sharing in One World Mission*, Para 2.6.

missionary from the South was appointed in 1979, and by 1983 five previous 'receiving' churches were now sharing missionary personnel with other churches. The Training in Mission (TIM) programme which focused on training a new generation of leaders for the church began in 1981. A three year programme on 'Ministry to the Urban Poor' ran from 1982 to 1985, and linked the CWM to much of the creative work that was beginning at that time in Urban Mission. During this period, three elements were identified as priority areas for CWM funding, namely, Outreach; Christian Formation (including Leadership Development); and Work with the Disadvantaged. In 1985 the Council also set in place an Education in Mission process, which we will reflect on in the next phase.

1.3. Discovering Diversity (1987 – 1994). In 1987, Christopher Duraisingh was appointed General Secretary, the first of three from the South who led the Council for the past twenty years. He served for three years until 1989. After a year with Aubrey Curry in an acting position, D. Preman Niles was appointed in 1991. During this period, the reality of being a community of diversity was beginning to be experienced, with changes in leadership at the London office being both a sign of wider changes and also a catalyst for such changes.

The ecumenical decade of solidarity with women had an impact upon the work of the Council which introduced the Community of Women and Men in Mission in 1991. In 1993, for the first time since 1977, the number of missionaries sponsored by CWM rose, illustrating just how long it took for the new vision to become a reality in the life of the partner churches.

In terms of the focus of the work of the mission, there was a strong focus on connecting mission thinking with the life and work of local churches, and the equipping of local congregations in mission. The Education in Mission process initiated in 1985 began to take root in this period. This process had a number of emphases, the most central of which was the primacy of the local congregation in mission. Other emphases included recognising that the mission of God sets the agenda for the mission of the church, and therefore for the "radical restructuring of local congregations for mission" where they are not mission enabling. There was a strong focus on partnership, equipping the faithful, and learning by doing, with a number of outcomes including "greater self-understanding of participants ... enriched and ever-widening understanding of the claims of the gospel ... [and] critical and creative use as well as the restructuring of resources at hand..."[10]

1.4. Stewards of Grace (1995 – 2003). Even though 1995 fell within the middle of the leadership period of D. Preman Niles, it is a natural division for the history of CWM. The first reason for this is that it was the bicentenary of the founding of the London Missionary Society, with the resultant reflections on the contemporary meaning of the missionary legacy, drawn together in the consultation "Perceiving Frontiers, Crossing Boundaries." Of greater significance, however, was the sale in 1994 of the Nethersole Hospital in Hong Kong for £135 Mil. This "gift of grace" saw the CWM's assets rise by £100 Mil, and this both enlarged the scope and scale of the CWM and the member Churches' ability to engage in mission, and placed more administrative demands upon the leadership of the Council. It is important to note that the CWM was always well managed from a financial point of view, but the sheer size of the financial resources at the command of the CWM required (and continues to require) a great deal of energy and attention from the leadership.

With the increase in financial capacity, this period saw a growth in the CWM sponsored initiatives, including Mission Education Schools I (1996) and II (1999), the Network Of Theological Enquiry (NOTE) in 1999, the Self-support Fund, and the Mission Programme Support Fund. The Mission Development and Education Unit replaced the Education in Mission programme in 1998. This period also saw a remarkable new and exciting range of initiatives such as Face to Face, ClergyXChange, strengthened Ecumenical partnerships, the revamped magazine, *Inside Out,* a new logo, and the global Youth Convention all seeking to resource the church for mission.

A key milestone was reached in 2000 when, for the first time ever, missionaries from the South (to churches both in the South and North) outnumbered those from the North. The vision of mission "from everywhere to everywhere" proclaimed in 1977 had taken almost half a century to become reality. In 1997 the CWM moved its London office from Livingstone House to Ipalo house and the general busyness of such changes and challenges of the 'gift of grace,' together with the

---

[10] Roderick Hewitt, "Equipping Local Congregations in Mission – the CWM Experience," *International Review of Mission* 81 no. 321 (1992): 82, 83.

bicentenary of the LMS just two years earlier, meant that the twentieth anniversary of the Council seems to have passed unnoticed!

Towards the end of this period there was a significant change in leadership in the CWM. Des van der Water from South Africa took over from D. Preman Niles as General Secretary (in Jan 2002), and with only one senior staff member remaining on, there was a significant change in leadership in the executive during that year.

1.5. Resourcing the Churches for Mission (Since 2003). There was a great deal of re-structuring work undertaken in the Council for World Mission after the year 2000, stimulated by three impulses. Firstly, the 'gift of grace' had brought with it a great deal of new work, new initiatives and new challenges, and these needed to be structurally integrated. Secondly, there were a whole range of financial and legal changes to the management of charities in the United Kingdom following the events of 9/11. Finally, there was an ongoing desire in the Council itself to ensure that the shift of power from the North to the South to represent the relative sizes of the member churches of the CWM was brought to fruition. All of this work climaxed in the constitutional changes to the Council and the inaugural Assembly of CWM in Ayr, Scotland in June 2003, around the theme, "Who is my neighbour?" The second Assembly was held in Ocho Rios, Jamaica in June 2006, around the theme, "Take home the good news."

At the end of 2007, Des van der Water had led the CWM for six years, and is in his second term of office. While it is difficult to gain a sense of historical perspective upon this period, it is clear that in the decade after the 'gift of grace,' the Council has managed to settle down to its new roles and responsibilities, and to continue in its main task of resourcing the churches for mission.

2. Shifts in the Mission Theology of CWM

As we have seen the CWM has been through a range of changes since 1977. Key changes include a shift in leadership coming from the South rather than the North, the unexpected financial strength of the organisation, and the resultant structural, management and programmatic changes that these have necessitated. The shifts have not just been at the level of organisation and practice, however. There have also been some significant shifts in mission theology within the organisation, and it is important to explore this by reflecting on the five key texts that outline the shifts over the past thirty years.[11] These texts are:

> 1977 *Sharing in One World Mission,* the founding document of the 'new' CWM.
> 1984 *The Handbook of the Council for World Mission,* explaining the new structures and underlying vision of the CWM.
> 1991 *The CWM Handbook.* This is a revised version of the 1984 handbook.
> 1995 *Perceiving Frontiers, Crossing Boundaries,* the report of a 'Partnership in Mission Consultation' on the occasion of the bicentenary of the LMS, and the 'Gift of Grace.'
> 1999 *World Mission Today.* This is the most comprehensive and all embracing missiological statement adopted by the CWM.

A close reading of these texts helps us identify three key shifts in the thinking of the CWM. The first concerns the weight given to the Bible in missiological thinking.

2.1. Sharing in One World Mission (1977). The second section in this the founding document of 1977, is headed "Theological Setting," and there is reference to the influence of the ecumenical movement and the work of the World Council of Churches, as well as the Lausanne Covenant. The heart of the theology is a confessional statement: "There is a central belief which is our guide and our hope. It is that Jesus Christ lives for all mankind."[12] The document takes a very broad approach to mission:

> There are many words and phrases which are used to express the nature and purpose of Christian mission. For example:
> > Conversion – forgiveness – new life – eternal hope
> > Reconciliation – peace –community
> > Liberation – justice – humanisation
> > Sacrificial caring – healing – wholeness

---

[11] For a greater engagement with the biblical shifts in this mission theology see my paper, "Reversing the Biblical Tide: What Kuruman Teaches London about Mission in a Post-colonial Era," *Acta Theologica* (2008).
[12] *Sharing in One World Mission,* Para 2.3.

> Preaching and teaching – baptism – church growth
> It is our belief that all these aspects of Christian mission are true to the New Testament and that none of them can be isolated from the others and made the one controlling emphasis for all missionary work.[13]

This text is foundational for the Council, and helps to set the missiological approach for the new organisation.

2.2. The Handbook of the Council for World Mission (1984). In this text, a key section lays out the theological basis for the work of the Council and draws quite liberally from the 1977 document, but there are some significant departures which suggest that a deeper theology of mission was being requested. We now read that "the source of CWM's understanding of mission is contained in the Bible," and a new paragraph is added with references to and a brief sentence about Acts 1:8, John 20:21,22: 2 Cor. 5:18,19 and John 17:21.[14] A strong theological statement is made:

> The expressed object of the Council for World Mission is "to spread the knowledge of Christ throughout the world." The CWM seeks to achieve this object by its member Churches assisting one another in:
> - Preaching the gospel and proclaiming the good news of Christ to all people in all places and in all situations where God's love in Christ is not known.
> - Incarnating the love of Christ to those who are in need
> - Demonstrating his love to the poor
> - Making his love real to those who are suffering any injustice – racial, economic, social or political
> - Working for reconciliation within all communities
> - Making the Gospel credible by working toward the unity of the Church

---

[13] *Sharing in One World Mission*, Para 2.2.
[14] *Handbook of the Council for World Mission, 1984* (CWM, 1984), Para 3.2.

This means bringing healing, wholeness, liberation and a sense of dignity and worth to every human being. Jesus who came proclaiming the kingdom of God has made plain that God's purpose embraces all humankind and all creation. God our creator is Lord of all. Those who are in Christ are new creatures and one day God will bring to completion his creation of a new heaven and a new earth.[15]

2.3. The CWM Handbook (1991). The Handbook was revised in 1991. In this document, the four biblical texts noted above become the framework for an extensive theology of mission, one that seeks to integrate some of the concerns of both *Sharing in One World Mission* and the 1984 Handbook. Acts 1:8 is taken as 'the basis of mission.' John 20:21 signals the 'Pattern of our Mission,' for it is the call "to do Mission in Christ's way," most importantly through working with the disadvantaged. II Corinthians 5:18 provides "the goal of mission." It is noted that "reconciliation is not possible without justice. Therefore, prophetic critique of unjust structures, solidarity and pain-bearing with the oppressed, envisioning the new possibilities in Christ and empowering people in their struggle are essential elements of the mission of the Church today."[16] Finally John 17:21 helps us see 'Mission and unity as inseparable correlates.' [17]

2.4. Perceiving Frontiers, Crossing Boundaries (1995). Four years after the 1991 Handbook, the CWM hosted a 'Partnership in Mission Consultation' at High Leigh, UK. A report was adopted, *Perceiving Frontiers, Crossing Boundaries*, which affirms much of what we have noted about the CWM's mission theology, but which also suggests new themes. There is a re-statement of the CWM's holistic understanding and practice of mission as noted above. Then three new themes and texts are introduced. First is the whole area of 'creation.' The text that is engaged here is Psalm 24:1.[18] "The second theme is the Reign of God as an alternative dimension of hope for resisting the threats to life," and this is rooted in Jesus' Nazareth Manifesto (Luke 4:18-19),

---

[15] *Handbook of the Council for World Mission, 1984.* Para 3.2.
[16] *Council for World Mission Handbook, 1991*, 8.
[17] *Council for World Mission Handbook, 1991*, 8.
[18] *Perceiving Frontiers, Crossing Boundaries* (CWM, 1995), Para 20.

and the Beatitudes in Matthew 5:3-10.[19] For the third theme, the document turns to the Great Commission in Matthew 28:18-20. The idea of 'the nations' which are to be baptised and taught, provides an opportunity to reflect upon the nation as an inclusive entity that should be non-fragmented, thus showing respect for "their identifiable religious cultures with which they have been endowed by God."[20]

2.5. World Mission Today (1999). This document, which was adopted by the CWM in 1999, is the most comprehensive and all-embracing missiological statement coming from the CWM. It acknowledges and accepts the previous statements that we have identified above, and then lays out new themes and challenges for mission. In doing so, it presents quite a different approach to missiological thinking by beginning not with New Testament texts about mission, but by beginning with the Old Testament. By gaining an understanding of God's work in the world, *the missio Dei,* the document roots mission in the doctrine of God, rather than the work of Christ or the Spirit. The feeling is that such an approach enables a theology of mission to deal with three pressing contextual issues, namely, globalization, the ecological crisis, and genuine respect for people of other faiths.[21]

> To address the implications and challenges of such a complex situation, we need an adequate theological framework for mission. To do this we turn to the biblical witness of the missionary God who reaches out in creation and redemption.[22]

The document then takes a Christological turn by seeing the incarnation of God in Christ as the full proclamation and pattern of God's work, and this parallels earlier statements by the CWM. However, a further new development is an eschatological vision which points to "people from every nation, tribe and language coming before God with their own gifts, their own voices and their own cultures" (Rev 7:9; 21:22-27).[23]

The document then turns to read the 'signs of the times' (Section 3), and then returns in section 4 to "Our Missionary Calling: Partners in

---

[19] *Perceiving Frontiers, Crossing Boundaries,* Para 21.
[20] *Perceiving Frontiers, Crossing Boundaries,* Para 22.
[21] *World Mission Today* (CWM, 1999), Para 2.1.
[22] *World Mission Today,* Para 2.2.
[23] *World Mission Today,* Para 2.14

God's Mission." This identifies four areas in which we are called to be partners in God's mission: (i) in being a sign of hope; (ii) in having a holistic understanding of mission; (iii) in having Christ's way as the model for our mission; and (iv) in forming wider partnerships for mission. Much of this is a restatement of the themes that have characterised the missionary vision of the CWM since 1977, although there is a greater openness to issues of creation and inter-religious dialogue.

3. Grounding the Mission Theology of CWM

One possible critique of the theology in the five documents that we have examined above is that they are elitist, emanating from the staff of the CWM or academic theologians, some of whom are not affiliated to the CWM member churches. Clearly, such a criticism does not invalidate the theology contained in the documents, but it does raise the question as to how far such thinking has been 'owned' and grounded within the life and practice of the Council and its member churches. In this section we shall approach this in two different ways. The first will be to look at the Assembly statements of 2003 and 2006, which emerge from the most representative gatherings within the life of the Council as a whole. The second will be to look at the work of the member churches as represented in articles in the magazine of the Council for World Mission, *Inside Out*.

3.1. Assembly Statements. The triennial the CWM Assembly is a relatively new structure in the life of the Council, having only come into existence in 2003, and having its second meeting in 2006. It brings together the family of the CWM churches from the six regions, and had 150 delegates at Ayr in Scotland in 2003, and 140 at Ocho Rios in Jamaica in 2006. Each assembly has released a 'statement' at the end, summarising the discussion and charting the way forward for the Council.

The 2003 Assembly gathered around the theme, "Who is my neighbour?" There was discussion about 'major new mission frontiers today' including health issues; multifaith, multicultural and multiethnic communities; abuse of God's creation; social and economic injustices; war and violence; breakdown of family life and marginalisation of women and youth. The statement calls for a commitment to 'innovative, creative and more effective means of evangelism,' practical expressions of solidarity with victims of human rights abuses, Christ-like compassion, respect for God's creation, becoming more caring, welcoming and healing communities, becoming more multicultural, engaging in inter-faith dialogue, and acting more strongly in favour of poor, deprived and disadvantaged communities. It then challenges the CWM itself to use its resources and influence to support the work of reconciliation, to build alliances with those who "share our values and visions for justice and peace and the integrity of creation," and to devise strategies that will "empower the churches, and disadvantaged individuals in the societies in which they work, to gain access to fundamental human and civil rights such as education, health, housing and employment opportunities."[24]

The 2006 Assembly gathered around the theme, "Take home the good news." The statement is shorter than the 2003 one, and is quite different. There is less discussion of missiological themes, a continuing commitment to the concerns identified in 2003, and then half the statement consists of a 'declaration.' The declaration begins with the surprising affirmation of the Great Commission (Matthew 28:16-20), surprising only in that it has thus far not figured at all in the mission thinking of the CWM, other than in a discussion about the meaning of the 'the nations,' a theme that is not picked up here. There is also an affirmation of Acts 1:8, which we have seen to be the most significant biblical text in the theology of mission for the Council. Some of the affirmations of the declaration are:

- We celebrate our common life as both hearers and bearers of the good news in our global, regional and local contexts.
- We commit ourselves to the interaction of gospel and culture as we seek new ways of following Jesus together.
- We acknowledge that mission 'embraces' local knowledge and local contexts and that the good news is already embodied locally.

---

[24] All quotations from the *CWM Assembly Statement* (Ayr Scotland, 25 June 2003. CWM, 2003).

- We commit ourselves to deepen the relations with our global, regional and local ecumenical partners.
- We affirm anew the conviction that the gospel invites all persons to experience fullness of life (John 10 verse 10).
- We pledge ourselves to a faithful prophetic and compassionate pastoral approach in pursuit of God's mission.[25]

It is clear from this cursory overview of these statements that the thinking and commitments of the delegates to the Assembly reflect a strong affinity to the mission thinking of the theological documents examined above.

3.2. The Work of Member Churches. The CWM is not just what the collective Council thinks and does, but it is embodied in the member churches that live out the vision and praxis in their own context. A survey was undertaken in September and October 2006 of the articles and reports about these churches that have appeared in *Inside Out*, the magazine of the Council for World Mission over the past years.[26] A database was created and all articles that referred to actual engagement in mission were captured around a series of categories to do with the details, target group, focus and methods.

574 entries were made, with a good spread from all the six regions (Africa 136; South Asia 97; East Asia 92; Pacific 85; Europe 83 and Caribbean 54), and all 31 churches were represented with the largest number of entries for the United Congregational Church of Southern Africa (41) and the smallest for the Naru Congregational Church (5). Some of the entries referred to ecumenical partners or to programmes that are housed in the CWM office in London. This provides us with a representative sample of what is going on in the churches, although it is recognised that not everything that happens in the member churches finds its way into the pages of *Inside Out*.

In terms of the focus of the work of the churches, the articles were entered in terms of six key categories. The divisions between these

---

[25] *CWM Assembly Statement* (Ocho Rios, Jamaica, 26 June 2003. CWM, 2006).
[26] This survey was undertaken and analysed by Susannah Steele, a CWM assistant, and myself.

categories were often difficult to sustain, and in many instances there were double entries as the article referred to a wide-ranging activity. The following intriguing picture emerged. *Evangelism*, which is underplayed in most of the missiological statements of the CWM, emerged as the major area in which churches engaged in mission, with 411 or 71.6% of the entries referring to evangelism or sharing Christian values. The second highest area of engagement was *Social justice and human rights*, with 261 or 45.4% of the entries. This covered such matters as education and literacy, general justice issues, equal rights, gender relations, and cross-cultural work. Third was the area of *Poverty and economic justice* with 224 or 39% of the entries. This included matters such as community development projects, unemployment, and micro-credit. Fourth was the area of *Health and wellbeing* with 199 or 34.6% of the entries. This included matters such as general health concerns, HIV and AIDS, nutrition, drug and alcohol abuse and reproductive health. The fifth area was *Violence, peace and reconciliation* with 134 or 23.3% of the entries. This included matters such as conflict resolution, disaster relief, domestic violence, crime and broken homes. The final area was *Nature, ecology and food security* with 65 or 11.3% of the entries. This included general ecological concerns, farming and agriculture and 'green programmes.'

It is clear that apart from evangelism, the other themes all emerge in the theological statements of the CWM, and reflect the broad understanding of mission within the Council and its member churches. However, an interesting tension lies around the new themes that emerge in the *World Mission Today* document, which grounds mission in the doctrine of God and creation in order to deal with the three themes of globalization, creation and respect for people of other faiths. These three themes have not really found an echo in the work of the member churches, as covered in *Inside Out*. A clear tension lies in the fact that *World Mission Today* speaks about respect for other religions and inter-faith dialogue, whereas many of the churches prefer to engage in evangelism. Also, the themes of globalization and creation are not strongly represented in the entries, which may point to a struggle for member churches to develop mission action around these large global concerns. These tensions represent an area for future reflection.

In terms of the target groups for such mission engagement, a wide-ranging set of beneficiaries were noted. The majority had a 'general' target group (256). Beyond this there was a strong focus on youth (120), women (70), school children (42), and families (35). Other key beneficiaries with more than 10 entries were orphans and vulnerable children (29), low income households (27), the disabled (20), men (19), survivors of natural disasters (17), the elderly (16), prisoners (16), drug addicts (15), street children (15), and the homeless (13), prostitutes (12), ethnic minorities (11), and victims of war (10). Again, this list of beneficiaries does bear some resemblance to the theological commitment to work with those on the margins, although it is also clear that the major work is with the categories of church membership – youth, women, children and families. It suggests that quite a few programmes of CWM member churches are aimed at equipping church members to engage in mission, rather than the mission itself.

The third major area of analysis was around the 'methods' used in the mission engagement. Here the following list emerged:

Method	Count
Teaching and awareness raising	251
Practical help and relief	197
Skills development	184
Sharing experiences	155
Building partnerships	89
Advice and counselling	88
Advocacy, lobbying and campaigning	60
Community groups	59
Support groups	47
Self-esteem/confidence building	44
Media	34
Leadership formation	24
Funding	20
Research	16
Performing arts	14
Fundraising	5
Sport	4

This list points to the broad engagement of the CWM member churches in mission work, using a number of different methods - many of which have to do with building partnerships, relationships and community.

As we draw this section to a close, it is clear that with some interesting anomalies, there is a strong congruence between the mission theology that the CWM promotes, and the practical concerns of the member churches and their representatives at the Assembly. The one large area that requires future work lies in the tension between inter-faith dialogue and evangelism, and it may be that greater attention needs to be given to this area of mission theology and practice.

4. Seeking Coherence in the Theology and Practice of CWM

This essay has argued that in the past thirty years, the CWM and its member churches have engaged in a wide range of theological reflection, organisational changes, and practical mission engagement, and that this experience of 'growing up and increasing and yielding' provides a rich narrative from which we can draw lessons and learning for future engagement. The story of the CWM over this period of thirty years is far greater than what can be represented in an essay of this nature; nevertheless even this cursory glance will raise a number of important issues.

By way of drawing this essay to a close, I propose to identify a series of affirmations that are drawn from the past thirty years, and that characterize the heart and soul of what CWM understands as mission – not just theoretically, but from the praxis of mission itself.[27] These themes are all rooted in the early vision of the CWM as noted in *Sharing in One World Mission*, but they have become real in the life and work of the Council since then. They are themes that emerge out of thirty years of 'new' mission praxis, and can contribute to contemporary missiological thinking.

1. *Local church as the bearer of mission.* The most significant change from the LMS to the CCWM in 1966, and then to the CWM in 1973, was the recognition that mission is not just the task of a few highly motivated individuals gathered together in an association or society. Mission is a fundamental task of the church, and the local church – the community of Christian people gathered in a local context – is the primary bearer of mission. As *Sharing in One World Mission* put it, "We believe that churches everywhere are the primary bearers of the

---

[27] As part of my work as a 'Scholar in Residence' these affirmations were shared with the CWM executive staff in October 2006 and formed the basis of their report to the Council in November of that year. They were affirmed in that context.

good news to each community."[28] The CWM has therefore never sought to take mission away from the churches, but to facilitate and support the work of the member churches themselves. This concern continues to be a major focus of the work of the Council.

2. *Breadth of mission engagement.* The CWM has, since the beginning, held to a broad notion of mission engagement, rather than to a narrow focus on one aspect of the Gospel. "As we recognise the variety of God's gifts to his servants and the multitude of human situations, so we seek to share in many-sided mission."[29] This is borne out by the survey of the witness of CWM member churches reported in *Inside Out*, which illustrated the breadth of such engagement: Evangelism, Social justice and human rights, Poverty and economic justice, Health and well-being, Violence, peace and reconciliation, and The earth, ecology and food security. It also remains the commitment of the Assemblies of the CWM in 2003 and 2006.

3. *Proclaiming Good News.* At the heart of the work of the CWM is a desire to share the Gospel of Jesus Christ with the world, and thus the object of the Council "shall be to spread the knowledge of Christ throughout the world."[30] This is a crucial part of the legacy, and has been kept up in the ongoing work of the member churches where evangelism has a high priority. This Good News is rooted in the contexts in which people live and work, thus "we believe that as we commit ourselves to him, the Holy Spirit enables us to share in the demonstration of his love, a healing love which is unsentimental enough, wide enough, patient enough, to change the world."[31] In recent years, the challenge has been to explore the tensions between evangelism and inter-religious dialogue in a global world in which religious intolerance is rising. As noted above, this represents a key area of reflection for the CWM and other mission organisations.

4. *Working with those on the margins.* To share the love of Jesus Christ with a world in need means always to bring a loving presence to those who live on the margins of society. *Sharing in One World Mission* ends with these words: "As the barriers of politics and race and culture confine men (sic.); as the modern 'principalities and

---

[28] *Sharing in One World Mission*, Para 2.5.
[29] *Sharing in One World Mission*, Para 2.2
[30] *Sharing in One World Mission*, Para 4.4.
[31] *Sharing in One World Mission*, Para 2.3.

powers' of world economics kill human hopes; as ideologies claim supremacy over people – at such a time we cannot withdraw into closed defensive camps."[32] Alongside the theme of Outreach, and Christian Formation, the CWM has consistently shared its resources in programmes that seek to deal with the survivors of conflict, and those living in difficult circumstances. The Council has also spoken on political matters where it has been deemed necessary, believing the Christ is the Lord of all life, and not just of a religious sphere.

    5.   *From everywhere to everywhere.* The clear movement in 1977 was to encourage an understanding of mission 'from everywhere to everywhere.' This means that proclaiming the Good News and working with those on the margins is not a paternalistic form of charity, but is something that engages people from both the North and the South. It recognises that the time has come for the South to contribute to sharing of the Gospel in mission. "No particular church has a private supply of truth, or wisdom, or missionary skills. So within the circle of churches which we serve we seek to encourage mutuality. This is a recognition that to share in international mission every church is both a receiver of help and a giver of its talents."[33] Thus over time, the CWM has seen a remarkable shift in the sharing of personnel from the South.

    6.   *Respecting cultures.* Because mission is from everywhere to everywhere, there is a recognition that the European cultural captivity of the Gospel is unhelpful for everyone. "All of us are still searchers. We have glimpsed the glory of God in the face of Jesus Christ, and what we know we love. But there are varieties of Christian experience and of Christian community we have not entered. There are doubtless many ways in which Christ comes to men that we have never seen."[34] Over the past thirty years, the cultural diversity of CWM has become a blessing to all involved in the work of the Council. Leadership has emerged from diverse regions, worship patterns have been enriched, new insights have been gained, and communities have been encouraged to find the reality of Christ in their own cultural context. The full implications for what this means for those cultures that do not acknowledge Christ remains to be explored.

---

[32] *Sharing in One World Mission,* Postscript.
[33] *Sharing in One World Mission,* Para 2.5.
[34] *Sharing in One World Mission,* Para 2.7.

7. *Community of women and men.* The first Chairperson of the new Council was a woman, Mrs. G. Gopal Ratnam from India, which is a clear reminder that the Council did not set out to diminish the role and status of women. However, in the early documents of CWM, there was no reference to gender equality, for this was something which still had to emerge. Since the 1990s, it became clear to the Council that there was a need to build a mutuality between women and men in mission. Since then, constitutional amendments and a range of programmes have been put in place to help the council in its task of building inclusive communities.

8. *Investing in youth.* There is no reference to young people or to youth work in *Sharing in One World Mission*. Yet, from 1981 the programmatic work with young people has possibly been the most exciting and creative work undertaken by the Council. The demographic profile of the countries of many of the member churches is one in which there are many young people, and they represent both an important focus of mission, but also a huge wealth of energy, enthusiasm and faithful commitment. Learning from young people, whilst sharing the wisdom of the ages has been a crucial focus of the Council.

9. *Ecumenical engagement.* Given its legacy in the LMS, the CWM has always been ecumenical at heart – seeking to share the gospel in partnership with other Christians, rather than to plant a certain form of the church. "It is emphasized that the new Council will be open to ecumenical development. Provision will be made for new participating bodies to be received and for ecumenical representatives to share in the meetings of the Council."[35] In truth, CWM has generally represented churches of the Congregational and Presbyterian tradition, although there are some exciting exceptions to this rule. Nevertheless, there has always been an engagement with the wider ecumenical movement, and an early principle of the Council was to share its finances ecumenically. Most recently there has been a good deal of work with the World Alliance of Reformed Churches, and partnerships with the church networks CEVAA and UEM.

10. *Catalyst, enabler and facilitator of mission.* Given all that has been said above, it is clear that the task of CWM in its administrative and programmatic structures is to act as a catalyst, an enabler and a

---

[35] *Sharing in One World Mission*, Para 3.3.

facilitator of mission undertaken by the churches and by their partners in mission. A key task of the new Council was "to help churches to proclaim the glorious Gospel of the blessed God and to share resources of people, money, faith and understanding in this work and witness."[36] At its founding, this was understood to involve missionary service (section 5), education and advocacy (section 6), and the sharing of finance (section 7), and this has continued and developed as the Council has grown in capacity and wisdom over the past thirty years. The role of the Council then is to be a 'space between' the churches, equipping and encouraging them for mission engagement in their own local context.

5. Conclusion

This essay has examined the way in which one global mission partnership, the CWM, has sought to change the way it understands and engages in mission. In the three decades between 1977 and 2007, it undertook a conscious pilgrimage from being a classic European 'sending' agency, to being a postcolonial partnership of churches of equal stature. This has not always been easy, but as we have noted, it has been undertaken with a great deal of passion and missiological reflection.

As a case study on one particular global partnership of churches in mission, it provides very important lessons for wider discussions about mission precisely because the CWM has sought to radically embody the shift from a colonial mentality about mission to a postcolonial one. The decision it took in 1977 was indeed a radical and exemplary one within the ecumenical movement; yet it is to be hoped that the wider movement can also learn from this more sustained reflection on the period since then. For indeed, "other seed fell into good soil and brought forth grain, growing up and increasing and yielding thirty and sixty and a hundredfold" (Mark 4:7, 8 NRSV).

---

[36] *Sharing in One World Mission,* Para 4.4b.

2

Council for World Mission:
A Case Study and Critical Appraisal of Postcolonial Partnership in Mission

Des van der Water[37]

Introduction

When the reconstituted[38] CWM was formed in 1977, the organisation held up *partnership in mission* as the key constituting factor of its identity as a new mission organisation. My objective in this paper is to critically appraise the missional journey of CWM over three decades, with particular reference to the *partnership in mission* motif and with special reference to power relations in mission within a postcolonial era.

Historically, within the global ecumenical community context, the term 'partnership' was first coined in 1928 at a meeting of the International Missionary Council (IMC) in Jerusalem. The adoption of a principle of partnership was, at the time, to a large extent motivated by the desire amongst delegates from the global South to reject all forms of 'religious imperialism.'[39] The phrase *partnership in mission* was however not formally used until after the 1947 IMC in Whitby, which

---

[37] Desmond van der Water is general secretary of the Council for World Mission.
[38] The Council for World Mission was established in 1973 already, after the union of Congregational and Presbyterian churches in England and Wales in 1972, as a successor to the Congregational Council for World Mission.
[39] Quoted in "Agreement on Partnership Relations Between Agusan District Conference of United Church of Christ in the Philippines and Koblenz District Conference of *Evangelische Kirche im Rheinland* (EKiR) in Germany" (unpublished paper).

had adopted the phrase 'partnership in obedience' to speak about relationships between churches.[40] D. Preman Niles[41] points out that questions around being 'partners in mission,' together with such issues as 'autonomy in government' and 'unity in life' had already been raised in much earlier times, namely at the 1910 IMC by V. Z. Azariah of India and C. Y. Cheng of China.[42]

It was, however, in 1987, at a meeting sponsored by the World Council of Churches (WCC), held in El Escorial Spain, that the understanding of ecclesiastical and ecumenical partnership was most comprehensively and clearly articulated. One of the important outcomes of the El Escorial consultation was the adoption of a set of Guidelines for the Ecumenical Sharing of Resources by the ecumenical organisations and churches that participated in the event. These guidelines, to which I shall return, were both reflective of, and influential to the CWM model of partnership. At the core of this model was a commitment to partnership in which all the member churches shared equal power and full ownership of the mission enterprise.

A Different Concept in Mission

The London Missionary Society (LMS), which is the CWM's oldest and main predecessor, was a pioneering and ground breaking 19th and 20th century Christian missionary organisation. The LMS approach, understanding and practice of partnership were however not free from the ingrained influences of colonialism, cultural imperialism and paternalism. When a decline of activity and enthusiasm had therefore set in during the modern missionary era, particularly after the Second World War, LMS missionaries also began to withdraw from 'mission fields.'

---

[40] Andrew Prasad, "Mutual Sharing in Mission: An Analysis of the Structures, Programmes and the Theological Statements of the Council for World Mission, 1977-2000," (Ph.D diss., University of Birmingham, 2006), 5. Prasad served CWM as Executive Secretary for Personnel & Training from 1989 to 1999.
[41] D. Preman Niles served CWM as General Secretary from 1991 to 2002.
[42] D. Preman Niles, "The Mission Thinking and Partnership Journey of CWM: A Review," (1995), End notes, 16. (unpublished paper). Niles expands on the historical importance of Azariah's and Cheng's critiques in his recent book, *From East and West: Rethinking Christian Mission*. St Louis, Missouri: Chalice Press, 2004, 51ff.

This withdrawal was also due to the call for a missionary moratorium[43] from Africa and Asia in the early 1970s. More significant however was the impact of the rising up of peoples and nations from the global South against colonialism.

As one era in Christian mission declined, a new era of *world mission*[44] and postcolonial mission emerged. The growing selfhood of the churches in the South and their desire to engage in mission, locally and globally, as full partners with their Western European and North American counterparts, marked the significance of the new era. The development of the modern ecumenical movement, commencing with the establishment of the IMC in 1910, also played a significant role in bringing about a paradigm shift in the understanding, agenda and structure of world mission. Fundamentally, world mission no longer meant West European and North American Christian hegemony in missionary movement and activity, but the participation of churches across the world in mission, with all six continents being the 'mission field.' And with this fundamental shift, the *balance of power* in global ecumenical relationships could no longer remain the same. The key issue of who wielded power in relationships is identified by Jet den Hollander in her summation of the continuity and change between the LMS and the CWM eras:

> However great the difference between what people saw in their task in 1795 and in 1975, the similarity is that on both occasions people had the feeling that their eyes were being opened...in 1795 the geographical frontier – to step out into the world, and in 1975 the frontier of power – to move to a position of shared decision making.[45]

---

[43] It important to note, as pointed out by Emilio Castro, that the call for a moratorium was a call *for* (world) mission, not a call *from* mission ("Structures for Mission," *International Review of Mission*, LXII, no. 248 (1973): 397.

[44] It was Emilio Castro, at the time the person who was to direct the WCC's Commission on World Mission and Evangelism, who made the very perceptive and prophetic statement: 'We are at the end of a missionary era: we are the very beginning of world mission.'

[45] Elizabeth Henriette ('Jet') den Hollander, "The Council for World Mission: A Viable Model for Contemporary Mission?" (Thesis, 1990).

It is therefore in the context of changing power relations in the early postcolonial era that the seeds were sown for the sprouting of a reoriented and reconfigured mission organisation - to be known as the CWM, with the core concept of *partnership in mission* as its structural, relational and organisational principle. A consultation held in Singapore in January 1975 proved to be the turning point in the journey of change and transformation, and led to the formal constituting of the Council two years later.[46] With the formation of CWM, the old missionary society ceased to exist and a new arrangement characterising itself as a *partnership in mission* had been founded. In the thinking of its founders, the organisation therefore represented a rupture and with the past and the formulation of a different concept in mission.[47]

The founding document of the CWM, *Sharing in One World Mission*, summed up the shifts in mission perspectives in the following ways:

- At the present time we are seeing a shift in the world church's centre of gravity from Western Europe to parts of Africa, Latin America and parts of Asia and the Pacific
- We believe that we become participants in mission not because we hold all the answers and all the truth, but because we are part of the Body of Christ. All of us are still searchers
- As one small section of the world church we are indebted to the ecumenical movement for helping us to understand aspects of mission as they become particularly significant at moments of history.[48]

Sharing in One World Mission mapped out the missiological way forward as running along three integrated tracks, namely a multi-faceted understanding of mission; a notion of the multi-dimensional sharing of material and spiritual resources; and an emphasis on the local church as primary agent of mission. The missional paradigm shift that

---

[46] "Record of a Consultation held by the Council for World Mission (Congregational and Reformed) at Singapore, 31 December 1974 – 6 January, 1975" (unpublished paper).
[47] Niles speaks about the formation of CWM as a 'New Arrangement for Mission' (Niles, *From East and West*, 47ff.).
[48] *Sharing in One World Mission: Proposals for World Mission*. CWM, 1975. 6-7.

came with the change from the LMS to the CWM was also reflected in a new understanding of the New Testament mission mandate as no longer only arising from Matthew 28:18-20, but also from Acts 1:8, John 20:21 and II Cor. 5:18-19. At the heart of the new theological mandate was the conviction that mission was fundamentally the work of the Triune God, and that the Holy Trinity is in essence an outward movement of God's love towards creation, redemption and consummation.

The new emphasis in the CWM theological equation was therefore on the church being a drawn into the *missio Dei*, and as such can at best only be an agent and an instrument in the movement of the Trinity. The CWM subscribed to the view that the church was a partner in God's mission and that the new organisation represented a partnership of churches in God's mission. The characterisation of the Council as a *partnership in mission* was also reflective of a new theological paradigm that emerged within the postcolonial era of shared mission thinking and practice.

Ten Years After: 'New Shoes or Stocking Feet'?

In his critique of the CWM after its first ten years, Jan van Butselaar, a Dutch missiologist, asked the question whether the structural changes that were introduced were in fact 'new shoes' or simply 'stocking feet.'[49] In other words, he was asking whether the new structures had changed anything significant as far as the prevailing power relations between former constituent churches and former associate churches were concerned.

Before attempting to answer the question raised by van Butselaar, it is appropriate that we reflect on the global ecumenical event that focussed on the partnership theme and which took place in the same year the CWM celebrated its tenth anniversary, namely the ecumenical consultation at El Escorial. As I mentioned earlier in this paper, the shaping of CWM had been significantly influenced by El Escorial, both by virtue of its participation in the event itself and also by one of the important outcomes of the consultation. The outcome referred to here is the formulation and adoption of the set of Guidelines for the Ecumenical Sharing of Resources, to which the participants and their principals committed themselves. These guidelines called for:

---

[49] Jan van Butselaar, "Structural Changes in Mission: New Shoes or Stocking Feet," (unpublished paper).

- All parties to be accorded the dignity and respect by which they would be recognised and regarded as equal partners
- Mutual trust, mutual affirmation and mutual accountability to characterise the processes of engagement by parties concerned
- A shared commitment to a global value system based on social and economic justice, peace and the integrity of creation
- The engagement in partnership relationships from the perspectives of an holistic understanding of mission
- The voices, needs and concerns of oppressed, marginalized and excluded groups to be heard and to be allowed to influence and shape decisions about policy, practice and priorities in the use and deployment of resources
- That the spirit and principles of ecumenical sharing be promoted at all levels of church life, namely national, regional and international.[50]

Even a cursory glance suggests that the above principles were entirely consistent and compatible with the vision and values of the CWM when the organization was constituted in 1977, particularly in relation to the sharing of common resources. The critical question however is to what extent the vision of *partnership in mission* translated into reality during the first ten years of the organization's existence, especially with regard to achieving the desired balance of power between former constituent churches and former associate churches.

To its credit the CWM, from its inception, recognised the importance of a regular review of its life, work and witness in relation to its founding vision, values and principles. Apart from the more formal review undertaken after every six years which focused on organisational structure and programmatic work,[51] the organisation also engaged in reviews and reflections of a more theological and missiological nature. In 1987, such an exercise was undertaken, whereby former and

---

[50] For the full text refer to *Guidelines for Sharing: WCC World Consultation on Koinonia, El Escorial*. WCC, 1987.

[51] With the adoption of a new Structure of Governance in June 2003 the core principle of regular review was maintained. However, the intervals between reviews no longer stipulated six years, with the idea being that reviews would be undertaken in both an ongoing and periodic fashion.

incumbent leaders shared their thoughts and reflections on the nature and shape of the organisation's journey as a *partnership in mission* after its first decade.[52] Their essays were subsequently published in the International Review of Mission (IRM).[53] In an attempt to answer the question I raised above, namely about the translation of vision into reality, I will identify and briefly comment on some of the major points of critique made by the contributors in the IRM journal mentioned above.

The first is the extent to which structural changes in an organisation such as the CWM were able to bring about the desired transformed orientation in thought, action and attitude. Eugene Stockwell[54] suggested that mission organisation structures, like secular bodies, are notoriously difficult to change for the simple reason that major changes threaten existing power relations. Bernard Thorogood, who served as the first General Secretary of the new organisation, conceded that after ten years of the CWM's existence, the 'historical imbalance of power is very with us still.'[55] A second point is the shift of the geographical centre of Christianity from Western Europe and North America towards the Southern Hemisphere and how this had impacted church life and models of mission in postcolonial times. In this regard, Thorogood had posed the question about the relevance of the concept of world mission in the prevailing era, given the fact that there was no locality then that looked 'like a central hub to the Christian wheel.'[56]

---

[52] The full list of contributors included: Eugene Stockwell (editor), Bernard Thorogood, Barrie Scopes, Maitland Evans, Christopher Duraisingh, Fred Kaan, Daisy Gopal Ratnam, John Smith, John Thorne, Albert Bowa, Samuel Ada, Marie Tobin and Walter J. Hollenweger. It is important to understand that all of these contributors were at various stages and in various capacities involved and active in CWM. As such, their critique and reflections arose both from the need to reflect critically on the mission work and witness of the organisation, but equally from the perspective of those who shared a deep commitment to and love for the objectives of the CWM.

[53] *International Review of Mission* 76/304 (1987).

[54] Eugene Stockwell, Editorial, *International Review of Mission* 76/304 (1987): 436-438.

[55] Bernard Thorogood, "Sharing Resources in Mission," *International Review of Mission* 76/304 (1987): 441. Thorogood was the first General Secretary of the CWM. He served the CCWM/CWM from 1970 to 1980.

[56] Thorogood, "Sharing Resources in Mission," 442.

I would imagine that there would have been questions raised at the time about the very desirability for another Christendom-style of dominance. The CWM itself was at the same time both a participant and a product of the demographic and ideological shift in the trajectories of the mission movement. A significant feature of this shift is seen in the new multi-directional movement of missionaries, epitomised in the phrase, 'from everywhere to everywhere.' This meant that power and control was no longer vested in a geographical centre.

A third point is the achievement, or non-achievement, of mutuality after ten years of partnership relations. It was always going to be a formidable challenge for the organisation to transform the nature and basis of relationships, whereby historically certain parties had been able to command and commit substantial funding resources to the 'common pool.' In 1977 all the parties concerned had signed up to the vision and principles of equality and mutuality. To have expected member churches to have fully bought into the notion of being both a giver and a receiver of resources a mere ten years later was always going to be unrealistic, given all the historical and ideological dynamics. This challenge was equally pertinent to those constituent bodies who had traditionally functioned as donors and to those who had been mainly regarded as recipients. The unlearning of past habits, attitudes and assumptions did not happen swiftly or smoothly. The addiction to power and control proved to be stronger than the desire to fully exercise mutuality in partnership.

The adoption of a principle of mutuality was, however, a step of huge significance. In Niles' estimation, it brought into the equation 'other forms of power besides the power of money,' namely that of 'gifts and resources for enabling (empowering) all churches engaged in mission.'[57] In his assessment, Christopher Duraisingh suggested that after ten years, the CWM had begun to understand its partnership-building role in a two-fold way: First, to encourage member churches 'to practice mutual responsibility,' and second to assist member churches "to experience a liberating interdependence in mission through a mode of common sharing of what the church is and has."[58] For Maitland Evans, the CWM *partnership in mission* experiment meant that member

---

[57] Niles, *From East and West*, 61.
[58] Christopher Duraisingh, "CWM's First Decade and Beyond," *International Review of Mission* 76/304 (1987): 475.

churches had been "summoned to be vulnerable stewards crossing ethnic and class frontiers under conditions that require common struggle for equality, and justice, and the commitment to affirming and sharing diverse gifts and resources that each brings to the partnership."[59]

A common thread that runs through the above points of critical appraisal is the assertion that the principle and practice of mutuality was meant to apply to all areas of the life and work of the organisation, and not merely in relation to the sharing of resources. However, it would have been unrealistic for the CWM to expect to have achieved the ideal of complete mutuality within the partnership, after only its first decade of existence. The question, however, is whether there were sufficient signs that the organisation was moving in the right direction. In answer to such a question, Evans was of the view that the organisation had taken "a timid yet positive step in the direction of partnership where needs, plans and projections are placed in faith on a common table."[60]

The fourth and final point of critique has to do with the question of whether the partnership principle had any significant bearing on notions of a theology of mission within the CWM and its member churches. Insofar as most of the CWM member churches were the products of the LMS, it would be reasonable to assume that those churches would have not had too much difficulty identifying with the new theological foundations that informed and shaped the basic missional thrust associated with the founding of CWM.[61] One of the New Testament texts that formed the core of the organisation's self-understanding as a *partnership in mission* and which formed the basis for its missiological mandate was John 20:21; 'As the Father sent me, so do I send you.' The clear and unambiguous emphasis here was the understanding of 'mission in Christ's way.'[62] While it is inconceivable

---

[59] Maitland Evans, "The Council for World Mission's Partnership in Mission Model: Experiences and Insights," *International Review of Mission* 76/304 (1987): 462. Evans was one of the founding members of the Council for Mission. He served as CWM Education in Mission Secretary from August 1981 to August 1983 and later as CWM Chairman from June 1989 to June 1993.
[60] Evans, "CWM Partnership in Mission Model," 461.
[61] Refer to *Sharing in One World Mission* for the full text of CWM's foundational theological position.
[62] In this regard CWM's missiological understanding was strongly influenced by the 'Ecumenical Affirmation' of the Conference on World Mission and Evangelism (CWME).

that any of the member churches would have had major difficulties identifying with this Christ-centred and holistic missiological perspective, the extent to which it had impacted the mission thinking and practice of member churches is not clear.

We return to the question posed by Van Butselaar. Did CWM, after ten years of its life and work, assume a character of 'stocking feet' rather than 'new shoes?' Van Butselaar suggested that the organisation still had a strong 'British scent'[63] ten years after its founding, by not reflecting, for example, the necessary cultural plurality that should have characterised relationships under the new *partnership in mission* arrangements. For Van Butselaar therefore, the presence of cultural imperialism in the CWM was still very much a challenge to the organisation. Cultural imperialism, however, represented only one aspect of multifaceted challenges that faced the CWM in its quest to become a mission partnership in which the ideals of equality, mutuality and accountability were fully realised. Hegemony in theological discourse, for instance, represented another major area of challenge for the organisation. Notwithstanding the fact that the majority of member churches in the CWM hail from the global South, the deep-seated theological influences of Western Europe and North America proved to be pervasive, despite the advent of radical changes in church and society that were inevitable within a postcolonial era. In this regard, Philip Wickeri suggested that 'Western Christianity and the theologies of the West are still seen as normative (implicitly more powerful) in academic circles' and that contextual theologies 'are somehow seen as less authoritative.'[64] Steve de Gruchy, reflecting on the journey of partnership in the CWM from a greater distance of years, observed that "it is clear that while the shape and vision of CWM changed in 1977, it took a long time for these to become reality in the life of the Council, not through intransigence, but simply through the sheer task of re-shaping an old organisation with much tradition."[65]

It is evident that some significant strides had been made and certain basic understandings of what it meant to be and become a

---

[63] Van Butselaar, "Structural Changes in Mission."
[64] Philip Wickeri, "Transforming Structures: From Partnership to Solidarity in Mission" (unpublished and undated paper), 15.
[65] Steve de Gruchy, "Continuity and Change in the story of CWM: First Thoughts," 2006 (unpublished paper).

partnership in mission had been gained. Although the question of power relations does not seem to have been prominent on the agendas of review within the CWM, there is no doubt about its underlying influence on the overall journey of partnership. If however our expectation of change after ten years of existence needs to be tempered by realism, to what extent did the organisation make greater progress its partnership ideals in the decade that followed? It is to this question that we now turn.

Destination Unknown?

For the purposes of this section I am using the year 1995, and not 1997 (i.e. a full ten years later), as the second moment of review. I do so because the year 1995 was the 200th anniversary of the LMS. The occasion of this anniversary also then presented an opportune moment to take stock and to review progress of the the CWM missional enterprise. Such an exercise was accordingly undertaken by the organisation in the shape of a *partnership in mission* consultation, held at Hoddesdon, England in April 1995.[66] This consultation set the following threefold objective:

- To review the mission thinking of the CWM in the light of its partnership journey
- Sharing and reflecting on the member churches' theologies of mission and experiences of partnership in mission
- Identifying the way forward for the CWM to become a community of churches in mission.[67]

In the introduction to the papers and reports on the Hoddesdon consultation, Roderick Hewitt suggested that 'in their urgent desire to learn about partnership by doing, member churches got onto a CWM bus without a clear understanding of where it was going.'[68] As far as Hewitt was concerned, by 1995 the organisation was still hampered by certain 'dysfunctional realities' that affected the Council's life, work and witness. At the heart of the 'dysfunctional realities' was the indistinctness and lack of clarity about the CWM's theology of mission

---

[66] Those who contributed articles were: Roderick Hewitt, Preman Niles, Dhyanchand Carr, Janet Wootton, Lourdino Yuzon, Sarah Mitchell and Samuel Isaac.

[67] Roderick Hewitt, "CWM Papers and Report of the Partnership in Mission Consultation" (1995) (unpublished), ii. Hewitt served CWM as Executive Secretary for Mission Education from 1986 to 1997.

[68] Hewitt, "CWM Papers and Report," i.

and the extent to which this impacted on the organisation's missional priorities. There would certainly have been fragments of that theology of mission in different places but it is clear that most member churches had by then not adequately understood, embraced or shared the basic tenets of an emerging corporate theological brand. This point about the vagueness of the organisation's theology of mission is also borne out by an observation made by Niles, with reference to the Six Yearly review process:

> Every six years there are reviews of the CWM's programmes to ascertain how they have enabled churches to grow together in partnership for mission. But these have not critiqued the CWM's theology; only assumed it.[69]

While some strides had been made by 1995 in relation to the principle of mutual accountability around the deployment of money, people and ideas, there seems to have been limited progress in regard to greater theological accountability within the CWM family. *Partnership in mission*, it appears, ran mainly along the trajectories of seeking to establish just relationships within the partnership and ensuring the equitable sharing of resources. Being and becoming partners in mission had, by and large, assumed the nature and status of an organising principle, albeit based on certain theological foundations. What it meant to be authentic partners also as far *a theology of mission* was concerned, and the power dynamics that also bear in this area, was as yet not prominently on the agenda. Almost twenty years after its founding, the Council had not been able to clearly articulate and engage in discourse on the basis of its own home grown theology/s of mission. In this regard the CWM could draw much more deeply on the strengths of contextual theologies which inform the mission thinking and action of member churches

Positively, progress made in such key areas as shared decision-making at the highest level of the organisation reflects a significant change in the balance of power associated with the one of the main thrusts of the postcolonial era. After two decades of its existence, there was a much stronger sense amongst the constituencies that genuine

---

[69] Niles, *From East and West*, 1.

power sharing was indeed achievable. The fact that each member body was constitutionally accorded an equal vote and an equal voice in all major decisions regarding the organisation's assets, policies and practices speaks of an unambiguous commitment towards achieving full power sharing. It is worth noting that this feature is reflective of one of the central principles adopted by the El Escorial consultation, namely the achievement of equal power sharing. Konrad Raiser, a former General Secretary of the WCC, summed up the spirit of this objective when he observed: "Sharing takes place in relationships which are truly reciprocal and free of domination, in other words, the test of sharing is ultimately the sharing of power, mutual empowerment."[70]

On the whole therefore, it could be said that, after about two decades of the Council's existence, there were positive indicators that the organisation had been moving in the direction of realising its ideal of being and becoming a *partnership in mission* in the sense in which it was intended. One of the clear signs of movement in the intended direction, which resonates with the postcolonial agenda, is that decisions about funding and personnel - taken together by all the CWM's partners - meant that decision-making had effectively been 'internationalised,' as recognised by Wickeri. It is in this regard that the CWM "embodies the spirit of the decisions made at El Escorial."[71] Notwithstanding such areas of progress, there was however still much room for improvement. For one thing, the half-hearted commitment on the part of certain member churches to sharing their respective resources and personnel in mission represents a significant drawback in the journey of partnership.

The Hoddesdon consultation had hoped, at the very least, that key signposts would be identified to map the way forward for the organisation in more direct and decisive ways. Whether that objective for the consultation was achieved or not is a matter that need not detain us here. What is before us at this juncture, namely about 15 years after Hoddesdon, is the question of where the organisation had journeyed to after three decades of being together in ministry and mission, as a *partnership in mission*. What, for example, are the dominant character

---

[70] Quoted in "Sharing Life" in *Official report of the WCC World Consultation on Koinonia: Sharing Life in a World Community*, ed. Hubert van Beek. Geneva:WCC, 1989: 18.
[71] Wickeri, "Transforming Structures," 15.

traits of the partnership at this juncture? And which are the factors that have worked to advance the partnership principle? Above all, as far as fuller power sharing was concerned, which issues continue to be a hindrance? I will devote the ensuing part of this paper to reflect on these and other related questions.

Strengths, Opportunities and Challenges
A Creative Space

The CWM as an unfettered ecumenical *place of hospitality* and as a dedicated *space for creativity in mission engagement,* has emerged as one of the key characteristics of the organisation after thirty years of its life and work. Therefore what must be celebrated, affirmed and strengthened is the nature and extent to which the organisation, in its being and its doing, has been an innovative, hospitable, creative and safe space for the partnership to flourish in its journey together of being churches together in mission. It continues to seek to be a secure space where networks of social capital are created and nurtured among and beyond the church member partnership. It continues to attempt to be a global space unencumbered by the clamour of many competing interests and where genuine cross-cultural encounter does take place. It will always aspire to be a space where non-judgemental interfaith dialogue and encounter is promoted.

A feature of the CWM's ethos of hospitality is that the organisation does not impose change, in the sense of trying to squeeze different views into one mould, but offers a non-manipulative opportunity where change can take place at the participants own pace and on the partners' own terms. It is a space where the individual partners are free to exercise the right and to demonstrate the power of singing their own songs in ministry and of dancing their own dances in mission. In a profound sense therefore, in the CWM equation, the journey of partnership is as important as the destination. This hospitable and creative space is the nexus through which the organisation's mission and ministry programme activities have been able to develop and grow to the benefit of all parties concerned, including the ecumenical partners beyond the Council's community of churches. The ways in which this space-creating feature of the organisation's mission identity has been experienced over the past three decades or more are, *inter alia*:

- An international, regional and local ecumenical space for engagement, encounter and innovation in Christian mission thinking and acting
- A mission movement that journeys with and accompanies other mission organisations on the basis of partnership and solidarity, not paternalism and charity and in which the ideal of partnership is seen not as a matter of expediency or functionalism but of principle, ecclesiology and missiology
- A relatively small but worldwide family of churches in which the quality of relationships in mission matter more than the orthodoxy of each member's theology, where hospitality rather than hostility prevails, and where all members of the family are accepted, affirmed, and treated with respect
- A place where the dominant style of the engagement is personal and pastoral rather than pragmatic or goal-orientated
- A global community of churches whose very being and *modus operandi* represents an antithesis of globalisation with its reductionism of people, communities and countries into entities of materialism, competition and consumerism
- A community of churches in mission together whose unity is enriched and not polarised by multinational, multicultural and multiethnic diversity

Reformed and Always Reforming

The principle of *reformata semper reformanda* has been relevant to the CWM since its inception, and not merely because most of its member churches are part of the Reformed family. When founded, the CWM expressed the intention to create a significantly different mission organisation that broke with colonial-era structures, arrangements, engagements and attitudes of the past, but which also had the flexibility and fluidity to undergo further changes as and when necessary. Since 1977, therefore, the organisation has, for instance, been engaged in processes of structural, administrative and organisational changes which sought to keep pace with transitions in society and with evolving contextual demands. By and large, such changes provided opportunity for the Council to reshape and reform itself, while at the same time it seeks to hold firm to its basic character of being a *partnership in mission*.

There were, however, ways in which things did not go according to plan and intention. This was the case especially in relation to CWM's structures of governance and systems of administration. It was no surprise, therefore, that the frustrations around the slow progress of discontinuity with attitudes and actions associated with the organisation's colonial predecessor, namely the LMS, surfaced quite strongly in 1997 at the CWM Council meeting in Gaborone, Botswana. It had become clear that after several years of the organisation's founding, there existed deep dissatisfaction amongst leadership from the global South, around unfulfilled expectations. The concerns expressed by delegates were heard and taken seriously by the Council meeting. One of the significant outcomes of that meeting was the adoption of a new structure of governance in June 2003, which was more in keeping with CWM's self-understanding and ethos of partnership, equality and mutuality.[72] The purpose of the new governance structure was twofold; firstly to ensure the fullest possible representation and participation of member churches on the organisation's decision-making bodies; and secondly to enable CWM to respond more faithfully and effectively to the mission challenges of the prevailing times. The question of the empowerment of those who were historically excluded was therefore at the heart of these structural changes.

Structures of Governance, Management, and Administration

Formulating new structures of governance and administration was not new in CWM. In 2003, however, the structural changes adopted sought to address the issue of power relations in a decisive way, while at the same time attempting to pay due attention to contemporary challenges of global and local mission. One of the significantly positive outcomes of the structural changes was that the processes of 'regional empowerment'[73] within CWM were given new impetus. The full impact

---

[72] Since June 2003, the CWM's governance instruments are the following: an Assembly (which meets every three years); a Trustee Body (which meets at least thrice between Assembly meetings); and an Officers Group (which meets as and when mandated by Trustees). In terms of the new model, the CWM has been constituted as both a charity and a limited company.

[73] This term 'Regional Empowerment' became more prominent following a decision, taken at the 2001 the CWM Council meeting, to allocate significant funding resources for the purposes of strengthening intra-regional networks and inter-regional participation. The funding resource that was designated for this purpose is known as the Regional Empowerment Fund. However, the concept

of the deployment of additional financial resources to regions has still to be assessed, but there are several positive indicators that this move is beginning to bear fruit.

One of the major benefits of regional empowerment is that member churches have been experiencing a greater measure of interdependence within any given region. It stands to reason that churches within a particular region share much in common by virtue of their traditions and cultures, social histories and geographical proximities, and are able to forge closer partnerships, than is the case within the larger family of the CWM. Whether the structural changes had intended to do so or not, another outcome was the decentralisation of decision-making and devolution of power to the regions. It was always the intention though that the global CWM values and ideals of *partnership in mission* would be at the heart of developments, be they structural or administrative, at whatever level of the organisation's life they occur.

On the whole, the new structure of governance has been functional and reasonably effective since its inception. In 2009, after about six years of being operational, the time had come for the CWM to do some in-depth assessment about the extent to which the core partnership principles of inclusion, equality, mutuality and accountability had been achieved, at both structural and relational levels. At this juncture, therefore, the organisation is engaged in comprehensive reviews, looking again at structures of governance. This time, however, the reviews are going beyond governance. By virtue of having adopted a new vision statement, a new mission statement and five 'expressions of mission,'[74] the organisation is also reviewing its management capability to deliver on its new mission direction. In addition, the CWM is examining how appropriate it is that the Secretariat remains in London.[75]

---

and practice of regional empowerment itself was not new, but in certain regions co-operation and collaboration had been operating on a limited scale.

[74] These are: building life-giving community; equipping for mission; seeking renewal and transformation; sharing common resources; engaging with the world.

[75] The CWM Trustee Body, meeting in Chennai, India in June 2009 mandated a small working group to undertake a review of the appropriateness of the Secretariat offices remaining in London.

The CWM's Mission Statement

Notwithstanding clear strands of discontinuity, the Council has consistently affirmed its historical and spiritual link with its founder and main predecessor, namely the LMS. The CWM has come to recognise, however, that in addition to the reviews mentioned above, the need had also arisen to reflect seriously on the language and terminology the organisation uses - particularly against the background of the postcolonial area - to articulate its reason for existence and its mission purpose. The LMS founding principle, which could also be referred to as its mission statement, namely 'to spread the knowledge of Christ among heathen and other unenlightened nations'[76] was simply not appropriate language to use in postcolonial times. For one thing, the language conveys certain values and assumptions associated with the colonial period's imperialist and expansionist ideology. For instance, the use of the term 'spread' in the mission statement betrays a specific notion about mission, and about evangelism especially, namely that the movement of mission proceeds from a certain geographical centre of enlightened religious and divine knowledge to other parts of the world not similarly enlightened.

In the CWM era we have been using the language of 'sharing' rather than 'spreading.' The use of 'sharing' is particularly relevant for the work of evangelism within the context of multi-faith societies. Likewise the use of the word 'knowledge' (of Christ) belongs more to the LMS era. Today we use the language of 'experience' (of Christ) rather than 'knowledge.' When the new mission organisation was formed however, the Council, for all its radically new orientation, felt that it could not abandon the fundamental aim expressed in the LMS principle, so a compromise was found in the modification of the language of the statement, to read 'to spread the knowledge of Christ throughout the

---

[76] R. Lovett, *The History of the London Missionary Society 1795-1895* (London: Oxford University Press, 1899), 30. The LMS founders did not articulate a Mission Statement in the way it is done by organisations today and it is clear that they did not distinguish between what they saw as their mission and what could be called their vision. The mission and their vision were fused into the one purpose for existing, namely a world filled with 'the knowledge of Christ,' as prophesied many centuries ago by the prophet Isaiah when he declared that the 'the earth will be full of the knowledge of the Lord as the waters cover the sea' (11:19).

world.' Some thirty years later the bold step has been taken to articulate a new vision statement and mission statement for the CWM that reflects contemporary and contextual realities in world mission, but which retains the organisation's own identity and unique vocation. The vision statement embraces universality, namely 'Fullness of life in Christ for all creation.' The mission statement expresses CWM's self-understanding, "Being called to partnership in Christ to mutually challenge, encourage and equip churches to share in God's mission."[77]

These statements also form the basis and foundation for the formulation of a new strategic plan for the organisation's mission work and witness for 2010 to 2019. Although these developments have not been expressly connected with postcolonialism, their effect is nonetheless that CWM is clearly moving further away from the ideologies and missiologies that guided and shaped its colonial past.

Partnership Beyond Self – An Ecumenical Imperative

One of the enduring and positive legacies bequeathed to the CWM by the LMS is the Council's ecumenical character. It is well documented that ecumenism and ecumenical partnership were foundational and fundamental to the way in which the LMS sought to function. The central importance of ecumenism is illustrated by Richard Lovett, who outlines this principle, and by quoting from the preacher's words at the LMS commissioning service:

> This sentiment was so universal, that when Mr. Bogue of Gosport, in the course of his sermon, said, "we are called together this evening to *the funeral of bigotry*, and he hoped it would be buried so deep as never to rise again," the whole vast body of people manifested their concurrence, and could scarcely refrain from one general shout of joy.[78]

The message in the above declaration was as clear as it was decisive: In the LMS missionary enterprise, there was to be no place for denominationalism. By implication, 'the funeral of bigotry' was also a new birth of ecumenism. Whatever else the LMS missionary forebears did wrong, they cannot be faulted as far as their ecumenical credentials were concerned. Denominational bigots they were not! The CWM has

---

[77] Adopted at the June 2009 CWM Trustee Body meeting in India.
[78] Lovett, *The History of the London Missionary Society*, 38.

sought to be true and faithful to this legacy. The organisation's founding document, *Sharing in One World Mission*, is therefore explicit in its recognition and appreciation of the influential role of the ecumenical movement in its self-understanding.

The above sentiments have been affirmed and repeated in all of the organisation's major documentation, if not always in practice, throughout its existence. One of the ways in which the CWM expresses its ecumenical commitment is by supporting global ecumenical initiatives aimed at promoting Christian unity in spiritual and material ways. At the same time, the organisation encourages its member churches to also engage in church union initiatives and ecumenical work within their respective geographical contexts, by providing dedicated resources for this purpose. A feature of the Council's ecumenical character has been its active partnership relationship with global, regional and national ecumenical partners in relation to the tasks and challenges of mission.[79] In terms of its worldwide membership, size and global reach, the Council is one of the smaller international ecumenical and mission organisations. Therefore, its active and long-standing partnership with global ecumenical and mission bodies has, amongst other things, served as a channel for expression of its world mission interest.

Over and above its partnership with global ecumenical movements, the CWM has also been working with certain denominations located especially in countries and continents where the organisation does not have a member church, such as in Australia and Canada. The nature and shape of collaboration with ecumenical organisations and united churches has, by and large, been in the nature of sharing mission personnel, sharing financial resources and sharing ideas in mission. The commitment to ecumenism, apart from being entrenched in its ethos, challenges the CWM to think and act on the basis of its *partnership in mission* principles in a way that extends beyond the inner circle of

---

[79] For instance the CWM has been collaborating over several years with the WCC, UEM and Cevaa to promote HIV and AIDS ministries, with particular reference to the work being done within Africa. In recent times the CWM has been working together with the WCC and WARC on a project called Oikotree, a web-based initiative aimed at promoting justice in economic systems and relationships.

member churches. Notably, the organisation's close journey with ecumenical organisations reinforces the principles and values promoted by ecumenism and associated with the postcolonial era, especially those of mutual respect, equality and power sharing.

Over the past decade or more, the CWM has been trying to shake off a rather unwelcome image, namely that of being an international donor agency. This image has emerged in the wake of a significant financial injection into the organisation coffers, following the sale of LMS-owned property in Hong Kong during 1994. The proceeds from this sale, dubbed a 'Gift of Grace'[80] enabled the CWM to be generous with sharing its largess with the ecumenical world. It is this generosity that, to a large extent, resulted in the organisation being seen as a soft touch for doling out funds to all comers. If, however, this unwelcome image has been conferred because the organisation had been erring on the side of generosity, it would be unfortunate if in trying to shake off this image, the Council becomes tight-fisted and uncharitable as far as ecumenical sharing is concerned.

In seeking to both clarify and affirm the principles that should guide ecumenical sharing beyond itself, the organisation has articulated a basic threefold principle that would govern and guide the nature, direction and scope of our partnerships at international, regional and national levels. These are:

- Journeying together and accompaniment in mission action (praxis) and reflection (theology)
- Mutual and equitable sharing of human, material and spiritual resources in mission
- Prayerful and practical solidarity in times of suffering, calamity and crisis.[81]

Being in the fortunate position to have substantial financial resources at its disposal, the CWM is constantly faced with the challenge of not acting towards its ecumenical partners in a way that smacks of a throw-back to colonial times. Moreover, a preoccupation with self and

---

[80] 'Gift of Grace' is the term that has been used to refer to the funds acquired from the sale of historic property in Hong Kong. For a full report on the background to this 'gift' refer to A. Andrew Morton (ed) & Julio de Santa Ana, *In All Good Grace,* CWM, 1996.

[81] CWM General Secretary's report to the Trustee Body meeting, June 2004.

own interests runs counter to the ecumenical spirit that is at the heart of the organisation's consciousness and character.

Partnership with the Poor

It is generally accepted that global ecumenical and mission partners with whom the CWM collaborates, are involved, in one way or another, with initiatives and efforts towards alleviating poverty and empowering poor people, especially in the global South. In this regard, the organisation's sharing of resources is of benefit to the poor beyond the circle of its own constituencies. In one sense therefore, the Council is in partnership with the poor, albeit in an indirect way. There is also another strand which could be considered a direct partnership that the organisation has with the poor, namely through the agencies of its member churches, most of whom are by and large located in poorer countries and in economically deprived communities.

Sharing resources with poor communities reflects an underlying commitment on the part of the Council to making a meaningful contribution to one of the major longstanding global mission challenges, namely that of poverty. This commitment is to be commended and affirmed. However, in a world in which the global economic systems are loaded against continents, countries and communities who are already disadvantaged, the organisation's contribution to this major challenge should go beyond mere sharing of financial resources with the poor, to more intentionally addressing the root causes of poverty and deprivation. Does the CWM's 'benevolence,' for instance, actually contribute towards the perpetuation of a dependency cycle, which the protagonists of postcolonial mission are so desperately trying to shake off? Moreover, while the Council has, over the years, made funding resources available, with the intention of benefiting the poor, the processes by which this has happened has been sporadic, rather than strategic. The organisation's partnership with the world's poor should, as such, receive greater priority and be more explicit within the bigger scheme of its stewardship of resources.

It is unfortunate that, in recent decades, so much of the mission activity amongst economically deprived communities and churches globally has come to be project-orientated and finance-driven. One of the negative consequences of this trend is that poor people are, by and large, still treated as the objects rather than the subjects of God's mission by those who control the mission agenda. The project-centred and fund-driven notions of mission not only go entirely against the spirit of postcolonial global mission, they also perpetuate a hugely flawed theological notion - that poor churches and communities, because of their economic deprivation and disadvantage, are not able to engage in mission. Needless to say, the New Testament witness refutes this notion emphatically. This is not to deny the importance of material resources in mission. But it is just as important that in this process, poor people should not be engaged with in neo-paternalistic ways by parties and agencies which command substantial material and financial resources. After more than thirty years of life and witness as an international *partnership in mission*, it is an opportune time for the Council to take stock of its policies and practices of *partnership in mission,* vis-à-vis both the economic and missiological empowerment of the poor.

Partnership with Women and Youth

The partnership concept and experience of the CWM is that it is and strives to be an inclusive community, where for instance the interests of both women and men in mission are taken on board as fully as possible in the task of mission and ministry. The CWM, by intentionally including women and youth within its decision-making and governing structures, and by establishing programme activities that engage women as fully as possible, seeks, firstly, to give assent to the equality of women and men in mission. Secondly, it seeks to avoid pitting the interests and concerns of women against men (and visa versa) and, thirdly, it seeks to overcome the gender barriers that limit God's grace, which extends to all equally. It is essential to the mission work undertaken by the CWM, both within its member churches and ecumenically, that in the process of building life-giving community, it avoids the exclusion of any of God's children, whether male, female, youth or children, as this significantly diminishes its witness. It had been recognised, however, that whilst the CWM has put in place well-established programme activity that directly engages women constituencies and youth constituencies, there is as yet nothing in place that draws children into the equation in a significant and transforming way.

Partnership means that all parties concerned bring their best to the table from the gifts and abilities that God has bestowed on each, irrespective of the age, sex, gender, class, caste, colour, or race. In the CWM, the additional element of immense cultural diversity adds another dimension to the richness of the partnership, which seeks to fully engage women, youth and children. Through such programmes like the building a Community of Women and Men in Mission, Women in Mission, Training in Mission, Youth in Mission and Mission with Children, the CWM tries to give substance to the full scope of its *partnership in mission* philosophy and principles. At the same time, CWM recognises that a huge challenge remains to engender and promote a fuller engagement of women, youth and children in mission with the member churches. As such this remains one of the ongoing priority areas in a mission in which much has been achieved, while at the same time so much more could be accomplished.[82]

Beyond Partnership: The CWM as Community and Family in Mission.

The *partnership in mission* principle, being at the heart of the CWM's self-understanding when it was constituted, meant that this key principle would energise, enthuse and shape the organisation throughout its missional journey. In the process, as much by default as by design, the organisation has also taken on the character of a *covenant community of churches in mission*. The general principles that govern partnerships, such as mutuality, equality and accountability – noble as they are – do not necessarily require parties concerned to commit to and be in a covenant relationship with each other. In this regard, Philip Wickeri observes that 'there are many ways of being a partner, and not all of them involve friendship.'[83]

The patterns of the engagement between the partners in the CWM are, if not always in practice but certainly in principle, driven by covenant and not by contract. This means, for instance, that the nature of trust within the organisation is based on the understanding that member churches, because they exist in covenant, relate to each other as members of a family. The first recourse to resolving disputes and differences between parties is therefore not to pursue legal and constitutional solutions. Accordingly, the manner in which the Council handles a breach of trust by one of its members is with a creative combination of

---

[82] For relevant surveys up until 2000, see the following Ph.D. theses, namely Andrew Prasad, "Mutual Sharing in Mission: An Analysis of the Structures, Programmes and the Theological Statements of the Council for World Mission, 1977-2000" (University of Birmingham, 2006) and by Andrew Williams, "Sharing People in Mission – Case Studies from the Council for World Mission." (University of Birmingham, 2004).

[83] Wickeri, "Transforming Structures," 10.

censure and compassion. Mere partnership would not necessarily require the exercise of such compassion and understanding.

The CWM's familial ethos has also been demonstrated in the organisation's capacity to constantly seek to embrace the full spectrum of cultural, national and theological diversity amongst its member churches, while at the same time trying to maintain a corporate identity as a global mission community. While a more precise definition and a more concise articulation of the nature of this theological and missiological identity has yet to emerge, the fact remains that notions of identity that exist have not compromised or alienated its constituents. Therefore, notwithstanding the organisation's flaws and failings to live up to its high ideals, there has been a genuine sense in which the *koinonia of covenant community* and the *intimacy of family* has been an integral part of the Council's missional journey.

The community character and family ethos of the organisation is also borne out by one of the central aspects of the way in which CWM proclaims the Gospel message, namely the creation of space and opportunities for *story-telling* and *experience-sharing*. The joys and sorrows, the hardships and the achievements that are told from the member churches' journeys of life, faith and ministry feature prominently in the narrative of the Council's missional story.[84] The stories told and the experiences shared do not seek to coerce, co-opt or control, yet they carry the transforming power of the Gospel to engage, convince and convict. The freedom and space for all concerned parties to share their own stories and experiences, not least of failure, without fear of rejection or ridicule, is one of the precious home-grown legacies nurtured and nourished by the nature of the CWM missional journey. The belief is that everyone has a story to tell about their journey of life, faith and ministry and that it is in the compassionate and non-judgemental listening to the stories and the experiences of others that their self-images and self-worth are enhanced.

Words and concepts that are used to describe the ways and places where people meet to hear and share their life and faith stories are different, but they all reflect an underlying attitude of hospitality. The showing of hospitality to stranger and friend is a characteristic that

---

[84] These stories are told when leaders, representatives, and participants from the member churches get together at the various meetings, consultations, and conferences.

belongs innately to the social and psychological make-up of most of the CWM member churches. In the Pacific, for example, there is the *maneapa*, which, in addition to its more formal social, legal and ceremonial role, is also the place where the stranger is welcomed. In south Asia the term *haat* is used to denote 'a meeting place to receive and share wisdom' and within a southern African context the word *imbizo* is used to refer to a time and place when and where 'the tribe or community gathers to confer and to consult' and where each one's voice will be listened to. The community and family ethos therefore adds depth and richness to the noble ideals of partnership in the CWM equation.

The experience of being a real part of a global community of churches, and the sense of the intimacy of family is therefore the benchmark by which CWM's *partnership in mission* is measured. This family and community ethos is not merely the product of the sum of all the parts. It is in a profound sense an outflow of the cultural, national and spiritual synergies drawn from the best features of the member churches. It is precisely this corporate entity called a *partnership in mission,* with all its uniqueness, that serves to encourage, challenge and inspire each individual member to realise more fully its own potential for mission.

Notwithstanding then, as Hewitt suggested, that after two decades CWM was still hampered by 'dysfunctional realities,' we could at this juncture state that after three decades of its existence, the CWM 'bus' is still very much on the missional journey as a *partnership in mission*. But it is clearly not a journey to nowhere. And one of the significant *places* at which the journey has arrived is the experiences, the engagements and the encounters of the organisation as a community and as a family. The CWM experiment and experience therefore is, in itself, a witness to the movement of global mission that is being constantly renewed, and which, in the process, is also shaking off the shackles of a colonial past.

Signs of the Times

The focus of this paper has been on the nature of the journey of CWM as a *partnership in mission* with particular reference to challenges of partnership and power in mission. A reflection of this nature must recognize and reckon with the fact that the world of today is a significantly different place to what it was in 1977. In the year when CWM was constituted, the global landscape was dominated by a different set of interests and preoccupations than at the present time. It is true that some of the major underlying issues that dominated the global headlines and drove the mission agenda in 1977 are still with us today, such as the quest for a justice and peace in the world. The struggle to overcome poverty in much of the two-thirds world remains as compelling and urgent as it was three decades ago. However, global events and their impact in the 1970s carried a distinctly different feel to that which occupies international interest and concern today. Accordingly, the nature and focus of mission thinking is being shaped by a different set of agendas, as the global ecumenical community recognises fully the contextual nature of mission and the extent to which mission engagement is shaped and influenced by world events, by international developments and by global trends.

In the era of its founding, the CWM's *partnership in mission* agenda had also been precipitated and influenced by a particular set of global, regional and national developments. Unlike the 1970s, today's global mission agendas have to grapple with major challenges such as the negative impact of neo-liberal economic globalisation on countries and communities in the two-thirds world; the wanton exploitation of natural resources and the degradation of the environment; the deterioration of international relations and growing hostile and provocative rhetoric between world leaders; the escalation of conflict in the Middle East; growing tensions between peoples of different faith communities; the prevalence of HIV and AIDS; and the emergence of other pandemics. Accompanying such macro issues are a number of developments and phenomena that characterise the post-modern age. These have to be taken into account when Christian mission organisations, including the CWM, set their strategies and priorities for the medium to long term.

The above mentioned are the 'signs of the times' that have a direct and indirect bearing on key decisions and directions taken by CWM as a *partnership in mission* at the present time and into the foreseeable future. The ongoing task facing the Council, and for that matter its ecumenical and mission partners, is to rightly *interpret* these 'signs of the times.' Its task is to charter a missional course that holds vital strands of continuity with the past in creative tension with an expression that is decisively contextual and contemporary. In the final analysis, that which determines the CWM's success or failure in fulfilling its objectives as *partnership in mission* is the degree of influence and impact it exercises on the mission thinking and action of its member churches. In this respect the ultimate test is the extent to which local churches, parishes and congregations have been enabled and empowered to assume their rightful identities as the primary agents of mission.

Conclusion

The postcolonial era of world mission, inaugurated in the early 1970s, is still relatively young, and many are the existing and emerging tasks, opportunities and challenges of world mission today. The CWM's missional journey of the past, present and future cannot be understood nor undertaken apart from the global ecumenical journey of partnership in mission. But the vision that gave birth to the *partnership in mission* witness in 1977 and which sustained it over three decades must find contemporary expression. It must also derive a new impetus, draw fresh inspiration and source untapped energies for the missional task ahead. It is a journey that can only be undertaken with the courage of faith, the fortitude of hope, and with the humility of love.

3

Partnership in Mission:
An Appraisal of the Partnership of Women and Men

Isabel Apawo Phiri[85]

The purpose of this essay is to provide critical reflections on the 'partnership in mission' founding principle of the Council for World Mission (hereafter CWM). This will be done in two ways – firstly a theological reflection on the concept of partnership; and secondly, an appraisal of the partnership of the women and men programme of the Council for World Mission through the lenses of an African feminist postcolonial theory. According to Musa Dube:

> The struggle for liberation of postcolonial feminist readers is located within the framework of resisting global and natural structures of oppression—be they politically, economically, socially, or culturally based. Since gender oppression pervades all sectors of life, postcolonial feminist readers add gender analysis to the struggle of Two-Thirds World communities of resistance to ensure that national and international efforts of establishing justice do not sideline gender justice. Postcolonial feminists thus ask how various forms of national oppression affect women and men, how international forms of oppression affect men and women, how gender oppression functions with other forms of oppression such as class, race, ethnicity, age,

---

[85] Isabel Apawo Phiri is professor in African Theology and Director of the Centre for Constructive Theology at the School of Religion and Theology, University of KwaZulu-Natal.

and sexual orientation. They also propose various ways of reading that will chart social justice and that take on gender justice in national and international relation.[86]

While Musa Dube was focusing on reading biblical texts and what she calls other "World" texts in communities of faith in Botswana, this essay will limit itself to the 'reading' of CWM and its member churches, focusing only on partnership in mission. Following Kwok Pui-lan's step of combining the feminist postcolonial theories with theology, I too will adopt a feminist postcolonial theological lens in my analysis.[87] In addition to using the theoretical work of Musa Dube and Kwok Pui-lan, my analysis of this topic is also influenced by my social location as an African woman theologian from the Presbyterian tradition.[88]

---

[86] Musa W. Dube, "Rahab Says Hello to Judith: A Decolonizing Feminist Reading," in *Toward a New Heaven and a New Earth: Essays in Honour of Elisabeth Schüssler Fiorenza*, ed. Fernando F. Segovia (Maryknoll: Orbis Books, 2003), 54-55.

[87] Kwok Pui-lan, *Postcolonial Imagination and Feminist Theology* (London: SCM Press, 2005), 126.

[88] As I reflect on the theology of partnership I am informed by my own experiences of partnerships as a Malawian Christian woman from the Presbyterian tradition who is teaching African theology at in the school of Religion and Theology at the University of KwaZulu-Natal. Therefore within the post colonial framework, my reflection on the theology of partnership is limited to my context with the hope that it points to universal dimensions which can be applied to other contexts. My own relationship with God is primarily informed by my experience of the Divine, in different contexts that I have found myself, which has also influenced the way I have received and interpreted the bible. The fact that I am Presbyterian is not by choice but by accident in that the missionaries who first came to my village happened to be the Dutch Reformed Church, who later formed partnership with the Scottish Free Presbyterian church and the Scottish Presbyterian church to form the Church of Central African Presbyterian (CCAP). The fact that I have remained a Presbyterian is by choice despite forming a marriage partnership with a husband who comes from a Pentecostal tradition. Throughout the twenty four years of marriage (by 2009), we have lived with the tension of both traditions whose expression is made even more complicated by living our lives within the African primal religion of our Chewa ancestors located in two countries. All this information is aimed at showing that for most of us, hybridity is not just an academic theory but a lived

Partnership in Mission 63

Musa Dube has identified seven guiding questions that she uses in her postcolonial feminist strategy of reading the bible. This study will only use three of her guiding questions as following:

- How does this text (CWM) construct difference: Are there dialogue and mutual interdependence or condemnation of all that is foreign?
- Does this text (CWM) employ gender representations to construct relationships of subordination and domination? If so, which side am I reading from: the colonizer, the colonized, or the collaborator? If I concentrate on patriarchal analysis of the text (CWM), does this translate to a decolonizing act?
- How can one reread this text (CWM) for relationships of liberating interdependence between genders, and among races and their social categories of our worlds? [89]

Thus, this essay will investigate the expression of powers of imperialism and patriarchy in CWM. It will also identify relationships that promote dignity of all humanity within the family of CWM as well as the "other." It will then reflect on what liberating partnership in mission could look like when just relationships have been mainstreamed in all CWM church members.

The concept of partnership, from a theological/missiological point of view

Andrew Kirk has stated that:

Within world Christianity, "partnership" expresses a relationship between churches based on trust, mutual recognition and reciprocal interchange. It rules out completely any notion of 'senior' and 'junior,' 'parent' and 'child,' or even 'older' and 'younger.' It is a term

---

reality that informs our perception of doing theology of missions. The perception itself is not linear but circular in that one's experience leads to reflection within a multiplicity of religious traditions. The reflection leads to theories, which returns to inform practice.

[89] Dube, "Rahab Says Hello to Judith," 56.

> designed to show how different parts of the church belong to one another and find their fulfillment through sharing a common life. It implies a relationship in which two or more bodies agree to share responsibility for one another, and in which each side meaningfully participates in planning the future of the other. Put in this way, partnership is an ideal to be aimed at. In practice, as we shall see, there are real difficulties in the way of a truly equal relationship.[90]

As shown in the introductory studies of this book, CWM was founded on the ideals of partnership as described by Andrew Kirk in the above quotation. By so doing, CWM was rejecting some of the values of the founding mission bodies[91] of the global North in relation to the mission churches of the global South. It was an act of rejecting imperialism as a guiding principle in the relationships of the churches in the global North and South. It was also an acknowledgement of the shift in the gravity of Christianity from the North to the South. With this shift came the renegotiations of power relations. Instead of the majority South demanding to have power over the North, there was a call for a different type of relationship based on different configurations of relationships and understanding of power. The new relationships were based on a new theology of the concept of partnership in mission. As with all new organizations, living up to the ideals of partnership in mission was a huge challenge for CWM as Evelyn Kamwendo describes in what follows:

> When my church - the United Church of Zambia - nominated me to the Council meeting in 1993, I knew very little about the Council for World Mission. The little that I knew was that it was an organization that funded member churches. My first experience at that Council was depressing. I witnessed how difficult it was to get those funds. I also saw tension, the bad language

---

[90] Andrew J. Kirk, *What is Mission? Theological Explorations* (Minneapolis: Fortress Press, 1989), 184.

[91] The London Missionary Society, the Commonwealth Missionary Society and the Presbyterian Foreign Missions Committee.

> used by the most influential churches. I concluded that it was meaningless for small churches to belong to CWM. I witnessed people crying when left out, while others rejoiced because they got their share. I asked: "Is it the way it is done"? [92]

Kamwendo's statement may also be a reflection of the struggle that the South went through in the process of transforming the old colonial mindset of partnership where the South was looking to the North as resources of funding. She then goes further to describe the transformation that has now taken place in the CWM, which has moved the churches closer to the ideal of partnership in mission. She says:

> There are no tensions in our meetings now. We all have a respect for one another, and are ready to listen and bear one another's burdens. Now there are situations where even regions care for each other and movements are taking place as it is said "everywhere to everywhere." I am encouraged because mission belongs to all. A sense of belonging has been established through CWM's sharing of all its resources. [93]

What we have here is the experience of one person. The value of this experience lays in the fact that she represents the often forgotten experiences of women from the third world as part and parcel of the whole experience of organizations like CWM and its member churches. She is a representation of the voice from the margins which has been brought to the centre to speak to power and claim that space for people of her kind. Her experience becomes important when reflecting theologically on partnership within the circles of CWM and its church members.

Drawing again from the work of Andrew Kirk, to theologically reflect on partnership in mission, he has also argued that:

> It may therefore be even harder to lay hold of the notion that 'partnership in mission' also belongs to the essence of the Church: partnership is not so much what the church *does* as to what it *is*. Churches (theologically)

---

[92] *Inside Out* The magazine of the Council for World Mission, 48 (2006), 18.
[93] *Inside Out*, 18.

belong to one another, for God has called each "into the fellowship (*koinonia*) of his son, Jesus our Lord' (1 Cor. 1:19). However diverse may be the patterns of worship, methods of evangelism, styles of leadership, involvement in society and ways of expressing faith, one baptism, one God, Father of all" (Eph. 4:4-5); 'in the one Spirit we are all baptized into one body... and we were all made to drink of one Spirit'" (1 Cor. 12-13). Partnership therefore is not a nice slogan that some clever committee has dreamt up: it is the expression of one, invisible, common life in Jesus Christ. [94]

CWM has clearly articulated its theology of mission in the recent document entitled Partners in Mission: The Practice and the Promise. This document is an outcome of the Singapore 2007 missiology consultation which was attended by the representatives of CWM member churches and ecumenical partners to celebrate the 30th anniversary of CWM. Of particular interest to this study is the section which states:

> As a partnership and a community of churches in mission, we therefore recommit ourselves to:
>
> - worshipping the Triune God, who invites us to be partners in God's mission
> - maintaining our missional vocation in response to God's redemptive grace known to us in Jesus Christ
> - reading the Bible in new ways to gain new insights for mission engagement
> - being open to the transformative work of the Holy Spirit in the life of every believer
> - calling people to faith and fullness of life in Jesus Christ
> - working and praying for healing and reconciliation, justice and peace
> - strengthening our unity amidst diversity, upholding the values of mutuality, equality, respect and power-sharing in just ways.

---

[94] Kirk, *What is Mission?*, 187.

- giving priority to local context in mission reflection and action
- deepening our fellowship, partnership and engagement with the world church and ecumenical community
- listening and learning from the voices other than our own
- ongoing mutual sharing of human, spiritual, material and financial resources
- exercising prophetic witness and pastoral solidarity in the face of oppressive systems and structures
- taking greater responsibility for the care of creation.

Thus what is clear here is the fact that the CWM concept of partnership has its foundation in scriptures. Although the actual biblical passages are not quoted to highlight the biblical basis of partnership in mission, the language used portrays a biblical foundation.[95] First, there is the theological affirmation that the Triune God is partnership based. As explained by Andrew Kirk, "the foundation of partnership is the model provided by the drama of the incarnation of Jesus Christ. God with us."[96] While Trinitarian theology certainly provides a model of partnership, this partnership is not always equitable, as, feminist theologians have argued. Christian tradition has consciously or unconsciously perpetuated sexist language in its symbol systems such as an all-male Trinity (Father, Son and the Holy Spirit). Catherine LaCugna has argued that, firstly, Trinitarian theology seems to compromise feminists' concern for the equality of women and men; thus reinforcing hierarchical male relationship among the divine persons.[97] The implication is the

---

[95] This is a CWM style of writing. The Bible is used but when writing they do not reference it. Is it a weakness or strength? Some churches, especially from the North, do not see the need for quoting directly from the Bible, while other churches, especially from the South want to see where the passage is in the Bible.

[96] Kirk, *What is Mission?*, 191.

[97] Catherine Mowry LaCugna, "God in Communion with Us: The Trinity," in *Freeing Theology: The Essentials of Theology in Feminist Perspective*, ed. Catherine Mowry LaCugna (New York: Harper San Francisco, 1993), 84-85.

understanding that man fully images God while woman images God by virtue of her relationship to man. Thus, this doctrine tends to support the subordination of women to men. Secondly, LaCugna notes, because God is named Father, Son and the Spirit, the doctrine of the Trinity has been used to reinforce solely masculine images for God, manifest particularly in liturgy and in theology. This contributes to an overwhelming understanding of God as male, and thus legitimizes patriarchy in the church in the sense that the human male is normative for all human experience. Therefore while the CWM affirms partnership in mission as based on the Triune God, it needs to show awareness of its possible negative interpretation to the humanity of women.

The second theological affirmation for partnership in mission is based on God inviting humanity to partnership through the incarnation of Jesus Christ. God is the one who initiates the partnership. The part played by humanity is to respond passively to this call. This understanding helps to take away the misconception that some people are called to mission from one location to another, which previously used to be from the North to the South. In postcolonial contexts where imperialism is resisted, it makes sense to have the CWM statement that "mission is from everywhere to everywhere." In so doing, everyone then should feel that God is calling them to mission, as affirmed in the quotations above from Evelyn Kamwendo and from the mission statement of the Singapore missiological consultation of 2007.

The third theological affirmation for partnership, which is also highlighted in the CWM documents, states that humanity (part of God's creation that is made up of male and female) is invited by God to be in partnership with the Triune God and with each other. It is partnership with each other which is being emphasized here. It is my opinion that when some of CWM partner churches refuse to affirm the humanity of women through ordination, they accept the partnership with God and reject partnership within the community of men and women as being the body of Christ together. The partnership that is affirmed by all CWM churches seems to be at a church level with all the thirty-one (31) churches that form the CWM and with its ecumenical partners. As a way forward, it then becomes important for CWM to revisit its definition of partnership to highlight, in a more visible and concrete way, that partnership with God also implies partnership within the body of Christ that is made up of the community of male and female. Perhaps this should be incorporated as part of CWM's identity.

The fourth theological affirmation is the sharing in a common project. This project is sharing the Gospel of Jesus Christ as part of partnership in mission. As affirmed in the documents of CWM, churches of the South work with the churches of the North in a partnership that benefits both sides, based on mutual sharing. It is well accepted that the concept of mutual sharing rejects the imperialistic tendencies of expecting the sharing to be one directional, which is based on the wrong assumption that only some people in the partnership have something to share and others have nothing. If the gospel is the common project to be shared, then it is now accepted that everyone has something to share because the whole world needs to be evangelized.

It is possible that the sharing in a common project is one directional because of the misunderstanding of what it is that needs to be shared. In the CWM statement quoted above, the sharing has been divided into two: the sharing of gifts and the sharing of material resources. In the case of the sharing of gifts, it is affirmed that the Holy Spirit gives gifts to all Christians so that the gifts can be used in the body of Christ. Scripturally, the gifts are given to the church to equip God's people in their work of building the church of Christ. This is also affirmed in the work of CWM, where partnership is seen as contributing to the lives of one another in such a way that the needs of all are met.

In the case of sharing material resources, it is based on the theological truth that the earth belongs to God and everything that is in it. Because of this truth, postcolonial social analysis, gives us the opportunity to argue that historically some countries of the North have accumulated wealth as a result of the enslavement of others from the global South. Churches from such countries have access to material wealth which was acquired through the suffering of others. Thus, as was the case of the early church as reflected in the book of Acts, in postcolonial partnership in mission, this historical truth should provide motivation for all the churches of CWM to put their material resources together for equal sharing. The story of Evelyn Kamwendo, when reflected upon in the context of sharing of material wealth, reminds one of Acts chapter 5 and 6, which demonstrate the struggles of a young church in its efforts to solve the problem of having everything in common.

One of the strengths of the CWM's partnership in mission is the rejecting of the "donor to receiver" model to one of sharing resources of money, human resources and spirituality from everywhere to everywhere. In some of the CWM documents it was mentioned that the major contribution of the global South to this partnership is spirituality and human resources. This is not to ignore those churches from the South that have also been contributing finances at par with the churches from the global North. The question that this scenario raises for CWM is how to continue promoting partnership in mission relationships of respect, integrity and mutuality in the context of economic injustice.

One aspect of sharing which is not highlighted by the CWM but is part of the CWM's practice of partnership in mission is the sharing in suffering. This is based on the theological truth that when one body of Christ suffers, the whole body of Christ suffers. Andrew Kirk has beautifully explained it as follows:

> Because it is also the suffering of Christ, every member of Christ feels the suffering of every other member (1 Cor. 12:26). In many ways this is the most profound and most difficult of all manifestations of partnership. When the church has learnt to share in this way, it has truly learnt what it means to be a *koinonia* in the Holy Spirit: Participation in suffering and struggle is at the heart of God's mission and God's will for the world. It is central for our understanding of the incarnation, the most glorious example of participation in suffering and struggle...[98]

The CWM team visits to troubled spots like Zimbabwe is one example of sharing in suffering. Whilst it has been a challenge to engage consistently with ecumenical organizations in solidarity with Zimbabwe, such as doing joint visits, the CWM has been collaborating well with the ecumenical community in placing the spotlight on the socio-political and economic situation in country. Moreover the CWM's particular role has been that of strengthening the witness of its member churches in the region.

---

[98] Kirk, *What is Mission?*, 191.

As a conclusion to this section then, when one analyses the policies of the CWM, one can strongly argue that its theological articulation of mission in partnership is sound. As shown in the few cases quoted above, theological articulations are not always put into practice - either in such a way that promotes dignity of all partners or in such a way that would strengthen the unity of the ecumenical movement in partnership in mission. A further exploration of the partnership of women and men programme of the CWM and its member churches is what we will turn to.

The Partnership of Women and Men Programme of the Council for World Mission

The CWM should be affirmed for having established in 1991 the Community of Women and Men in Mission Progamme. This programme was formed for two reasons. The main reason was in response to the World Council of Churches' Ecumenical Decade of the Churches in Solidarity with Women 1988-98. This call gave rise to the second reason which was in response to the question on how the 'church can practice partnership when many women feel that their gifts and talents are not fully acknowledged within their churches.'[99] It took the CWM fourteen years for it to accept that having an organization that was based on partnership in mission did not automatically translate to the formation of partnership between women and men in all the CWM churches. Therefore the aim of this programme is "to promote equal partnership between women and men within the CWM member churches to empower women and end discrimination and violence against women."[100] As a result of the realization that some churches are doing well in living a life of partnership between men and women and others are not, a need was felt to share information, skills and resources as well as raise awareness of gender issues, as they affect all the CWM member churches and the society in which these churches are found.

---

[99] Council for World Mission Community of Women and Men in Mission Newsletter no.1 (1993), 1.
[100] Council for World Mission Community of Women and Men in Mission (CWMM) Global workshop on Gender Issues 6-10 October 2008 in Hsiinchu Taiwan, Theme: Review Gender Justice and Renew Mission Practice. A Reflective Report.

Insaka

In order to fulfill its information sharing aim, a newsletter was introduced in 1993 by the name of *Insaka*.[101] The newsletter of the Community of Women and Men in Mission (CWMM) is also meant to show where the inequalities between men and women are, and to inspire them to act for gender justice. Initially the newsletter was to be produced quarterly. In reality, in some years there are more issues than others. The issues raised in *Insaka* so far highlight gender, leadership and power in the church and society. In the case of church issues, it raises issues of: stories about the role of women missionaries; ordination of women and general participation of women in leadership positions; Women in theological education; spouses of pastors, and church women organizations. Within the societal issues, there is a wide range of topics which can be summarized as follows: education of women and girls; violence against women and children; human sexuality; economic injustice; and issues of masculinity. The information is presented in the form of commissioned short articles, Bible studies and stories. It would be necessary to have an in-depth analysis of all issues from 1993 to the present so that there is a systematic address of gender issues in the church and society for a lasting impact.

The articles, stories, and bible study materials are all from a gender perspective. Thus the newsletter is an important expression of the existence of patriarchy in the church and society. The articles are written by church practitioners and academic scholars[102] in a language that is accessible to the majority of church people who can read in English. This

---

[101] *Insaka* is a word that comes from the Bemba of Zambia, which has multiple meetings as follows: "a village council where women, men and youth meet to discuss issues affecting the community; a community court; a place for communal meals; and it can refer to skills and instructions given as a preparation for adulthood."

[102] Some of the contributors include: Cheryl Dibeela, a minister from the United Congregational Church of Southern Africa; Lindsey Sanderson a mission enabler for the Synod of Scotland of the United Reformed Church; Steven Titus when he was the General Secretary of the United Congregational Church of Southern Africa; Bob Franklyn from New Zealand; Atalua Taniel from Congregational Christian Church in Samoa; Monica Melanchthon from India; Lucy Kao from Taiwan; Bishop Samuel Amirtham of the Church of India.

guarantees that the articles are of good quality. The idea of having a newsletter that is dedicated to discussion of issues that affect men and women in the church and society is a very good one. The question it raises is whether the targeted people in the member churches actually read the information that is in the *Insaka*. The facts that the newsletter is co-edited by a man and a woman[103] and that they are contributors of information in all three categories of issues are a strong motivation for women and men from the member churches to engage the issues raised in the newsletters. It is also encouraging to note that in the main bi-monthly magazine of the CWM, *Inside Out,* has a dedicated page to women issues but not gender issues. It would be interesting to find out how many of the subscribers to *Inside Out* actually read the women's page(s). It would also be very important to find out who is actually reading *Insaka* and the women's page in *Inside Out* and how the contents thereof has helped them in their understanding of the partnership of women and women as mission.

A reflection on the contents and readership of *Insaka* and *Inside Out* calls for a need to elaborate on the difference between women's issues and gender issues. Globally, conscientised women and men are concerned that the structures of race, class, religion, nationality, sexuality and region subordinate and oppress women.[104] Their goal is to end the invisibility, marginalization and subordination of women in religion and society. The category of gender emphasises a focus is on how society and religion have constructed women and men in their power relationships. The mistake that is made is that many people associate gender issues with women and not with the power relationship between men and women. Hence, the concern here about the readership of *Insaka* and *Inside Out*.

---

[103] The editorial names say something about what CWM understood to be the role of the Newsletter. Initially there were individuals who took the responsibility of editing *Insaka*. Ekei Etim was the first editor. For a number of years (1994-2000) Francis Brienen took the responsibility of editing Insaka. There seems to have been a gender reflection on the editorial team because one then notices gender balanced editorial teams from 2000. The names included Francis Brienen and Nick Sireau; and Elizabeth Joy and Beccy Beard.

[104] Rita Nakashima Brock, "Feminist Theories" in *Dictionary of Feminist Theologies*, eds. Letty M. Russell and J. Shannon (Clarkson, Loisville: Westminster John Knox Press, 1996), 117.

Team Visits

Team visits were identified as another method that would assist the CWM to share information about the concerns of the Community of Women and Men programme with the CWM member churches at a church level. The purpose of the team visits is:

> to bring together men and women from each of the CWM's six regions to help churches build a new community of women and men in mission. They aim to:
> • Share experiences, promote understanding, provide encouragement, challenge one another and share working methods.
> • Appreciate the benefits to the churches from building this community;
> • Root the journey in the gospel call to build a community of women and men by engaging one another with different visions of gender equality;
> • Share stories which help through the barriers of culture and tradition.[105]

The idea of choosing mostly people who are in decision making positions to go on team visits is a strategic one, with the intention that when such people see the positive side of partnership in mission between men and women, they would be in a position to influence policies and action in their own churches.

By 2005, an assessment of the reports of the team visits from initial phase revealed that:

> • The churches have indeed made progress in the increased participation of women in the church's life.
> • In the majority of churches, women still continue to hold a subordinate position and violence against women is very much a reality at varying intensities.
> • Even in the churches that have a higher representation of women in many of the decision marking bodies, we do not see a visible change in the life and witness of the church as there is no change in the

---

[105] *Insaka,* August 2005, 3.

mindset of these women. Most of them blindly and spontaneously follow the patriarchal models, thus perpetuating the subordination of women.
- The churches which have advanced in gender participation still have issues such as under-representation of women at the tip of the hierarchal structures.[106]

CWM needs to be affirmed for its ability to self- evaluate so that they can measure whether their programmes have an impact at the grassroots level or not. While the newsletters are very good for the societies that have a high rate of literacy, it is the team visits that I would assume to have a higher impact in communities where the majority of the people do not have literacy skills. Therefore, team visits should be encouraged on a bigger scale than what is the case currently. Of particular interest to this study is the theology that under-girds the partnership in mission of women and men in the CWM.

The Theology of the Partnership of Men and Women

CWM has declared that the partnership of men and women in mission is an anthropological one. The major question that bothers many churches who refuse the participation of women in leadership positions is whether women also reflect the image of God. These member churches are not sure that women reflect the image of God. They hold on to biblical passages like 1 Cor. 11, which at face value seem to be saying that only men reflect the image of God. Some leaders may have studied in theological colleges where they were introduced to the work of the early fathers, who also did not believe that women on their own reflected the image of God. They only reflect the image of God when they are attached to men.

It is arguments about women not reflecting the full image of God that lead to the subordination of women in the church and society, which is reinforced by patriarchy. In the WCC Sheffield report, Jürgen Moltmann is quoted to have stated that "patriarchy is a very ancient and widespread system of male domination that was not introduced by Christianity but that Christianity proved incapable of successfully

---

[106] CWMM reference group meeting minutes of 11 to 14th April 2005.

opposing it."[107] In the case of Africa, culture has been used as to be the major reason why the majority of Mission churches do not ordain women. This has also been the reason used by some churches in India for the rejection of the ordination of women. The challenge for CWM then, is to come up with a postcolonial method to engage culture in the pursuit of gender justice.[108] This is particularly important in the light of the CWM Assembly statement which acknowledged the marginalization of women and the youth and affirmed the need to "consistently keep the issues presented by women and youth high on our agendas in our common bid to give full recognition to all members that constitute the Body of Christ."[109]

Those churches that have accepted women as reflecting the image of God base their arguments on Genesis 1 and Galatians 3. For feminist theologians, the central question here is: what does it mean to be human? This question is important because of the way women have been constructed both by society and the church. The issue at hand is that throughout the ages, both society and the Christian religion have denied the full humanity of women, bringing negative consequences upon the dignity of women. The goal of Christian feminist anthropology therefore is the restoration of the full humanity of women as created in the image of God.

Accordingly, the CWM established the Community of women and men programme based on the theological truth that "as human beings created in the image of God, women and men are empowered by God to be instruments of God's mission in affirming the dignity and worth of all people."[110] This means that while one may use the bible to discredit women's participation in leadership positions, the same bible has been used by the CWM in a liberative way to embrace the full humanity of women and men to partnership in mission.

Therefore, armed with this positive theology of the humanity of men and women, the CWM 'acknowledges that many women experience

---

[107] Constance F. Parvey, ed., *The Community of Women and Men in the Church: The Sheffield Report* (Geneva: World Council of Churches, 1983), 4.

[108] See Musimbi Kanyoro, *Introducing Feminist Cultural Hermeneutics: An African Perspective* (Cleveland: Pilgrim, 2002).

[109] CWM Assembly Statement Scotland, 27 June 2003.

[110] Council for World Mission Community of Women and Men in Mission Newsletter, 1 (1993), 4.

pain because the dignity and worth given to them by God and the opportunities to fulfill the call to be part of God's mission are denied to them by traditions and structures, prejudice and language, and the attitudes of both men and women."[111] Thus it is for this reason that the CWM felt that partnership in mission can only be complete by including the contribution made by women on an equal basis with men. The CWM went further to invite its member churches to join the "Ecumenical Decade: Churches in Solidarity with Women" by taking measurable steps. Many people in CWM and in the ecumenical movement have talked about the success of this decade, although it is also argued that it was more in line with women in solidarity with the churches than the other way round.

Conclusion

This essay has tried to show that the question of partnership in mission, when approached from a postcolonial perspective, shows that it is an issue of social justice. Unjust relations of the past missionary enterprise, framed in modernist framework that made one group of people take control of missions based on their material worth and gender, has been rejected by CWM. New relationships based on postcolonial just relationships have been promoted cross-culturally and between genders. The issue of gender justice has been the hardest for the CWM to address. However, through the use of different strategies, efforts are being made to promote gender justice in all the CWM churches. The team visits have been highlighted as being very effective in picking up the vibes of what is happening in the local churches in the building of communities of women and men. In this essay, we have dwelt on the theology of anthropology to be the source of the subordination of women. Using a feminist anthropology, a positive construction of women and men is possible which can lead to partnership in mission. Perhaps it is too limiting to only focus on the theology of anthropology when dealing with issues of partnership in mission. In further studies, the focus should also be a combination of feminist anthropology and ecclesiology in seeking partnership of men and women in mission.

---

[111] Council for World Mission Community of Women and Men in Mission Newsletter, 4.

4

Building Communities of Hope:
A Case Study in Postcolonial Mission

Roderick Hewitt[112]

My formal introduction to the CWM came in June 1984 when the United Church in Jamaica and the Cayman Islands sent me for missionary service along with my wife and two children to serve the United Reformed Church (URC) in the United Kingdom. I was placed at South Aston URC in Birmingham as an associate minister to serve a multiracial congregation and community. The Rev Dr Fred Kaan, the famous hymnodist and former Moderator of the West Midlands Province of the URC, conducted the induction and welcome service. I can still vividly recall the warm reception that I received from the Imam of the local Mosque as he embraced me and said: "Brother Roderick I pray that Allah will bless your work amongst us." I was catapulted into a multi-faith and multi-cultural environment that exposed the limitation of my restrictive embedded Christian faith and invited me to engage in new missional learning. This Jamaican missionary needed another conversion experience in order to cross new frontiers in mission!

Mission engagement within the community of South Aston brought into sharp focus issues that impacted on the capacity of people to experience fullness of life. The local church had to work out what it was

---

[112] Rev Dr. Hewitt is a minister of the United Church in Jamaica and the Cayman Islands. He lectured at the International University of the Caribbean and the United Theological College of the West Indies/The University of the West Indies. Dr Hewitt recently joined the staff of the School of Theology and Religion at the University of KwaZulu-Natal in South Africa. He has held a number of leadership positions both in the local and international ecumenical organisations.

called to be and do within a multi-faith/multi-cultural environment with high unemployment, high incidents of crime and poor educational resources. How should the bible be read and understood in such a context? What is the good news that the church is called to proclaim and practice? How should the church respond to issues of racial, economic and social injustice? The two years spent in the context taught me that the church's mission is not a pre-set and pre-determined reality. The classical colonial understanding of mission was irrelevant in this context.

I wish to recall another significant event that opened my eyes and ears to new missional learning. My ministerial colleague, Peter Loveitt, shared with me the story of how the local Imam's daughter was ill and he was requested to visit their home to offer prayers of healing. He was somewhat wary of the invitation and the consequences should the girl's condition deteriorate after his visit. However, he went and prayed for her. After one week he saw the Imam and sought information about his daughter's health. He responded: "She is fine thank you! The Prophet, peace be upon him, said that Allah honours the prayers of those who follow the prophet Jesus!" The confidence that was demonstrated in the efficacy of the Christian's prayer strengthened the local church in their ministry of prayer within the community.

The mission of the church is concerned with building communities of hope as it forges risky engagement with the joys and sorrows of ordinary people. The community of South Aston became for me the new face of CWM, a postcolonial discourse in seeking to build a community of hope. Over the past twenty five years I have served CWM in various capacities as missionary, executive staff and the moderator of its Trustee Body. It has afforded me a unique opportunity to participate in shaping the identity, vocation and witness of this global mission enterprise. In this chapter I will therefore attempt a missiological reading of selective "stepping stones" along the CWM journey and reflect on the ways in which this family of churches has or has not functioned in building communities of hope.

Reading Signs of the Times

The missional experiences that I encountered in Birmingham are replicated in different ways and in diverse communities all over the world where the 31 member churches of CWM engage in ministry and mission. Their different contexts for mission are shaped by plurality and contradiction within difficult living environments. Fear has become a tangible global force that is affecting how nations organise their way of life. The 2008 crash in the global financial market graphically illustrated how interconnected our world is and how economic confidence or lack of it can create stability or instability within nations.

Health concerns such as HIV/Aids, Avian flu, H1N1(Swine flu) and other forms of diseases have threatened the capacity of nations to cope. New forms of social barriers are being established by nations, especially those in the North, to keep out persons (those from the South) that are considered economic migrants. Fear of the other (xenophobia) is now a hard currency that is being used openly by nations under the pretext of protecting their national interest.

Finally, religious fears have catapulted our world into a siege mentality. Global ambiguities and contradictions have raised questions as to whether humanity has a future with hope. In spite of great advances in science and technology in boosting human self-confidence in controlling and exploiting nature, the world is increasingly becoming fragmented with persons living on the margins, being excluded from economic development. It is this ideology of exclusion of the many from economic progress that constitutes seeds of destruction for the hope of humanity.

A Movement for Greater Human Solidarity

The most pressing need in our contemporary world is for greater human solidarity because there are increasing vulnerabilities within the environment, ecology and economy that threaten the very survival of humanity. Climate change that has resulted in global warming is already having a catastrophic impact on islands of the Pacific and Caribbean regions.[113] Vulnerable communities are facing increasing health and food security risk. Theologian Phillip Wickeri identified the future of religion to be dependent upon engagement in fostering true human solidarity and helping various communities to meet and interact through effective

---

[113] Kate Markes, "Pacific Islands to Sink Under Global Warming," nzherald.co.nz,
http://www.nzherald.co.nz/world/news/article.cfm?c_id=2&objectid=10407508. (accessed 12 August 2010).

participation, thus creating a different order in the world.[114] Building solidarity with all people within the sphere of the church's mission must be a key feature of the hope that is pursued. Building communities of hope requires transformative justice that empowers people to experience life in all its fullness (Micah 6:8; John 10:10).

Common Witness as an Instrument of Hope

The dilemmas and contradictions found in the human condition motivated the vision of the ecumenical movement for greater human solidarity. In diverse contexts where plurality in cultures posed significant challenges for the churches' identity, vocation and witness, there was an urgent desire for common witness in order that they may function as effective instruments of hope. The quest for unity in mission was ignited by the nineteenth century missionary movement. The churches embraced joint action in mission as a concrete expression of God's purpose for the world. The formation of the World Council of Churches (WCC) in 1948 placed the agenda of Church unity as a priority.[115] The formation of the Church of South India in 1947 and the Church of North India in 1948 became potent signs of hope within their religious and ethnic plural societies.

Other unions within South Asia helped the church to function as an influential minority faith within dominant Islamic, Hindu and Buddhists' cultures. Without church unity, witnessing within these different countries would be severely weakened. After the 1961 New Delhi Assembly of the WCC, an upsurge in organic church union happened in Jamaica and the Cayman Islands, Zambia, Southern Africa, Madagascar, Papua New Guinea and the Solomon Islands. The ecclesiological movement towards union by Congregationalists, Presbyterians, Methodists and later Churches of Christ became a stepping stone for unity in mission.[116] The experiences of these churches in crossing new frontiers in mission laid the foundations for the Council

---

[114] L. P. Wickeri, ed., *The People of God Among All God's Peoples: Frontiers in Christian Mission* (Hong Kong: Christian Conference of Asia; London: Council for World Mission, 2000).
[115] *Hard Facts of Unity* (Geneva: WCC Publications, 1961), 35.
[116] Roderick Hewitt, "A Missiological Exploration into the Identity, Vocation and Witness of the United Church of Jamaica and Grand Cayman: A Gospel and Culture Exploration" (PhD diss., Kings College, University of London, 2001).

for World Mission (CWM) coming into existence. These united churches recognised that they had to function as hope-building faith communities wherever they served, in spite of their diverse cultural backgrounds and ecclesial traditions, because ecumenism and mission belong together.

Real Roots or Potted Plants?

Missionaries sent out through the London Missionary Society (LMS) in the 19th and 20th century founded churches that were developed with inherited seeds of a colonial culture fused with missionary Christianity. The strategic principle of the LMS stated that it would endeavour not to evangelise people into sectarian or denominational commitments but to allow the people to choose the ecclesial structures that they wished to govern their lives.[117] In theory the vision was laudable. However, in practice, the missionaries that represented the LMS did not leave behind their European denominational allegiances. They "proclaimed the gospel" and planted churches that developed bipolar identities with roots that were not fully earthed into the local soil. Caribbean theologian Ashley Smith questioned whether this developmental identity of the Churches should be described as "Real Roots or Potted Plants."[118] Colonialism and Church development were not practiced within an environment that nurtured mutuality in relationships between the colonisers and the colonised. They had different visions, expectations and needs of the context in which they lived. The priority of those who benefited from the colonial system was to facilitate the maintenance of the dominant Euro-centric world view concerning how church and society should be ordered. The faith communities that they built replicated this goal, and were therefore limited in their missional scope. The inherited missionary engagement was uni-directional: from Europe/eans to the rest of the world and was therefore flawed. The 1975 *Sharing in One World Mission* document described the historical setting that catapulted CWM into a new mission paradigm as an untenable and restricted understanding of the missionary task.[119] The global evangelisation strategies of the missionary

---

[117] Richard Lovett, *History of the London Missionary Society,* Vol. 2 (London: Oxford University Press, 1899), 50.

[118] Ashley Smith, *Real Roots or Potted Plants* (Jamaica: Mandeville Publishers, 1984).

[119] *Sharing in One World Mission* (CWM, 1975), 2.

organisations were supported by Churches and coincided with tacit alliance with the advocates of colonial expansion. This resulted in cultural, political, economic and religious relationships that lacked reciprocity. Although many churches were built, and political, educational and health services developed, the churches developed deficiencies bequeathed through the practice of un-just relationship in mission.

A Quest for Just Relationship in Mission

When the leaders of the churches that constituted the CWM gathered in Singapore in 1975 to discuss the future of their organization, the meeting was not meant to sever the ecclesial umbilical cord that connected the churches in a shared missional history. However, their political and ecclesial settings had radically changed. The decolonisation movement that gained momentum after the Second World War resulted in political and religious struggles of liberation that conscientized and empowered local leaders to call for a new order, based on just relationships.[120] Global mission organisations were not excluded from this anti-colonial critique. The aftermath of the 1910 Edinburgh Mission Conference had sown seeds that called for new ways of thinking about the mission of the church.[121]

Rethinking Theologies of Mission

At the World Mission Conference in Willengen, Germany, a significant shift took place in the understanding and practice of mission. The dominant paradigm up to that time was church-driven mission (missio-ecclesia). The conference rejected this restricted perspective and called on churches and mission organisations to embrace the idea of *"missio Dei"* because mission is not only revealed through the church. The following ecumenical and missiological documents gave shape and form to the formation of CWM and its early mission thinking and practice: *Sharing in One World Mission, Mission in Six Continents, the Missionary Structure of the Congregation* and the Bangkok papers on *Salvation Today*. The LMS, in a policy statement of June 1952, stated that the total work of the church at home and abroad must be recognised

---

[120] Jose Miguez Bonino, *Doing Theology in a Revolutionary Situation* (Philadelphia: Fortress Press, 1975), 2-20.
[121] *International Review of Mission* 76/342 (1997): 210

as a unity.[122] Historian David Thompson describes the CWM paradox as an ecumenical achievement and a misfit as it seeks to give reality to the unity of the church's mission throughout the world.[123] The "missio Dei" understanding of mission debunked the out-dated thinking of the global South as the object of mission and expanded to embrace mission in every continent. This paradigm shift emboldened the selfhood of those who, for centuries, were viewed as the recipients of mission, to become full and equal actors in the missionary calling of the church. This meant that every church must be missionary and that ministry and mission is the responsibility of the whole people of God and not for a few enthusiasts.

Building a Global Community of Partners in Mission

The transformation from the LMS to the Congregational Council for World Mission (CCWM) and finally into the CWM involved each organisation demonstrating a willingness to die to their old identity in order to give birth to something new that would make the mission of the church more effective. They demonstrated a willingness to change because they were uncomfortable with the unjust status quo. They all embraced opportunities for renewal and transformation. The birth of the new CWM in 1977 represented a journey that resulted in a more just relationship among the community of churches. They opted for mutuality over moratorium in mission. Although the churches were at different stages of missional readiness, they journeyed at a speed that left no one behind. Each church would contribute as it is able and the value of each gift would be equally appreciated and respected. According to David Thompson the new structure embodied the principle of partnership between the churches for missionary work.[124] Their response was undergirded by new theological awareness, heightened ecumenical engagement, renewed commitment to service and greater sense of identity.

The steps that were taken to form the CWM were not simply a minor repair job to an old mission structure. The goal was a thorough moral makeover in the structures of relationships that would debunk donor/recipient relationship in mission, reject London and other

---

[122] Bernard Thorogood, *Gales of Change: Responding to Shifting Missionary Context* (Geneva: WCC Publications, 1994), 225.
[123] Wickeri, *The People of God*, 286.
[124] Wickeri, *The People of God*, 286.

metropolis as "the centre" for decision in mission and embrace the witness of local churches as the first base for mission understanding and action.[125] This new mission perspective broke the nexus between concentration of power and money as the primary influence in mission action at the expense of the role played by the resources of faith, ideas and personnel for mission.[126] In seeking to build this new hope-giving community committed to partnership in mission, there was deep consciousness that years of ecclesial relationship built on injustice and inequality would not fundamentally transform behaviour over a short period of time.[127] The emerging mission theology placed the local church as the primary agent for mission and not the CWM as an international mission organisation. Its core purpose for existing is to facilitate churches to carry out their missionary mandate. Central to its missional mandate is the task of proclaiming the gospel with openness whilst learning from others. This commitment to the gospel necessitates sacrificial service and bold acts of justice and mercy that help people to experience fullness of life.

The CWM community of churches covenanted to be partners together in Christ's mission, to share justly between and beyond themselves their resources of people, money, gifts, faith and understanding.[128] It is a practice of partnership that best expresses the principle of sharing through giving and receiving according to each one's needs. The idea of pooling resources together for the common good was rooted in the biblical paradigm of "Pentecostal economics" as practiced by the early church. (Acts 4:32-35) This Christian community claimed to have within it the ability and capacity to reconcile the tensions between

---

[125] The LMS and CCWM had set the stage for radical change through previous major reforms in 1966 and 1972 and 1975 in which the discontinuity of structures once revered led the missional community to give birth to a new form of mission understanding and practice for a new era.
[126] Eugene Stockwell, *International Review of Mission* 76/304 (1987): 436, stated that in preparation for the 1987 El Escorial Consultation on Resource Sharing that an American Church leader wrote that the conference was doom for failure because new and improved patterns of sharing resources called for nothing less than a radical change of human nature. The existence of CWM proved that this Church leader was not totally right.
[127] Preman Niles, *From East and West: Rethinking Christian Mission* (St Louis, Missouri: Chalice Press, 2004), 59-64.
[128] Roderick Hewitt, *CWM Partnership in Mission* (London, 1995).

pluralism and equity by living out a unity-in-diversity. The new ecclesial community was born and took root among a people who were nearly hopeless and passionless in despair. In the sacramental traditions of the church, it is the movement and work of the Holy Spirit that builds unity amid the disruptive divisions within the church and the world. The CWM being a small missional instrument, seeks to be a potent sign of hope in a deeply troubled world and to facilitate people of faith to put up resistance against all forces that deny fullness of life.

The new model of mission engagement represented a fundamental break with the traditional Euro-centric missionary model by creating a community of diverse churches serving in religiously plural societies, but committed to practicing partnership in mission. Some churches in the South were psychologically addicted to being carried by churches in the North and this resulted in mal-formation that bequeathed the following dysfunctional developments:

1. Confused identity, vocation and witness in which some churches emerged with *weakly-indigenized ministry*. According to Lewin Williams the metropolitan tradition and the pressures of the new society created the socio-economic, political and religious condition, which in turn delayed the "indigenous backlash."[129] Williams argues that the slow process of change by these churches to become what is perceived to be 'authentically local,' is attributed to the fact that 'the roots of missio-colonial control are not dead.'[130]

2. *Inadequate investment in leadership development.* Colonial missionary strategy of local leadership development was not designed to give birth to a fully indigenised church that was self-administering, self-propagating and self-financing. Rather many local leaders inherited ecclesial institutions with structures that were unmanageable because of inadequate human and financial resources.[131]

---

[129] Lewin Williams, *Caribbean Theology* (New York: Peter Lang Publishing, 1993), 6.
[130] Williams, *Caribbean Theology*, 7.
[131] L. Philip Wickeri, K. Wickeri, D.P. Niles, and M.A. Damayanthi, eds. *Plurality, Power and Mission: Intercontextual Theological Explorations on the*

Learning Mission as Reciprocity

For some churches in the Global North, this new missional instrument meant that it required a willingness to have less authority than what they had in the colonial past and relinquishing their veto power to those who were historically considered not to be their equal. They became missionally disabled because they were ill equipped to engage in relationships in which they were not the dominant partners giving resources to financially weak churches. These churches were mis-educated to regard themselves only as donors. The change for some churches in the global South involved a painful journey of psychologically eschewing a mis-evangelised conditioned state of dependency. They had to learn how to take full responsibility for their engagement in local and global mission.

Reciprocity is Not a Cheap Option in Mission Engagement

Prior to the birth of the CWM, sending and receiving churches engaged in mission out of tradition and obligation. The years of relating together through the CWM mission empowerment instrument has, to some extent, changed their raison d'être of mission engagement. The CWM partnership model helped to weaken the "Lone Ranger" or individualist model of doing mission in which the economically powerful churches of the North would set terms for engagement with economically poorer churches of the South. Such relationships lacked mutuality and reciprocity. The churches arrived at an understanding that the gospel also speaks about power and its use, especially within the Christian community. Money, knowledge, property, national identity and ecclesial tradition bequeath power to Christian institutions and those who control them. At the core of the CWM identity is a strong imperative to share power as widely as possible by holding as much financial resources 'in common' and by valuing the different ways in which churches bear witness to Christ's mission. The CWM's partnership in mission model challenges, encourages and equips churches to share in God's mission throughout the world with the following five-fold objective: making offerings to assist each other in local mission; multi-directional exchange

---

Role of Religion in the New Millennium (London: Council For World Mission, 2000), 7.

of personnel; engaging in joint witness together; stimulating solidarity in Christian fellowship and understanding more deeply the gift of God in Christ.[132]

Mission in Contradiction

During the first ten years of the CWM journey, many un-sung and un-named persons engaged in selfless and sacrificial service, taking risk, crossing difficult missional frontiers and creating stepping stones as they went beyond self in order to hear afresh what God in Christ was calling the Church to be and to do. They were aware that the change envisioned was fraught with challenges that could not be glossed over. The churches were rooted in diversity and contradiction that made the quest for partnership in mission look like a distant dream. However, they were convinced that a different quality of relationship was necessary in which all participants would experience equal dignity and respect and be mutually accountable and affirmed. This missional relationship was built with an understanding that every church would embrace an intentional preferential bias for the needs of the poor and the marginalised.

The high rate of change of key administrative leaders within member churches has posed a major challenge to the strategic development of the CWM. Many of the new leaders who were given the responsibility to shape the future development were not intentionally groomed by their predecessors into the CWM ethos.[133] Some of them viewed the CWM as a funding agency to which they lobbied for resources and not as a partnership in mission enterprise to facilitate fullness of life. Missional leadership formation that gives attention to building communities of hope became essential in the CWM's priorities in mission.

Mission Action with the Whole People of God

In the early years, mission action through the CWM was restricted to the roles played by executive decisions, the appointments of missionaries and limited transfer of funds to churches in the South to help maintain their ministry. If the Churches were to become truly "missionary churches" and communities of hope, then they had to

---

[132] Niles, *From East and West,* 59-64.
[133] Maitland Evans, *What is our Partnership, Cost of Partnership* (1981-3 Report of The Council for World Mission, London, 1983), 4.

embrace a fresh understanding of the laity as the primary resource for mission action. New thinking on the missional role of ordinary people in local congregations, such as children, young people, women and men, was needed. An intentional learning process had to be developed to prepare new personnel for mission. Programmes such as Training in Mission (TIM), Mission to the Urban Poor, Leadership Development and Working with the Disadvantaged became important first steps in concretising the CWM's vision of building communities of hope.[134]

Having embraced an alternative way of relating in mission, the churches had to face up to the issue of how their local congregations were organised for ministry and mission. The recognition that mission was not the responsibility of a few enthusiasts but the very essence of being church, meant that an educational process of equipping local congregations in mission was needed. Bernard Thorogood described the challenge that the CWM partnership of Churches faced as a journey from standing in a circle facing each other to standing in a circle facing the world.[135] If the churches exist for the sake of the world, then their engagement in mission should begin right where they are in their local context. This way of being in mission requires churches to put into practice their belief in "the priesthood of all believers." However, their model of ministerial formation and theological education produced a strong clergy-centred understanding of ministry that contributes to the de-skilling of members in local congregations.

Transforming Theological Formation for Mission

In the critical area of ministerial formation, some of the CWM member churches had accepted a paradigm that was stuck in a maintenance culture. They uncritically embraced high-cost residentially-based, university-determined theological programmes that were, to some extent, unrelated to the daily realities of congregational life and faith. In 1988 CWM facilitated discussions on ministerial formation that allowed churches to share their experiences and was exposed to new perspectives on the subject. This resulted in bilateral relationship between the Presbyterian Church in New Zealand (PCUNZ) and the United Church in Jamaica and the Cayman Islands (UCJCI).

---

[134] *Beyond Ourselves, Report of the Secretariat of the Council for World Mission*, 1991-1993.
[135] Niles, *From East and West*.

Rev Dr Maitland Evans, who was General Secretary for the UCJCI, invited Dr Sarah Mitchell, who was Principal for Knox Theological College in Dunedin, New Zealand, to share their experiences in the new pedagogical instrument in ministerial training that strengthened the formation of students for ministry. The model allowed students and lecturers to spend significant time away from the College, with selected teaching congregations acting as learning centres. This allowed the students to be a better fit for ministry. The information inspired the UCJCI to critique its own contextual model that resulted in the formation of the Institute for Theological and Leadership Development (ITLD) in 1989. This is now a constituent college of the International University of the Caribbean.[136]

Between 1997 and 1999, CWM facilitated dialogue between the churches and the theological institutions that they use for training ministerial leadership. A decision was taken to invest in strengthening selective regional centres of excellence in the Pacific, Asia and the Caribbean. Many of the churches from the global South are addicted to sending their leaders to universities in Europe and USA for postgraduate training. This is based on the premise that such universities offer better quality training. In order to redress the major flow of human and financial resources from the South to the North, the CWM targeted a number of regional theological institutions in the South for significant capital investment, to strengthen their capacity to better compete and attract the CWM scholarship funds for undergraduate and post graduate studies.[137]

Ecumenical Engagement for Transformation of the World

The contemporary phase of the CWM's journey affirms a commitment to wider ecumenical engagement. Whilst maintaining a posture that critiques ecumenical instruments that veer away from serving the evangelical mandate of the church's calling, the CWM advocates that the church exist not for itself but for the transformation of

---

[136] Rev Dr Maitland Evans who is the President of the International University of the Caribbean was the first Education in Mission Secretary for the CWM and he later served as Chairman for the Council.

[137] The institutions included United Theological College of the West Indies in Kingston Jamaica, United Theological College in Bangalore, South India, and Pacific Theological College in Fiji.

the world. The threats to life in the world and the growing climatic and environmental crisis necessitates that the church's mission embraces healing of all creation. A significant percentage of its common resources are spent addressing the impact of environmental problems on vulnerable communities in eco-sensitive regions around the world, especially within the Pacific and the Caribbean.

Mission Emphasis with Children

For the CWM to build communities of hope, it had to respond to the powerful impact of conflict that is left unchecked in human community. Many churches carry out their ministry in communities saturated with human-induced tragedies that destroy hope. Children constitute a vulnerable group that suffer the most from human induced violence.

At the 2006 CWM Assembly, delegates called for greater emphasis to be placed on mission with children. Their wellbeing became an important agenda concern. Many developing countries have children living on the streets who engage in begging, theft, drug trafficking, prostitution, and other desperate measures to survive. Such children are threatened by moral, social, and economic forces that threaten their future. As poorer nations cut their social services to balance their budget, or to pay debts to richer countries, it is the welfare of children that suffers the most. They need a secure and stable family life, but that is hardly available to them because of the awesome pressures that families face. The consumerist culture that globalization has unleashed has severely weakened family life.

The CWM family of churches claims that children are central to their ministry, however reports suggest that children do not view the churches as welcoming, celebratory and friendly.[138] Sadly, children exist in many churches as objects of faith and not as subjects and partners. They are not respected and protected and their wholesome development in society is not treated as a priority in mission. The CWM helped to facilitate the Presbyterian Church of New Zealand with its Kids Friendly Church programme, and the Congregational Union of New Zealand with

---

[138] *CWM Mission with Children Consultation* (Auckland, New Zealand, May 2007).

its promotion of responsible parenthood and the development of healthy family life as central to the church's mission within the community.

Child Resiliency Programme

One concrete expression of this new emphasis of mission with children is expressed in the United Church in Jamaica and the Cayman Island's Children Resiliency Programme. One of its congregations, the Hope United Church, realised that the traditional approach to work with children could not prevent high risk behaviour among children within the communities that it served. After in-depth research work, it built partnerships with the local schools in identifying those children practising high risk behaviour. They formed a mission team of well-trained volunteers, headed by a professional doctor with specialization in adolescent health, to implement six components in repairing their high risk behaviour:
1. Spiritual empowerment that helps kids to embrace Jesus as their friend
2. Life Skills Training and Mentorship
3. Academic support (primarily increased literacy)
4. Creative expression activity to reinforce life skills
5. Physical team playing activity and nutrition
6. Parenting/Family support training and counseling

No Child is Irredeemable

Four years of doing this after-school programme with about 60 children has demonstrated that a holistic approach to children work within the community constitutes a viable way to engage children who have not been part of the church's ministry and mission. The programme serves to instill positive socialisation to the children whose early development in life was blighted by dysfunctional parenting and inadequate community support. The programme also offers opportunity for university students to do quality voluntary work and for retired members to get involved in mentoring children.[139]

---

[139]See http://childresiliency.org/; The Child Resiliency Programme of the Hope Counselling and Wellness Centre is an outreach programme of the Hope United Church, Kingston, Jamaica.

Using the "Gift of Grace" to Build Communities of Hope

Up to 1995 the significant financial contributions to the CWM came from European member churches and income from property and investments. Although all churches, according to their means, gave to the "Common Pool" of resources, it was quietly acknowledged that the churches from Europe had greater influence in the organisation in the setting of policy and deciding how and where financial resources are allocated. During this period, expenditure on missionary sharing remained static whilst expenditure on churches' special projects grew.[140]

The sharing of resources of money took a significant turn in 1995 when the CWM received significant financial resources from the sale of a piece of land in Hong Kong. This unexpected blessing that was recognised by the community as 'a gift of grace' was due to the global financial impact on the price of limited land resource in Hong Kong. After much to and fro between the local church leaders and the CWM, an amicable solution was found for the allocation of the funds. Within the CWM family there was much debate concerning how best the funds should be used. Some leaders argued that it should be divided up among the churches in the regions. There was a strong possibility that if the funds were not managed properly it could transform the CWM family into a dysfunctional partnership.[141]

It was agreed that the investment from the proceeds of the sale would be used to empower the churches. 5% of the amount was set aside for ecumenical work and an agreed amount was divided equally between all of the member churches, regardless of their size or economic situation. A self-support development fund was established for churches to access after their mission audit has determined their priorities in mission. The CWM expanded its common programmes to support churches work with HIV/AIDS, and to demonstrate its solidarity with economic justice for the poor by allocating £5m to the Oikocredit movement founded by the World Council of Churches.[142] A strategic decision was taken by the CWM in 1996 to increase the financial resources shared with global ecumenical bodies from 2% of available resources to 5%. This enabled historic ecumenical partners like the World Council of Churches and the World Alliance of Reformed

---

[140] *Report of the Secretariat of the Council for World Mission 1991-1993*, 12-13.
[141] Niles, *From East and West*, 99.
[142] Niles, *From East and West*, 103-104.

Building Communities of Hope 95

Churches to expand their work. In addition, international mission partners such as the Caribbean and North America Council for Mission and the CEVVA received one-off strategic support to consolidate their work.

The gift of grace is still serving an important purpose in helping financially dependent churches to restructure themselves for ministry and mission. The dependency issue constitutes more than a financial problem but it also involves "a debilitating weight of structures inherited from the past."[143] Through the launching of the Mission Support Programme, the CWM facilitated Churches to engage in strategic planning and to develop priorities in mission before certain common funds could be accessed. This was intended to facilitate churches to move from a maintenance and survival mode to strategic growth and development.[144]

Economic Justice: Indispensable for Hope-building

Another key area of hope-building for the mission of the church is that of economic justice. Since 2002, the CWM has used significant financial resources to partner ecumenical bodies in the common quest of addressing economic justice. Active partnership with the World Alliance of Reformed Churches and its Accra Confession and the WCC Agape movement has resulted in joint action in addressing global challenges. In the 2004 Accra Confession, the group affirmed that global economic justice is essential to the integrity of confessing the Christian faith. The church must take sides in challenging all economic and political systems that create relationships that destroy human beings and the integrity of creation.

The growing fragmentation of human societies and families are caused, to a great extent, by the impact of economic absolutism that claims there is no alternative to the neo-liberal economic model that is controlling the world's economic order. The advocates of this model declares that "there is no alternative" (TINA), and invites people to offer their blind allegiance. The development of the Oikotree project by CWM, WCC and WARC constitutes an example of how laity around the

---

[143] *Partnership in Mission: The Harvest and the Hope* (Council for World Mission, London, October 2008), 79. Quoting from Roderick Hewitt article: *Growing Up into Mature Partnership* (1994).
[144] Jooseop Keum, *Partnership Support Programme Handbook* (London: CWM, November 2006).

world can engage in sharing stories concerning actions taken to address economic justice.[145] The global economic dis-order is the system that is guilty of making the poor poorer and denying them fullness of life. On this core issue, the CWM has taken sides because neutrality is not an option in the quest for global economic justice and human rights. Indeed, it is the CWM's solidarity with Churches during their time of struggle with anti-justice forces that best demonstrate the strength of the partnership. The testimony of the Presbyterian Church of Taiwan during the 1980's, the Presbyterian Church of Myanmar during military rule, and the Churches in South Africa during the era of Apartheid all attest to this indispensable partnership. If the church is to be an effective instrument in building communities of hope, then it must be willing to explore and face up to the contradictions that are preventing many people from experiencing hope in our world.

Hope-building: A Risky Business

If the CWM is to continue functioning as a hope-building community, then it must ally itself with those that affirm the human capacity to overcome life-denying forces. This is risky business for any church that wants to be maintainers of the status quo, and thinks and acts only in terms of law and order. If the church dares to be a hope-building community, then its ministry and mission will be turned inside out or even upside down! Because to engage in hope-building is to be open to a life full of surprises, amazement and wonder. Hope-building upsets the readymade scripts of the church.

The poor are generally resilient people. Their way of life speaks to not giving-in to the calamities and pains of life. After the floods and droughts, they are ready to pick up the pieces and start the rebuilding process. The effective use of the CWM's Solidarity and Action fund over the years, to respond quickly to the suffering of people around the world, demonstrates how resources can be used by the churches to help the most vulnerable within their respective societies. The hope-building challenge that the churches face requires that they embrace a practice of power that is accountable, enabling and eschews coercive, manipulating and domineering models. Our world is hungry for alternative models of hope that frees people to become what God has purposed for their lives. It is

---

[145] See http://www.oikotree.org/default.aspx.

for this reason that the CWM uses most of its financial resources to empower churches and strategic ecumenical instruments to engage in God's mission for wholeness of life.

Overcoming Fear with Hope

Over the past 30 years, the CWM has honoured a noble tradition of non-interference into the internal affairs of member churches. However, there have been occasions when churches invite the CWM to journey with them during periods of societal upheaval. The crisis that has enveloped Zimbabwe since the year 2000 constitutes an excellent example of the CWM's capacity to journey alongside suffering people. The Uniting Presbyterian Church of Southern Africa (UPSA) and the United Congregational Church of Southern Africa (UCCSA) undertook a joint initiative that lobbied the CWM to embrace the Zimbabwe humanitarian crisis as a mission priority. In solidarity with the Zimbabwe Presbytery of the UPSA and the Zimbabwe Synod of UCCSA, the 2003 CWM Assembly expressed compassion for and solidarity with the people of Zimbabwe in their suffering and their urgent pleas for economic and humanitarian aid, for democracy to be upheld and for peace to be restored.[146]

This happened at a time when other global ecumenical organizations were hesitant to engage because of the controversial nature of the problem. Solidarity visits were made to hear what was going on within the country and to expose reported atrocities. With millions of Zimbabweans forced to migrate in order to keep themselves and their families alive, the CWM offered financial support for local pastors to ensure that their leadership would remain in local communities. Regional and international support was mobilised when a Zimbabwe summit was organised in Johannesburg in July 2007. Using the theme: "Overcoming Fear by Faith: Churches in Solidarity with the Peoples of Zimbabwe," Zimbabweans told their stories of the atrocities committed by the Mugabe Zanu PF regime against the people.[147] Through the presence of keynote speakers, significant press exposure was given to the summit

---

[146] Declaration of solidarity with churches in Zimbabwe 22/7/2003 (accessed 12 July 2010). http://www.cwmission.org/statements/declaration-of-solidarity-with-churches-in-zimbabwe.html.

[147] Documents relating to this summit can be access from the CWM website: http://www.cwmission.org/press/zimbabwe-summit.html.

and the need for urgent action to resolve the crisis. Finally, significant funds were made available to the churches in Zimbabwe to purchase seeds for local people to plant when the rains arrived. The stories from local people who received these seeds confirmed for them that the CWM is in the business of building communities of hope.[148]

Hope-building: An Apostolic Mandate

What is the CWM called and sent to do at this *kairos* moment in history? What are the essential non-negotiables that Christ has authorized, empowered and sent the CWM to be and to do? The apostolic mandate to the church implies that it would be better to risk failure than to settle for non-involvement. This authority that is bequeathed to the church and mediated through human leadership requires that the institutional manifestation of being church must be under the leading and teaching of the Holy Spirit in order that its ministry and mission may be empowered. The equipping of every local congregation in mission constitutes the most urgent task of ministerial and diaconal leadership, if the vision of being a hope-building community is to be realised.

Using the "Gift of Grace" to Share the "Good News"

Of major significance was the action taken to support the work of the Church in China. There is a strong but false perception among the religious right that ecumenical mission organisations engage only social justice issues and shy away from direct evangelization. Most of the CWM member churches, especially those in Asia, identify themselves as evangelical and have identified evangelism as one of their core priorities in mission. This corporate commitment to evangelism was demonstrated in the use of resources from the Gift of Grace. The CWM allocated £1m to share with churches in China for their work of evangelization and church-building programmes. In 2007, I joined a team of church leaders from the East Asia region of CWM to visit some of the newly built churches in China that received financial resources from the CWM. We

---

[148] In August 2009, Rev Dr Desmond Van der Water, Rev Dr Roderick Hewitt, Rev Dr Prince Dibeela and Rev Dr Jerry Pillay visited Zimbabwe to assess progress made. The report is available at "Inside Out, Solidarity with Zimbabwe," http://www.cwmission.org/features/solidarity-with-zimbabwe-one-year-on.html. (accessed 12 July 2010).

saw communities of hope that demonstrated life-giving testimonies on how they worked together and bore witness to the love of Christ within their context.

Always Reforming

The significant changes to the CWM governance structure that were made in 2002 saw each member church having one trustee named to the new the CWM charitable trust. This was viewed as a major achievement because it gave the churches a greater sense of ownership of the enterprise, regardless of their numerical strength or historical legacy. Armed with strong financial resources, and what was supposed to be a better mission-enabling governance structure, it was expected that the CWM would be better able to facilitate the churches in their mission.

The CWM 2003 Assembly at Ayr, Scotland entrusted the responsibility of managing this new Trustee Body, with Roderick Hewitt from the United Church in Jamaica and the Cayman Islands serving as its Moderator, and Robin Thompson from the United Congregational Church of Southern Africa serving as Treasurer. Four other Deputy Moderators from the regions were chosen to form the officers' corps. It was a critical time for the CWM because for the first time in its history, the key positions of Moderator, Treasurer and General Secretary were occupied by leaders from churches in the global South.

There were apprehensions from a few European church leaders that the team would follow policies that would result in the erosion of the CWM's strong financial base. Most of the persons appointed to be Trustees were new to the CWM experience. Ensuring that the historical memory of the CWM's identity, vocation and witness were effectively communicated to the new leaders and spending quality time learning about managing the CWM as a Trust, were paramount.

The General Secretary, Rev Dr Desmond Van der Water, took on the mantle of leadership at a time when some churches were concerned about how much the administration valued their participation and contribution. His academic and pastoral finesse that were shaped within the diverse South African context made him a great facilitator. His multicultural administrative team were guided to place the mission of the church at the centre of the CWM's life and work. The policies shaped by the Trustee Body and the vision given by the Assembly were given programmatic expressions that demonstrate a commitment to member churches becoming home-based expressions of good news.

The detractors within the family who expressed doubts whether the Officers and Trustees were capable of giving sound oversight to the Gift of Grace were silenced. Some had feared that the resources would be wasted and the future work of the CWM would be severely compromised. They were proven wrong. Although the period 2003 to 2009 saw the stock market move from boom to bust, the sound financial policies that were put in place ensured that the CWM resources grew and enough funds were found to meet the request of member churches and the ecumenical community. Unlike other charities that compromised their finite resources through greed for high returns, the CWM remained steadfast in its commitment to ethical investment and was not tempted to succumb to the snare of high risk returns investment accounts.

Strategic Framework and Plans for 2010 and Beyond

The CWM has a noble tradition of creating space for self-critique and has demonstrated a willingness to cease existing in order to give birth to something new. In order to respond more effectively to the mission of the church and to function as a hope-building community, a six-yearly review model was used to assess its missional performance and to determine new paths for the future. Having restructured the organization in 2002, the 2008 Trustee Body opted for the development of a Strategic Framework that would guide the work of the Council from 2010 to 2019. The process used to arrive at the final document involved global consultation with the member churches and ecumenical partners, the Trustee Body and administrative staff. The process confirmed an urgent need for review of the CWM's governance arrangement. The Strategic Framework document that was adopted by the Trustee Body sought to give clarity to the CWM's name, mission statement, organizational values and five faces of expressing its mission.[149] Out of this framework, it is expected that a CWM Strategic Plan will be emerge.

---

[149] The Strategic Framework Planning Group was chaired by Chris Nichol from the Presbyterian Church in New Zealand and the document was adopted by the Trustee Body Meeting in June 2009 in South India.

Refocus on Equipping Congregation and Theological Education

During the period 1989 to 2006, the CWM embarked on a fundamental policy shift in giving attention to an education in mission emphasis, to equip congregations in mission and theological formation for ministry and mission. This policy emerged from the churches' assessment of their priorities. This programme was abruptly discontinued after the Gift of Grace was received. The lure of money shifted attention from the fundamentals of the pedagogical imperative of moving congregations from maintenance to mission. Church leaders became more preoccupied with writing projects to get additional funds for maintenance of bureaucracy than the transformation of the churches for ministry and mission. Ministerial formation and theological education also became less of a priority. At the administration level of the CWM, the secretarial personnel with responsibility for Education in Mission was not replaced and a Secretary for Mission Programme was recruited to help Churches assess their priories and to write their mission programme before they could access funds from the CWM.[150]

The future of CWM's effectiveness requires that it return to these two fundamentals. If it exists for the missional empowerment of the churches then it must move beyond resourcing the headquarters of churches to the equipping of congregations in mission. Secondly, the deskilling of local congregations and their lack of numerical and spiritual growth is due in part to the quality of theological education that is serving the churches. Unless consistent attention is given to the theological education that is producing ineffective leadership within the churches, then they will forever be addicted to a maintenance culture.

The Next Phase of the Journey

The way ahead suggests that the CWM will need to reassess its staff appointment and job description to give attention to these two priorities. The CWM has depended on "Northern bias" ecumenical theology to shape its own theological emphasis. That is no longer sustainable. Its partnership in mission experiences over the past thirty years has given it some unique theological insights that require a disciplined approach in researching, recording and educating the member churches. Without this development, the CWM will be reactive rather

---

[150] Keum, *Partnership Support Programme Handbook*.

that proactive in missiological perspectives and practices. The plan that will emerge from the strategic framework must therefore give attention to these core areas of the CWM's life and work. Failure to do so will produce a CWM that lacks unique identity and praxis. Empowerment of the people of God in local communities constitutes the best action in building communities of hope.

Part Two

5

Constructing Postcolonial Mission in World Christianity[151]: Mission as Radical Affirmation to the World

Namsoon Kang[152]

> Mission is God's "yes" to the world.
>
> David Bosch

> Thought is no longer theoretical. As soon as it functions it offends or reconciles, attracts or repels, breaks, dissociates, unites or reunites; it cannot help but liberate and enslave. . . .thought, at the level of its existence, in its very dawning, is in itself an action—a perilous act.
>
> Michel Foucault[153]

---

[151] There are scholars who often use the term "world Christianity" to indicate Christianity in non-Western world such as Asian, Latin American, or African Christianity, whereas they use "Christianity" without "world" to denote Christianity in the West. I do not align myself with such a use of "world Christianity." My use of world Christianity here is to emphasize the worldly-interconnectedness of the Christian reality especially since the Western imperialization of the non-West. For a more detailed discussion about the new meaning and implication of "world Christianity," see Namsoon Kang, "*Whose/Which* World in *World Christianity*? Toward *World Christianity* as Christianity of *Worldly-Responsibility*, in *A New Day: Essays on World Christianity in Honor of Lamin Sanneh*, ed. Akintunde E. Akinade (New York: Peter Lang Publishing, 2010).

[152] Associate Professor of World Christianity and Religions, Brite Divinity School, Texas Christian University, USA.

Revisiting Mission and its Colonial Residue

In the twenty-first century, defining Christian mission is extremely complex as the Christian churches, institutions, and organizations have overloaded and misused the term "mission." The popular perception of mission that people in the church may have is a *foreign* enterprise. The mission trip is typically an exemplary program, which many churches in the developed countries often sponsor over the summer vacation. The typical mission trip would mean "sending" Christians to the *foreign* countries to "help" and "spread" the Gospel to the *heathen* people in the underdeveloped countries. Through the popular perception of mission in the mission trip, the binary of "sending and receiving" becomes a norm in the formulation of mission discourse in most churches. One of the most popular biblical texts that these churches use for this "mission" trip is in Matthew: "Go therefore and make disciples of all the nations. Baptize them in the name of Abba God, and of the Only Begotten, and of the Holy Spirit."[154] Christians have misinterpreted and misused this text to promote a "Crusade mentality" that resembles the colonial mentality of expansionism and triumphalism, suppressing religions other than Christianity. Unfortunately, one cannot deny that the Crusade mentality, which aggressively condemns and demonizes religious neighbors, is still actively present in the understanding of mission in the life of the church. In this context, "Christian mission has no role to play in a religiously plural society" and "the term mission is, in this sense, equated with religious propaganda, with proselytism, with an assault perception of truth, with intolerance towards people of other faiths, atheists or agnostics."[155]

Furthermore, since the sixteenth century, one cannot think of the history of Christian mission in the context of world Christianity without connecting it to Western imperialism through the global design of colonization of the "non-Western" world. Civilizing the "non-Western" world under the modern European model is a formal rationale for the

---

[153] Michel Foucault, *Language, Counter-Memory, Practice: Selected Essays and Interviews* (Ithaca, NY: Cornell University Press, 1980), 5.

[154] Matthew 28:19. *The Inclusive New Testament* (Brentwood, Maryland: Priests for Equality, 1996).

[155] Christine Lienemann, "Impact of Religious Plurality on my Life, my Work and Thinking," *Current Dialogue* 34, no. 2 (1999):16.

European colonization of the "non-western" world, and the Christian missional project coincides with this Western colonialism. Starting with sixteenth century Europe, the religious project of the Christian mission as Christianizing the non-Christian *heathens* and the secular project of civilizing the "primitive" non-Western world had one thing in common in their epistemological ground: expansionism with Westcentric superiorism. The origin of the word "mission," in fact, "presupposes the ambience of the west's colonization of overseas territories and its subjugation of their inhabitants."[156] The sense of Western superiorism was evident in how missionaries treated the "indigenous" culture and language. For instance, Spanish missionaries used the "possession of alphabetic writing" as a barometer to determine the rank of "human intelligence and civilization."[157] The absolutization of the alphabetic writing by the Christian missionaries in the sixteenth century can be an exemplary case for "subalternization of knowledge" of the non-western world. Through this absolutization of the alphabetic writing and its culture, the "indigenous" culture and knowledge automatically became *inferiorized* to the Western knowledge and *ethnicized* as static, backward, and primitive. Western missionaries hardly doubted the "validity and legitimacy" of colonialism. The following remarks written by John Philip in 1828, a superintendent of the London Missionary Society [hereafter LMS] at the Cape of Good Hope, can be an exemplary case for the consciousness of missionaries about colonialism and their perception of the colonized as "savage":

> While our missionaries . . . are everywhere scattering the seeds of civilization, social order, happiness, they are, by the most unexceptionable means, extending British interests, British influence, and the British empire. Wherever the missionary places his standard among a *savage tribe*, their prejudices against the colonial government give way.[158]

---

[156] Bosch, *Transforming Mission*, 303.
[157] Walter Mignolo, *Local Histories/Global Designs: Coloniality, Subaltern Knowledge and Border Thinking* (Princeton: Princeton University Press, 2000), 3.
[158] Cited in Bosch, *Transforming Mission*, 305. Italics mine.

Considering this colonial mind set of the missionaries, it is not surprising to learn the nature of the statement made by a Catholic missiologist in 1913:

> It is the mission that subdues our colonies spiritually and assimilates them inwardly . . . it is. . . the mission which must assist in securing the deeper aim of colonial policy, the inner colonization. The state can enforce physical obedience with the aid of punishment and laws; but it is the mission which secures the inward servility and devotion of the natives. We may therefore turn Dr Solf's [German Colonial Secretary]. . . recent statement that "to colonize is to missionize" into "to missionize is to colonize." [159]

It is, however, significant to acknowledge that there are "missionaries who accept" and "missionaries who refuse" the Western colonialism, just as Albert Memmi makes an important distinction between "the colonizer who accepts" and "the colonizer who refuses."[160] It is not difficult to imagine that even those missionaries from the West who refuse colonialism must have lived and worked in painful ambiguity in a time of Western colonialism. In this sense, it is important to note that the missionaries and their works in various regions of the world were never unitary but extremely varied and that one should not simplify the assessment of missionary-colonial interaction.[161] There are two extremely polarized views about the missionary work in relation to colonialism: extremely negative and uncritically positive. Although these extreme assessments reveal a part of what has happened and thereby may have its own "truth-claim," the reality in which the missionaries worked was far more than simple and monolithic. The missionaries, who differ from one another in personality, educational background, theological orientation, or vocational zeal, were not a unitary, homogenized entity

---

[159] Cited in Bosch, *Transforming Mission*, 306.
[160] Cf. Albert Memmi, *The Colonizer and the Colonized* (1965;Boston: Beacon Press, 1967), 19-76.
[161] Brian Stanley offers a reassessment about the nature of the missionary-colonial interaction in a more complex way. Cf. Brian Stanley, *The Bible and the Flag: Protestant Mission and the British Imperialism in the Nineteenth and Twentieth Centuries* (Leicester, UK: Apollos, 1990).

and they reacted to colonialism in diverse ways. They could have "supported imperialism" through the mission schooling, for instance, that made the colonized people "turn their backs on their own past and their own peoples," and at the same time, they may have supported "the efforts of ordinary people to arrive at a free and just society in the face of Colonialism."[162] Enrique Dussel maintains that the Spanish colonization of Latin America was to create a colonial Christendom, and goes on to argue that "the Church itself identified its life with that of Spanish civilization and its culture."[163]

Despite the complexity and multiplicity of the nature of missionary works especially in their relation to colonialism, the identification of Christianity with Western civilization seems a general attitude that spread through the colonial period. There is also a paradoxical interrelation among the missionaries, the colonial administrations, and the colonized people in the sense that the missionaries and the sending churches often had to sanction the colonial regime in order to work because "the state supplied the ships and financed the ventures."[164] Moreover the control by the colonial regimes "extended from the most basic issues of building the first churches to such matters as paying the clergy, nominating bishops, approving documents, selecting sites for convents and to almost all areas of Church concern."[165] There were, however, missionaries who harshly criticized the colonial policies through the "local" and international media and provided the colonized people with a significant source of resistance to the colonial administration by supporting the resistance groups with medical goods and humanitarian aid, risking the danger of the expulsion, detention, and murder.[166] In this regard, the interaction between the missionaries and the colonial regimes was significantly varied.

---

[162] Clayton G. Mackenzie, "Demythologizing the Missionaries: A Reassessment of the Functions and Relationships of Christian Missionary Education under Colonialism," *Comparative Education* 29, no. 1 (1993): 46.
[163] Enrique Dussel, *History and the Theology of Liberation: A Latin American Perspective* (New York: Orbis Books, 1976), 84.
[164] Thomas C. Bruneau, *The Political Transformation of the Brazilian Catholic Church* (Cambridge: Cambridge University Press, 1974), 13.
[165] Bruneau, *Political Transformation of the Brazilian Catholic Church*, 13.
[166] Mackenzie, "Demythologizing the Missionaries," 50.

It seems, therefore, theologically and politically correct when Des van der Water, the general secretary of the Council for World Mission [hereafter CWM], intentionally chooses the word "sharing" over the word "spreading" the Gospel and differentiates its identity from the LMS in terms of its colonial practice through the missionary movement during the colonial era. Van der Water contends:

> The LMS founding principle, namely "to spread the knowledge of Christ throughout the world" is what we today characterize as a mission statement. In other words, this founding principle also contains the LMS reason for being, or its essential purpose. . . . This LMS foundational principle remains intact and has continued to be the fundamental reason for being also with the formation of the CWM. It is evident however that the language and symbolism of the LMS mission statement. . . is reflective of the colonial period's imperialist and expansionist ideology. [167]

Claiming one's identity, whether individual or collective, in an absolute and fixed manner is dangerous because it does not allow one to grow, evolve, multiply, or transform. Van der Water, as the general secretary of CWM, posits that the CWM's "identity does not necessarily fall into a tidy definition or fit a neat and compact category" but does carry "a multi-faceted and mosaic identity."[168] The "multi-faceted and mosaic identity" of an ecumenical and worldy missional body such as the CWM opens up a space of contestation, persuasion, self-criticism, and transformation of Christian understanding of "world mission," transforming its missional task from the *mission-as-it-is* to *mission-as-it-ought-to-be*. Ashis Nandy contends that the carriers of what Nandy calls "the second wave of colonialism," such as Christian, humanitarian, social and medical mission, "were people who, unlike the rapacious first generation of bandit-kings who conquered the colonies, sought to be helpful." Those carriers of the second wave of colonialism were "well-meaning, hard-working, middle-class missionaries, liberals, modernists, and believers in science, equality and progress," but they "released forces

---

[167] Des van der Water, *From Ayr to Ocho Rios—CWM's Mission Journey from 2003-2006*, (CWM, 2006), 20.
[168] Van der Water, *From Ayr to Rios*, 20.

within the colonized societies to alter their cultural priorities once and for all."[169] It is hard to deny that the Christian missionaries in world Christianity were and still mostly are playing the role of well-meaning "carriers of the second wave of colonialism" and they look like what Albert Memmi describes:

> We sometimes enjoy picturing the colonizer as a tall man, bronzed by the sun, wearing Wellington boots, proudly leaning on a shovel—as he rivets his gaze far away on the horizon of his land. When not engaged in battles against nature, we think of him laboring selflessly for mankind [sic], attending the sick, and spreading culture to the nonliterate. In other words, his pose is one of a noble adventurer, a righteous pioneer.[170]

The reason we still concern ourselves about "colonialism" and its residue in mission when the era of colonialism seems over is that the colonial mentality resides in the very act of well-meaning mission, charity, or philanthropy. Even though the modern form of colonialism, which required a territorial occupation by the colonizer, mostly ended since the Second World War, a new form of colonialism, a "neo-colonialism," has emerged and permeated every sector of people's life in the world, without having to invade the physical territory of the colony. In this sense, the neo-colonialism people experience today is formless, forceless, and thereby invisible. The residue of colonialism is strongly influential on the construction of discourses and praxes, education, language, culture, geopolitics and economy, and so forth. The colonial mentality and its practice are still present in the mission discourse and practice in the life of Christian churches. In this regard, it is extremely timely and urgent to deal with the issue of "postcolonial mission" in the context of world Christianity. As long as people try to *patronize*, *dominate*, and *control* others, whether based on gender, race and ethnicity, sexuality, religion, nationality and citizenship, age, or social class, the colonial mentality permeates and operates in the very act of mission. Therefore, I adopt the notion of *colonial mentality* in a critically broad way in terms of its application and connotation in the life of

---

[169] Ashis Nandy, *The Intimate Enemy: Loss and Recovery of Self under Colonialism* (Delhi: Oxford University Press, 1988), x-xi.
[170] Memmi, *Colonizer and the Colonized*, 3.

Christianity, as it involves not only a socio-geo-political realm but also an interpersonal, institutional, or theological realm of discourse and practice.

It is my conscious intention to use the term "indigenous," and other words such as "non-west," "native," or "local," in quotation marks because the presupposed meaning and connotation of the very term is fundamentally problematic, which implies the Westcentric colonialist view of the world. Using the term "indigenous" or "local" for the "non-western" world and culture perpetuates the Westcentric view by making the West still the normative and *universal* and the "non-West" the deviant and *particular*. In the very naming of the "non-Western" countries "indigenous," "native," or "local," the colonial mentality implicitly resides. The very naming of the other is the heart of the colonial construction of the image of *the other*, and a "Western style for dominating, restructuring, and having authority"[171] over *the other*. Theologians and practitioners, both from the West and the "non-West," have been uncritically using these terms. In the context of colonization, the colonizer portrays what the colonizer is Not. Through the very act of naming, the construction of *the colonized other* becomes materialized. I am adopting the analysis of the colonized and the colonizer in the context of Christian missionary movement that came along with the Western colonization of the "non-Western" world.

According to Albert Memmi, the colonizer always perceives the colonized as "Not," as lacking the qualities the colonizer possesses.[172] In this sense, the word the "non-West" is an exemplar for how "the West" becomes placed discursively and politically at the center and the "non-West" on the periphery, perceived as "Not." One can apply the dichotomous distinction of "A and Not-A" to various socio-political relations of gender, race, religion, or sexuality, and "all dichotomous distinctions are not necessarily phrased as A/Not-A." [173] The problem in this dichotomous distinction between "the West (A) and the non-West (Not-A)" is that it portrays the "non-West" the "lesser West." If I apply the A and Not-A distinction as "Asia and non-Asia" to denote the entire world as in the "West and the non-West," the political implication of

---

[171] Edward Said, *Orientalism* (New York: Vantage Books, 1979), 3.
[172] Memmi, *Colonizer and the Colonized*, 83.
[173] Nancy Jay, "Gender and Dichotomy," *Feminist Studies* 7, no. 1 (Spring 1981): 44

power differential between A and Not-A does not have the same effect with the latter. In mission discourse and practice, such dichotomous distinction as "Christians and non-Christians" precisely captures the implication of the dichotomous distinction of A and Not-A. It makes "non-Christians" as those who are lacking some valued qualities that "Christians" have and therefore they become "lesser Christians." The very naming of the religious neighbors as "non-Christians" perpetuates Christian-centric worldview and it resembles colonial mentality of superiorism over the colonized other. Constructing a postcolonial mission in the contemporary world requires a fundamental change in the language that the Christian mission discourse has uncritically adopted and used. The "non-Christians" are simply the "religious neighbors" in the faith journey. Therefore, it is extremely important to critically and constantly create the alternatives to the colonial way of naming and constructing the "other."

In the eyes of the Christian missionaries, the religious and cultural "others" in the "non-Western" countries are an anonymous collectivity, carrying "the mark of the plural."[174] In this context, Jean-Paul Sartre states, "the European has only been able to become a man [sic] through creating slaves and monsters," who belong to a "race of less-than-humans."[175] Revisiting the history of Christian practice of mission requires scrutinizing the colonial mentality and practice because the initial Christian missionary movement in world Christianity cannot separate itself from compliance with the European colonialism and its mindset. In this context, how Christian churches in the global North would respond to the following remarks by Franz Fanon is not only a political but also theological and missional matter: "The well-being and the progress of Europe have been built up with the sweat and the dead bodies of Negroes, Arabs, Indians, and the yellow races. . . . Europe is literally the creation of the Third World. The wealth which smothers her is that which was stolen from the underdeveloped peoples."[176]

A new construction of Christian mission as theological discourse and practice needs what Cornel West calls a "prophetic criticism," which unveils, negates, and problematizes "the complex dynamics of

---

[174] Memmi, *Colonizer and the Colonized*, 85.
[175] Jean-Paul Sartre, Preface to *The Wretched of the Earth,* by Frantz Fanon (New York: Grove Weidenfeld, 1963), 26.
[176] Frantz Fanon, *The Wretched of the Earth*, 96 & 102.

institutional and other related power structures in order to disclose options and alternatives for transformative praxis."[177] In constructing a "postcolonial mission" in the context of world Christianity, postcolonialism seeks to "dislocate" the existing mission discourse and practice in order to raise theological questions regarding how dominant mission discourses and practice "have themselves been implicated in the long history of European colonialism."[178] As a dominant religion in the world with the past of colonizing force, Christianity must engage in *unlearning* its own privilege and power so that its mission becomes an instrument for promoting the equality and liberation of the individual humans in the every region of the world.

Colonial Mentality and Postcolonial Criticism in Christianity and its Mission

The term "postcolonialism," like other post-discourses such as postmodernism and poststructuralism is extremely difficult to define due to the complexity and wide-ranging use of the notion itself. Some people, especially political scientists and economists, use the term with a hyphen—post-colonialism--, to refer to the period "after" colonialism. Others, since the late 1970s, have adopted unhyphenated "postcolonialism" for a more wide-ranging way.[179] I use "postcolonialism" without the hyphen because I do not heavily rely on a "chronological" implication of colonialism, but do adopt it as a critical discourse of resistance and liberation in various realms of reality. "Postcolonialism," without a hyphen, seems to gain more popularity in various fields nowadays. As one can see in the very way the term is written, scholars have used postcolonialism in various ways. One of the common misunderstandings of postcolonialism is the prefix "post" in postcolonialism. Simply speaking, the "post" in postcolonialism denotes neither "after"-colonialism nor "beyond"-colonialism. In this sense,

---

[177] Cornel West, "The New Cultural Politics of Difference," in *Out There: Marginalization and Contemporary Culture,* eds. Russell Ferguson, Martha Gever, Trinh T. Minh-ha, and Cornel West (New York and Cambridge: The New Museum of Contemporary Art and MIT Press, 1990), 31.

[178] Robert Young, *White Mythologies: Writing History and the West* (New York: Routledge, 1990), viii.

[179] Bill Ashcroft, Gareth Griffiths, and Helen Tiffin, eds. *Key Concepts in Post-colonial Studies*. London and New York: Routledge, 1998), 186-192.

Constructing Postcolonial Mission in World Christianity 115

postcolonialism is not to denote post-independence. The misunderstanding often arises when one assumes that the "post" in postmodernism and the "post" in postcolonialism are the same.

The *postcolonialism* that I adopt here is "the discourse of oppositionality which colonialism brings into being,"[180] and it functions as the discourse of critical resistance against and liberation from colonial confinement and oppression. There are two positions among the postcolonial scholars regarding the question as to whether postcolonialism should imply certain historicality, pertaining to a specific time and space or it entails transhistoricality.[181] For me, "colonialism" or "colonial mentality" is about various kinds of socio-political, economic, symbolic, or religious oppression, domination, power, and control, which does not necessarily pertain to a specific historical context. Although postcolonial discourses have been based primarily in the specific historical context of Western colonialism/imperialism, the postcolonialism that I employ, as a discursive analytical tool, entails the nature of transhistoricality that moves beyond specific historicality, without excluding it. One can say that postcolonialism as a concept is "like the concept of patriarchy in feminism"[182]—a universal concept although one's experience of patriarchy varies according to one's socio-cultural and historical location. Postcolonial discourse offers a critical analytical tool to dismantle the implicit or explicit colonial mentality and practice. Today scholars and practitioners in various disciplines adopt postcolonial discourse to deal with issues such as representation, identity, migration, oppression and resistance, difference, race, gender, place, and responses to the grand discourses of imperial West such as theology, philosophy, history, or linguistics, etc.[183] Postcolonial perspective offers one an analytical lens through which one can approach the issue of power, domination and subjugation, or marginalization and resistance in a

---

[180] Bill Ashcroft, Gareth Griffiths, and Helen Tiffin, eds. *The Post-Colonial Studies Reader* (London and New York: Routledge, 1995), 117.
[181] One can see these two different positions of the postcolonial scholars in the collection of essays on postcolonialism such as *The Post-Colonial Studies Reader*.
[182] Stephen Slemon, "The Scramble for Post-colonialism," in *Post-Colonial Studies Reader*, 50.
[183] Cf. Ashcroft, Griffiths, and Tiffin, *Post-Colonial Studies Reader*, 1-11.

critically sophisticated way, which is extremely significant in creating an alternative world of justice, equality, and peace of all living beings.

Some social groups, based on gender, race, ethnicity, nationality, and so forth, have argued that they are "marginalized." When we say "marginal" however, we must always ask, marginal to what? But this *what-question* is difficult to answer. The place from which the human exercises power is often a hidden place. When we try to pin it down, the center always seems to be somewhere else. Especially when the power is hidden under the canopy of the "Divine," it is very hard to pinpoint where the center is and how one is socio-politically marginalized and psychologically, theologically, and institutionally colonized. In this regard, it is not surprising that the majority of women in the church, for instance, hardly think that they are "marginalized" and excluded from the center because the center is so hidden, invisible and unnoticeable, especially in the contemporary world, where the externally visible mechanism of sexism seems completely abolished. Generally speaking, "colonial mentality" is about power and ruling, and thereby about domination and subjugation. The colonial mentality has been firmly grounded on the *logic of power and domination*, and often accompanied in the fundamentalist notion of "mission." In this fundamentalist notion of mission, people understand Christianity in an extremely exclusive way as "the only true" religion in the world and portray God as the mirror image of Emperor of the world. I would argue that how one perceives God provides a ground for how one understands Christian mission, and that the Christian construction of the image of God as Father, Lord, or King, for instance, carries the colonial image of the Emperor with an untouchable absolute authority. For those who keep their perception of God in an exclusive, militant, hierarchical way, Christian mission would always mean dominating and colonizing the religious or cultural others and the "heathen in foreign land." According to the exclusive perception of God, it is inevitable that Jesus Christ is the King/Emperor of the world because he is the very incarnation of God.

Human beings have expressed their ultimate concern "symbolically." Since humans are finite, they can express their ideas about the infinite being only through "symbolic" language, not through "factual" language.[184] Therefore, the religious symbols provide a "model of" and a "model for" human reality. According to Clifford Geertz, religious symbols give meaning to existence by providing a "model of the reality-as-it-is" and a "model for the reality-as-it-ought-to-be." Geertz relates the symbol most closely to what it signifies, and he observes that the symbol system is the framework for all.[185] In this sense, religious symbols can function in both ways: as reflector of the existing reality and as producer of the new reality. One can ask what kind of reality the Christian symbols for God, such as Father, King, or Lord, could offer. Following this analysis of religious symbols and their relation to the construction of human reality, it is obvious that the symbols for Christian God as Father, King, or Lord, constructs and naturalizes patriarchal, imperial, and hierarchical reality, respectively. Moreover, the Christian notion of God as such constructs a Christian conceptual framework that influences the construction of "mission" in reality. Even when Christians adopt the notion of "missio Dei" in their notion of mission, the way they discern what kind of mission God would want us to participate in depends on the perception of God that they have. Although Christians have claimed that God is beyond human attributes such as gender, race, sexuality, or age and beyond human comprehension, it is hard to deny that people shape and mediate the symbol for God by the values inherent in a social matrix, in which the values of patriarchy, hierarchy, or colonial mentality prevail. As Tillich posits, "God is a symbol for God."[186] However, Christian theologians and practitioners tend to confuse "symbol" with "fact," and use the masculine symbol for God as a divine ground for men's superiority over women. After analyzing the 328 hymns, Brian Wren concludes:

> If male and female humans were really believed to be created as an equal partnership in the divine image, one would expect to find both feminine and masculine pronouns chosen for divine action. This is not so. In the 177 texts carrying pronouns, there are 1,423 pronouns

---

[184] Paul Tillich, *Dynamics of Faith* (New York: Harper & Brothers Publishers, 1957), 41.
[185] Cf. Clifford Geertz, "Religion as a Cultural System," in *Anthropological Approaches to the Study of Religion*, ed. Michael Banton (New York: Travistock Publications, 1966), 1-46, 97.
[186] Tillich, *Dynamics of Faith,* 46.

for the divine. One is neuter, none are feminine, and 1,422 are masculine. . . . We know that human languages (like our own) draw on the experience of their speakers and blow powerful uprights or downrights on thought and behavior. The fact that the genderless Trinity is prayed to and depicted in exclusively male images and pronouns must give humans a hooded or one-eyed vision of God.[187]

The literal and factual association of God with maleness has been prevailing in Christian tradition and churches and it has given a distorted perception of God as male. Furthermore, the problem of the notion of God is not only with the "gender of God," but also with the "race of God." In the history of Christianity, people have conceived God not only as male, but also as white. In her well-known novel *The Color Purple*, Alice Walker, a womanist writer, illustrates how a black woman perceives God as male, white, and old, even when she has suffered for her entire life from the oppression of white and males:

> Tell me what God look like, Celie.
> Aw naw, I say. I'm too shame. Nobody ever ast me this before, so I'm sort of took by surprise. Besides, when I think about it, it don't seem quite right. But it all I got. I decide to stick up for him, just to see what Shug say.
> Okay, I say. *He* big and *old* and tall and graybeard and *white*.
> *He* wear white robes and go barefooted.
> Blu eyes? She ast.
> Soft of bluish-gray. Cool. Big though. White lashes, I say.
> She laugh. . . .
> Then she tell me this *old white man* is the same God in church, Celie, she say, that's who is bound to show up, cause that's where *he* live. . . .

---

[187] Brian Wren, *What Language Shall I Borrow?: God-Talk in Worship: A Male Response to Feminist Theology* (New York: Crossroad, 1991), 118.

> When I found out I thought God was white, and a man, I lost interest. [188]

The exchange of "God-talk" between two black women reveals the fact that the perception of God that many people usually have is not a divinely given, but has been shaped in the image of those who have "power" to produce knowledge about God, reflecting the socio-cultural milieu and value systems in which they are located and positioned. The perception of God as male, white, and King is too easily compatible with sexism, racism, and imperialism, which has formed a conceptual framework of "mission" with colonial mentality of various types. Leo Perdue contends that "missionary religion has legitimated the exploitation and dehumanization of colonialism and imperialism, i.e. through the portrayal of an all-knowing, all-seeing, bearded, white, male deity 'from far'" and some churches "have largely ignored social issues in order to proclaim a white, male, supremacist deity who offers eternal life in the next world." [189] In the history and documents of CWM, the issue of gender exclusive language has not been on the surface, and all the documents have used masculine symbols and pronouns without any critical awareness. In the Theological Statement in 1991 by CWM, for instance, it says: "the Council embarked on an Education In Mission programme which is intended to. . . . discuss anew the ways in which God is at work in the world which *he* loves and how *he* invites *his* people to be partners with *him*."[190] The 2006 CWM Assembly Statement states its commitment to "addressing issues of masculinity and male concern," [191] which stimulates in the construction of mission discourse and practice in world Christianity. However the CWM needs to further elaborate what the "issues of masculinity and male concern" are, *whose* interests and *what* ends they would serve, and what theological and missional implications the CWM's commitment to the "issues of masculinity and

---

[188] Alice Walker, *The Color Purple* (1982; London: The Women's Press, 1983), 165-66. Italics mine.
[189] Leo G. Perdue, *Reconstructing Old Testament Theology: After the Collapse of History* (Minneapolis: Fortress Press, 2005), 280 & 281.
[190] CWM, "Theological Statement," in *Missiological and Theological Statements and Position Papers: 1975-2006*, unpublished manuscript. Italics mine.
[191] CWM, "CWM Assembly Statement," in *Missiological and Theological Statements and Position Papers: 1975-2006*.

male concern" would offer in the lives of Christian churches and theological institutions in the world.

As long as Christian understanding of mission is grounded in this notion of God as the male and the omnipotent King of the world, the colonial mentality resides in the very act of "mission," whether it takes the form of proselytization, evangelization, education, liberation, and so forth. If one portrays God in an anthropomorphic way, i.e. the gender of God as male or the race of God as white, then one has to come up with the answer to the question: What would be then the sexuality of God, heterosexual or homosexual? Needless to say, the anthropomorphic construction of the "knowledge" of God has been closely linked to the "power," and "power" and "knowledge" are two indivisible foundations of colonial mentality. Constructing discourses that justify and perpetuate the superiorism and expansionism of the colonizer and disseminating the colonizer's religion, culture, language, literature, education, or customs is the foundation of maintaining the colonial power. As Michel Foucault rightly points out, the center of power and knowledge overlaps, and "truth isn't outside power or lacking power."[192] When the mission resides in the colonial mentality of domination and control on various grounds, mission establishes its authority through the differentiation of identity and difference, and Christian churches and members insist on their religious difference from the "non-Christians" as a way of legitimizing their own superior position and identity in society. When the dominant "knowledge" about God takes a form of superiority of one group over the other, whether it is based on gender, culture, race, sexuality, or religion, "power" as a dominating and controlling force emerges and operates in every aspect of Christian mission. The dominant doctrines and practice have silenced the voices of the powerless and the marginalized. The task of theologians and practitioners in mission is therefore "to listen to the voices of those who are silent and silenced" in the Bible, in the church, and in society, such as the poor, the uneducated, women, racial *others*, religious *others*, or sexual *others* (LGBT-lesbian, gay, bisexual, transgender) and "to take that experience, that life, that story, as a crucial

---

[192] Michel Foucault, *Power/Knowledge: Selected Interviews and Other Writings 1972-1977*, ed. Colin Gordon, trans. Colin Gordon, Leo Marshall, John Mepham and Kate Soper (1972; New York: Pantheon Books, 1980), 131.

source for reflection."[193] The initial step for constructing a postcolonial mission is to fundamentally rethink what it means to be simply human, to see others simply as human as everybody else, and to determine the powers, practices, and doctrines that prevent one from being simply human, no matter who one is, what one is, where one is, or how one is.

Constructing *Postcolonial* Mission in World Christianity as Discourse and Movement
Postcolonial Mission as Transformative Boundary-Crossing

We are living in a world in which the "power disparity" between and among people of different group still exists. Engaging in the context of "power disparity" for a transformative Christian mission, the "boundary-crossing" can be a significant metaphor for postcolonial mission and has so many different implications. To determine the nature of the boundary-crossing, therefore, one must raise such questions as: Who is crossing the boundaries?; What kind of boundaries?; What ends the boundary-crossing entails?; What consequences will the boundary-crossing bring? ; Whose interest does the boundary-crossing serve? Jacques Derrida rightly says:

> The absolute victim is a victim who cannot even protest.
> One cannot even identify the victim as victim.
> He or she is totally excluded or covered over by
> language, annihilated by history,
> a victim one cannot identify.[194]

In this sense, those who are able to cross the boundaries, whether the boundaries are physical, epistemological, geopolitical, political, cultural, religious, or metaphorical, are not, at least, the "absolute victim." Instead they have a power and responsibility to persuade others to cross the boundaries to act for justice in an unjust world. Here, Christian theologians and practitioners should explore the ways in which

---

[193] Steve de Gruchy, "Human Being in Christ: Resources for an Inclusive Anthropology," in *Aliens in the Household of God: Homosexuality and Christian Faith in South Africa*, eds. Paul Germond and Steve de Gruchy (Cape Town & Johannesburg, South Africa: David Philip, 1997), 235.

[194] Jacques Derrida, "Passages--from Traumatism to Promise," in *Points. . . Interviews, 1974-1994*, ed. Elisabeth Weber, trans. Peggy Kamuf et al. (Stanford, CA: Stanford University Press, 1995), 389.

they could actively produce, promote, and mobilize the passion for transformation and justice in the life of Christian churches and people within particular socio-geopolitical contexts, beyond the boundaries of gender, race and ethnicity, religion, citizenship, or sexuality. Moving beyond the various boundaries for transformation and justice is what I would call a "postcolonial mission of boundary-crossing." Those who have a history of being marginalized on the basis of their skin color, gender, class, sexuality, or any other axis of categorization are reading, writing, and theologizing in the interstices of dominant culture, moving between the language of the center and that of marginality. Similarly those who have an experience of crossing the borderline between the cultures, languages, and the various configurations of power and meaning in complex hegemonic situations possess, what I call, *boundary-crossing consciousness*, or *liminal consciousness*. This consciousness is a *consciousness of interstice* or *in-between consciousness*, and could give one the ability to see things from multiple perspectives, not from a monolithic perspective that sees things from a binary juxtaposition of superior-inferior, civilized-primitive, good-bad, reason-emotion, spirit-body, men-women, white-black, Christian-non-Christian, or the West-the Rest, and so forth.

Being and living the multiple boundaries and borders, and multiple interstices, one may have the potential to lock oneself away in isolation and hopelessness as well as the potential for critical consciousness and particular creativity in thinking, observing, and being engaged with the complex reality. Rather than being trapped in anger or pain from different forms of oppression, a person who develops this "boundary-crossing consciousness" in a creative way has the potentiality for resistance against hegemonization and homogenization of the marginalized and a possibility of forming solidarity with the racialized, ethnicized, genderized, sexualized, or religious *other*. In this sense, crossing the various borders can be a *dangerous* act because the moment one crosses the boundaries and borders, one begins to question the invisible assumption of the dominant power, and the questioning the invisible assumption and the fixed "boundaries" is the beginning of resistance for liberation.

The phrase "crossing boundaries" appears in the CWM discourse in 1995. The report of the "Partnership in Mission Consultation" held in Hoddesdon, UK, April 3-7, 1995, has the title "Perceiving Frontiers,

Crossing Boundaries." The meaning of "boundaries" in the report seems to indicate merely geographical boundaries, not in the sense of the "boundaries" with metaphorically complex connotations. In the use of the phrase "crossing boundaries," the report does not offer any self-critical assessment as to how the act of geographical boundary crossing by Europe to Caribbean, Africa, Asia and the Pacific results in the colonialization of those regions, and how Christian missionary zeal "to send the Glorious Gospel of the Blessed God" [195] legitimizes and supports the Eurocentric superiorism and expansionism in the name of mission. The meaning of "crossing-boundaries" in this CWM 1995 report is utterly simplistic: "Ships were built. Seas were crossed. . . . boundaries were crossed. The gospel was preached. Schools were founded. Hospitals were established. Many people received the gospel. . . . It depicts a great missionary movement . . . ." [196] However, it is significant to note that the consciousness of "crossing-boundaries" begins to appear in the CWM mission discourse despite its being uncritical and simplistic. For it opens up the possibility of enhancing, broadening, deepening, and sophisticating the meaning and implementation of the missional act of crossing various boundaries, not only geographically but also metaphorically, socio-geo-politically, and theologically.

Postcolonial mission today should be a discourse and practice of "boundary-crossing," through which people acknowledge and experience multiple locations and realities of the different parts of the world. The boundary-crossing as mission is not merely physical or geographical crossing, but engaged, committed crossing through which people are able to get geopolitically, socio-culturally, religiously engaged in the reality of different religions, contexts, identities of the world and people in it. In this sense, the boundary-crossing functions to promote solidarity, equality, justice, and peace between and among people of different gender, race and ethnicities, culture, ability, religion, or sexuality. In so doing, Christian postcolonial mission can be a movement and practice of geopolitical alliances across the globe, transcending boundaries between

---

[195] CWM, "Perceiving Frontiers, Crossing Boundaries," The Report of the Partnership in Mission Consultation of the Council for World Mission, High Leigh, Hoddesdon, UK, 3-7 April 1995, in *Missiological and Theological Statements and Position Papers 1975-2006*, unpublished manuscript.
[196] CWM, "Perceiving Frontiers, Crossing Boundaries."

different identities, nations, cultures, or religions: Participating in God's "yes" to the entire world and to humans. What is crucial in such a vision of the postcolonial mission is the belief that we must not merely change the discourse of the mission, but fundamentally transform our sense of what it means to be "Christians" in other times and different spaces, crossing various rigid boundaries that divide world and humans, classifying humans into certain stereotypes and marginalization, and negating the full humanity of others. In this sense, "doing" postcolonial mission would mean a "dangerous boundary-crossing" in order to understand and feel in what kind of life situation the marginalized and ostracized people are positioned due to their certain gender, race, age, ability, class, religion, or sexuality, and how mission, as an act of participating in God's "yes" to the world, can offer a vision for the better world to the church and society.

Postcolonial mission, as *radical boundary-crossing,* provides us with the vision we need to dismantle the colonial mentality and come up with a liberative mission that makes possible a *trans-boundary-solidarity* across different religions, genders, races, and regions in the world. If we carefully examine the way Jesus interacts with people of different races, religions, classes, and genders, it is not difficult to conclude that Jesus is a radical boundary-crosser, and that this *radical boundary-crossing* is in fact an act of radical neighborly and divine love. In this sense, Christians, whose primary religious identity is to identify with Jesus Christ, are called to play the role of "radical boundary-crossers," who envision an alternative reality through the visions of God's "yes" to the world. The postcolonial mission is grounded in a new notion of God and Jesus Christ. Perceiving Jesus as a "radical boundary-crosser," as one can see in Jesus' encounter with the Samaritan woman at the well in John 4: 3-30, where Jesus crosses the boundary of gender, religion, race, and class, for instance, offers a new meaning of a "Christocentric" view of mission. When "Christ" becomes "doctrinated" as the "exclusive" Redeemer who condemns people of other faiths than Christianity, the Christocentric view of mission grounded on the so-called "Great Commission of our Lord Jesus Christ" ends up fostering the colonial way of mission and completely distorts Jesus' life and teaching of endless love and compassion for the "neighbors" and God's love for and "yes" to the world. The de-doctrinization of Jesus Christ and the de-patriarchalization of God opens up a new horizon of the question, "Who is my Neighbor?" which CWM chooses as its 2003 Assembly theme. Needless to say, the category of "neighbor" is not as self-evident as it looks. In this sense, the question of "who is my neighbor" is a significant and timely invitation to fundamentally re-think and re-address the perception of neighbor in the light of justice for and equality of all beings.

The perception of neighbor was once based on an ethnicity in Jesus' time and Jesus breaks the traditional boundary of neighbor through his life and teaching, as we can see in such stories as the story of the Good Samaritan. Christianity has broadened the category of "neighbor," moving beyond the ethno-centric perception, but there are still certain groups of people whose "neighbor-ship" the churches have denied based on their sexuality, their race, their ability, their gender, or their religion. The mission of colonial mentality is grounded on the dualistic mode of thinking of "logic of domination." It produces and re-produces the mentality of superior-inferior, normal-abnormal, inclusion-exclusion, neighbor-stranger, orthodoxy-heterodoxy, redemption-condemnation, but it overlooks the greatest commission of *planetary-neighborly-love* as we can see in the Jesus' parable of the "Last Judgment" in Matthew:

> I was hungry and you gave me no food;
> I was thirsty and you gave me nothing to drink;
> I was a stranger and you gave me no welcome;
> Naked and you gave me no clothing.
> I was ill and in prison and you did not come to visit me.
> .... The truth is, as often as you neglected to do this to one of the least of these,
> You neglected to do it to me.[197]

Constructing postcolonial mission requires re-visiting and re-theologizing the function of "doctrines" of Christianity. Although Christian doctrines are important in the lives of Christian community, it is hard to deny that the "absolutization" of doctrines and their institutional practices have sanctioned Christian exclusion and condemnation of "others." However, we must remind ourselves of the simple truth that Jesus clearly indicates to us that the barometer of the

---

[197] Matthew 25:43 & 45. *The Inclusive New Testament* (Brentwood, Maryland: Priests for Equality, 1996).

"Last Judgment" for the redeemed or the condemned, and what differentiates the sheep from the goats is not according to whether one believes a certain set of doctrines, whether one has a membership to the Christian churches, which religion one belongs to, or which sexual orientation one has. Instead, the divine Last Judgment is based on how one relates oneself to others in need, how one takes one's responsibility for and solidarity with the others, or how one regards one's "neighbors" and practices neighborly love towards them. In this context, I would suggest that Jesus' parable of the "Last Judgment" in Matthew should be a signature "mission text" for constructing postcolonial mission, and that the traditional mission texts such as Matt 28: 16-20 and Acts 1: 8 need to be re-visited and re-theologized in the very light of the Last Judgment, not in the light of "religious doctrines." [198]

Postcolonial Mission as God's *Yes* to the World

The statement of "go and make disciples of all the nations," from Matthew 28: 18-20 has been a principal "mission text" from the end of the nineteenth century.[199] CWM re-confirms the well-known two biblical texts, Acts 1:8 and Matthew 28: 18-20, as its "mission texts" in the 2006 CWM Assembly Statement, whereas it chooses Acts 1:8 over Matthew 28:18-20 in the 1991 Assembly.[200] However, what matters most is *what function* the specific biblical text would play in one's perception about others. If people interpret these two bible texts in the same expansionist way, whatever text one chooses as a signature "mission text," it does not fundamentally make a shift in the formulation of mission discourse. The idea of "*missio Dei*" appears only in 1952 at the Willingen Conference of the IMC (International Missionary Council), and its concept has been modified since then.[201] Moving from an *ecclesiocentric* to a *theocentric* notion of mission may have contributed to de-centering the church as the sole generator of mission, but it has not fundamentally dismantled the Western hegemonic role in mission in the world Christianity. Christian churches in most parts of the world have

---

[198] Cf. CWM, *Missiological and Theological Statements and Position Papers: 1975-2006*.
[199] Bosch, *Transforming Mission*, 341.
[200] Cf. "Council for World Mission Handbook 1991" in *Missiological and Theological Statements and Position Papers: 1975-2006*.
[201] Cf. Bosch, *Transforming Mission*, 389-393.

maintained their understanding of mission as what David Bosch describes:

> [M]ission was understood in a variety of ways. Sometimes it was interpreted primarily in sotereological terms: as saving individuals from eternal damnation. Or it was understood in cultural terms: as introducing people from the East and South to the blessings and privileges of the Christian West. Often it was perceived in ecclesiastical categories: as the expansion of the church (or of a specific denomination). Sometimes it was defined salvation-historically: as the process by which the world—evolutionary or by means of a cataclysmic event—would be transformed into the kingdom of God.[202]

In this respect, it is extremely important to keep reminding ourselves that the church is not the *center* of the mission, but simply one of the many instruments for the mission of God. De-centering the location of the initiative of mission leads us to the following theological question: What is or would be the mission of God in the twenty-first century in our concrete reality? How does one know whether it is the mission of "God" or an arbitrary human construction of the mission? David Bosch articulates thirteen key elements of mission: Mission as the church-with-others, mission as *missio Dei*, mission as mediating salvation, mission as the quest for justice, mission as evangelism, mission as contextualization, mission as liberation, mission as inculturation, mission as common witness, mission as ministry by the whole people of God, mission as witness to people of other living faiths, mission as theology, and finally mission as action in hope.[203] Although each element of mission would require an in-depth contextualization and theological interpretation in order to fully comprehend the missional implication, Bosch's articulation indicates to us the profound nature of mission as theological discourse, movement, and practice, moving beyond the colonial mentality of domination and control of one over against the other. In the light of the key elements of mission by Bosch, it becomes clear that "to think of church as the prior category and mission

---

[202] Bosch, *Transforming Mission*, 389.
[203] Cf. Bosch, *Transforming Mission*.

as one among several functions of the church"[204] is not right because mission is itself what constitutes the church and its existence.

If mission is God's "yes" to the world, as Bosch so eloquently puts it, the trajectory of Christian mission needs to take a transformative form to wrestle with the issues that pertain to the radical affirmation of the world, where the issues of migration and refuge, human trafficking, poverty and war, and various form of hate crimes, deny God's "yes" to the world and people in it. Angelus Silesius, a German mystic and poet, interprets God as "I-am-yes," in his rephrasing God's encounter with Moses in Exodus 3:14. According to his interpretation, "Jahweh spricht nur immer 'Ja,'" ["Jahweh always says only 'yes'"]: "Jah"-weh means, I am (*jah*, Hebrew) "yes" (*Ja*, German).

> God said to Moses "I am *yes*.." ...
> Thus shall you say to the Israelites, "I am *yes* has sent me to you.
> The Impossible, the Incoming"" [205]

When we perceive God as "I-am-yes," the radical affirmation of the world, humans and nature, and Jesus as God's incarnation, we could not use the Christian theo-centric or Christocentric approach to others as an exclusivist notion of people of other faiths and religions, or of other sexuality than one's own. In this sense, it is important to remind ourselves that one of the key principles of the CWM as a "community of churches in mission" is "openness to others."[206] Here the CWM needs to further elaborate, in terms of its theology and practice, two concepts: "openness" and "others." Acknowledging the significant concepts in the CWM's vocabularies is extremely important, but at the same time, the question we must continue to wrestle with is: What constitutes "openness" and to whom among the "others" are we open? Religious others, sexualized others, genderized others, physically-challenged

---

[204] Wilbert R. Shenk, *Changing Frontiers of Mission* (Maryknoll, NY: Orbis Books, 1999), 7.
[205] Cited in John D. Caputo, *The Prayers and Tears of Jacques Derrida: Religion without Religion* (Bloomington: Indiana University Press, 1997), 26.
[206] Cf. Preman Niles, "The Mission Thinking and Partnership Journey of CWM. A Review," 1995, in *Missiological and Theological Statements and Position Papers: 1975-2006*. The other key principles of CWM are "mutuality or sharing in partnership" and the "ecumenical character."

others, or cultural others? Does "openness" mean just "having-tea-together" with others or granting them their full rights, personally and institutionally, and fully accepting them into our community of faith? How does one move, as an individual and a community of faith, "Beyond Ourselves," which the 1993 the CWM theme indicates?

We are called to commit ourselves to demystifying and indicting colonialism and its inhumane brutality. One of the current tasks of the postcolonial mission is to go through the history of colonialism and Christian complicity with the construction and maintenance of colonial mentality and its empire in the name of mission in order to denounce the colonial mentality and practice and to create anew a liberative discourse and practice of mission, by which I mean "postcolonial mission." Postcolonial mission is a discourse and practice of resistance to reject "all ideas of empire which subvert God's sovereignty over life and which act contrary to God's just rule,"[207] as the CWM reaffirmed in 2006. We are living in the world where injustice is so extensively widespread that it seems there is no way to live free of the chain of injustice around us. The passion for the "postcolonial mission" is grounded in the painful awareness of the reality of injustice and our complicity with it, wittingly and unwittingly. The need for the postcolonial mission is out of an awareness that

> My first cup of coffee each day represents a decision to accept the benefits of unjust labor practices in the so-called third world. . . . The cotton blouse that I wear is a constant reminder of the history of slavery in the United States that made cotton "king" and put cash in the pockets of white people at the expense of black people's lives. . . . My every breath is a compromise with injustice.[208]

The primary goal of the "postcolonial mission" in world Christianity is to join in the spirit and work of *missio dei* by scrutinizing Christian complicity with various forms of injustice through its colonial

---

[207] Cf. CWM, "Living out the Accra Confession," Joint Statement with WARC, Kuala Lumpur, Malaysia, May 2006, in *Missiological and Theological Statements and Position Papers: 1975-2006*, an unpublished manuscript.
[208] Karen Lebacqz, *Justice in an Unjust World: Foundations for a Christian Approach to Justice* (Minneapolis: Augsburg Publishing House, 1987), 10.

mentality. Moreover, it is also to create a community of resistance, justice, compassion, and solidarity in an unjust world, where there is a shocking disparity between Christian ideals of neighborly love and the tragedy of Christian complicity with various forms of injustice based on religion, gender, race and ethnicity, sexuality, nationality, citizenship, or ability, not only in the past but also in the present. The postcolonial mission is a radical affirmation that mission is not simply a Christianization of the world but *God's yes* to the world--*God's yes* to every individual human being, *God's yes* to the entire living beings in the world, regardless of who/what they are.

6

The Bible *In* and *For* Mission:
A Case Study of the Council for World Mission[209]

Sarojini Nadar[210]

In 2008, my uncle passed away. At his funeral, the pastor who happened to be from a South African Indian independent Charismatic church, preached at length about how important it was that the Hindus and Muslims who were present (a sizeable number of those present were Hindu) repent of their sins and accept Jesus as their personal Saviour or they will all indubitably go to hell. Then at the cemetery before the casket could be lowered, the pastor once more made an altar call for all those 'non-believers' who wished to be assured of a place in heaven to raise their hands, and by so doing indicate that they would accept Jesus and thereby have guaranteed eternal life. By the end of the funeral, the Hindus and Muslims who were present were offended beyond measure, and as a Christian, I almost felt responsible for the pastor's offensive remarks, so I decided to challenge him in a private conversation.

During this conversation he scolded my "lack of knowledge of what the bible says" and pointed me to the great commission in Matthew 28:18. But when I pointed him to Jesus' un-condemning, inclusive, embracing, and affirming ministry, particularly to those who were not Jewish, he emphatically responded: "I would rather kick people into heaven, than pat them into hell!" The pastor's understanding of the great commission in Matthew 28 was that people should be guided to heaven, no matter what this entails.

---

[209] This article was first published in *Missionalia* 37, no. 2 (2009): 210-228.
[210] Dr Sarojini Nadar is Senior Lecturer at the School of Religion and Theology at the University of KwaZulu-Natal, and Director of its Gender and Religion Programme. She can be contacted at nadars@ukzn.ac.za.

The three-fold concerns of the authority of the bible and the un-critical and un-contextual uses of the bible in mission, as the above example illustrates, raise important questions about the role of the bible in and for mission. This article aims to examine the role of the bible in mission through a case study of the ways in which a mission organisation, namely the Council for World Mission (CWM) uses the bible in and for mission. While the analysis will make reference to the work of CWM in terms of its historical background to its predecessor, the London Missionary Society, and other mission organisations as well, the focus of this article will be on the ways in which the bible has been appropriated in the CWM since the year of its inception in 1977, and when it celebrated three decades of existence in 2007. This period has been termed the period of conversion from colonial to postcolonial mission.[211]

In his reflection on the Council for World Mission's history of 30 years between 1977 and 2007, Duraisingh makes a point of noting that the "CWM from the very beginning, located its primary mandate in the Acts of the Apostles 1:8 and not in Matthew 28:18."[212] "The commission in Acts 1:8 is not to become busybodies in mission. The promise is that you cannot but be propelled into mission when the Spirit comes,"[213] he argues.

In the opening illustration, the pastor, like the CWM, derived his mandate or motivation for mission from the bible. However, as Niles notes in a review of the mission thinking and partnership journey of the

---

[211] For an excellent account of the manner in which this 'conversion' occurred and is ongoing, see D. Van der Water, "Council for World Mission: A Case Study and Critical Appraisal of the Journey of Partnership in Mission," *International Review of Mission* 97 (July–October 2008): 305–322.

[212] See Acts 1:8 (NRSV): "But you will receive power when the Holy Spirit has come upon you; and you will be my witnesses in Jerusalem, in all Judea and Samaria, and to the ends of the earth." See also Matthew 28:18–20 (NRSV): "And Jesus came and said to them, 'All authority in heaven and on earth has been given to me. Go therefore and make disciples of all nations, baptizing them in the name of the Father and of the Son and of the Holy Spirit, and teaching them to obey everything that I have commanded you. And remember, I am with you always, to the end of the age."

[213] C. Duraisingh, "From Everywhere to Everywhere," http://www.cwmission.org.uk/theological-papers/from-everywhere-to-everywhere (accessed 29 April 2009).

CWM, while the CWM increasingly views mission as an identity rather than an assignment, the pastor in the example views mission or witnessing as an assignment not as an identity.[214] How can the CWM and this pastor both derive their mission mandate from the same bible and yet derive such different principles concerning mission? Or are their principles truly different? What is the role of the bible *for* and *in* mission? Does the bible contain examples of what true mission is? These are some of the questions that this article seeks to address. These questions are answered in three ways:

- by surveying the biblical texts that the CWM has used as its raison d'être for mission;
- by probing the challenges that mission faces in the context of globalization and increasingly conservative uses of the bible for mission; and
- by examining possibilities of using the bible not just *for* mission, but *in* mission, through a case study of a Contextual Bible Study (CBS) on Mark 7:24–30.

Theoretical and Conceptual Positions

The above questions are engaged through a theoretical and conceptual framework of analysis. In terms of a theoretical analysis, the contours of postcolonial biblical criticism that Sugirtharajah, the doyen of postcolonial biblical scholarship, has outlined are used. Sugirtharajah states:

> The greatest single aim of postcolonial biblical criticism is to situate colonialism at the centre of [both] the bible and biblical interpretation …What postcolonial biblical criticism does is to focus on the whole issue of expansion, domination and imperialism as central forces

---

[214] Preman Niles in a review of the mission thinking and partnership journey of CWM refers to "being witnesses is not our assignment, it is our identity." G. Hunsberger, "Is There a Biblical Warrant for Evangelism? *Interpretation* XVLVIII, no. 2 (1994): 131–144.

in both the biblical narratives and in biblical interpretation.[215]

First, using Sugirtharajah's framework, both kinds of biblical narratives that are used for mission are probed, as well as the ways in which they have been interpreted. This framework is engaged particularly in the last part of the article, which deals with the text of the Syrophoenician woman in Mark and Matthew, as a text that can be used for mission.

Second, because it is far too tempting, in terms of a conceptual framework, to work within dualistic paradigms of analysis, particularly between the colonial and postcolonial, the continuum mission model proposed by Kritzinger is used to analyse some of the ways in which the bible has been used in Reformed mission.

Kritzinger's Typology of a Mission Continuum

Liberationist/Activist	Conversionist/Evangelistic
Gaining credibility for the gospel locally	'Saving the lost'
Worldwide communal structural emphasis	Individual emphasis
Conscientisation regarding injustice	Fostering a 'burden for the lost'
Empowerment for transformation	Boldness to call others to conversion
Prophetic confrontation	Evangelistic confrontation
This-worldly	Other-worldly

Kritzinger explains the choice of the above continuum thus:

> By constructing a continuum I avoid the language of polarisation between 'ecumenical' and 'evangelical' tendencies that David Bosch used some years ago. I am not describing 'warring factions on the ground.' This continuum is a construct, attempting to open up space

---

[215] R.S. Sugirtharajah, *The Postcolonial Biblical Reader* (Oxford: Blackwell, 2006), 17.

within which the wide variety of Protestant missions may fruitfully be described.[216]

Kritzinger's continuum model of Protestant mission is certainly helpful for describing and analysing the cosmopolitan, globalized Christianity within which the world operates at the moment, particularly "when a shift in the world church's centre of gravity from Western Europe to parts of Africa, Latin America and parts of Asia and the Pacific"[217] can be seen.

Within this cosmopolitan, globalised Christianity at least three important factors concerning the role of the bible in mission can be detected. These are clearly reflected in the pastor's views on his missionary 'mandate' to Hindus and Muslims in my opening paragraph:

- the authority of the bible in Protestant mission;
- the uncritical use of the bible in mission; and
- the un-contextual use of the bible.

Authority of the Bible in Protestant Mission

Escobar argues that the "first principle of Protestant mission was that they [the subjects of mission] should have the bible in their own hands in their own language at the earliest possible date."[218] Having the bible in one's own hands, rather than having it interpreted, was the one defining characteristic of Protestant mission compared to Catholic mission. As Lenchak notes, "The Roman Catholic Church is not particularly known for its use of the bible in mission and ministry. It has a reputation for discouraging – even forbidding – the reading of Sacred Scripture. In the post-Reformation period the church's missionary strategy laid no particular stress on translating, publishing and distributing the sacred text."[219] Similarly, Kritzinger argues that "The

---

[216] J.N.J. Kritzinger, "The Function of the Bible in Protestant Mission," in *Scripture, Community and Mission: Essays in Honor of D. Preman Niles*, ed. P.L. Wickeri (Hong Kong: The Christian Conference of Asia and the Council for World Mission, 2002), 19.

[217] Van der Water, "Council for World Mission," 306.

[218] S. Escobar, *The New Global Mission the Gospel From Everywhere to Everyone* (Illinois: IVP Academic, 2003), 130.

[219] T. Lenchak, "The Function of the Bible in Roman Catholic Mission," in *Scripture, Community and Mission: Essays in Honor of D. Preman Niles*, ed.

centrality of the *Sola Scriptura* adage in the Protestant movement has made the bible a key feature of Protestant mission."[220] The *Sola Scriptura* adage to which Kritzinger refers has seen the bible assume an authoritative status in the practice of Reformed mission, far beyond what the reformers would have intended.

Uncritical Use of the Bible in Mission

Moreover, having the bible in one's own hands did not come without a price. It often meant that the bible was in the hands of people with little or no theological education, contributing to rather exclusive and often dehumanising tendencies in mission. As Bonino notes of the case in Latin America during the late nineteenth and early twentieth centuries: "Lay preachers many times without theological or even secular education became powerful evangelists resting their authority solely on the bible."[221] This was certainly the case with the pastor in the above example, who very proudly indicated to me that he was not in possession of any formal theological qualification but that he did possess a more important qualification – a BA (Born Again!).[222]

Un-contextual Use of the Bible

Not only did the pastor's way of reading the bible take little cognisance of critical interpretation, it also ignored the contextual nature of interpretation, thereby engaging in what postcolonial critics have termed a *mimicry* of the Western missionary tendency to demonise local culture and to read the bible through Western cultural lenses. While the concept of *mimicry* conveys the meaning of a direct imitation of another, it is defined by the postcolonial theorist Bhabha as "a subject of difference that is almost the same, but not quite."[223] This 'not quite' in

---

P.L. Wickeri (Hong Kong: The Christian Conference of Asia and the Council for World Mission, 2002), 1.

[220] Kritzinger, "The Function of the Bible," 18.

[221] J.M. Bonino, "Main Currents of Protestantism," in *Integration of Man and Society in Latin America*, ed. S. Shapiro (Notre Dame: Notre Dame University Press, 1967), 193.

[222] This is not to deny that even people with theological education hold uncritical views of the bible and its authority. However, an anti-intellectual stance regarding the bible has been proven to fuel fundamentalism (see M. McClintock Fulkerson, *Changing the Subject: Women's Discourses and Feminist Theology* (Minneapolis: Fortress Press, 1994), 280.

[223] H.K. Bhabha, "Of Mimicry and Man: The Ambivalence of Colonial Discourse," in *Tensions of Empire: Colonial Cultures in a Bourgeois World*,

the subject under current discussion refers not so much to difference, but to a 'pushing of the envelope.' In other words, the over-zealous appropriation of the missionary ways of reading the bible, present in the pastor's sermon above, goes beyond even the missionary endeavour to condemn and convert 'the heathen.' The attachment to a reading of the bible through cultural forms that are not one's own had caused this pastor of Indian descent to identify more with the ways in which the missionaries viewed Hinduism and Islam, than the ways in which Indians view themselves.

In this respect, Escobar notes:

> Though the bible was given to thousands of new communities, tribes and nations in the mission fields, the way of reading the bible communicated by the missionaries was heavily conditioned by their own culture. This retarded the possibility of gaining new insights from people of different cultures reading the bible with their own eyes. Even worse, it retarded the possibility of the new churches developing a proclamation of the gospel and pastoral practices geared to their own culture and community.[224]

It would be a helpful exercise to evaluate the way in which CWM shares or distances itself from endowing the bible with sole authority for missional practice, and further the way in which critical and contextual methods of interpretation of the bible are employed in the work of CWM.

Survey of Biblical Foundations for the Work of CWM

The 1984 *Handbook of the Council for World Mission*[225] contains the bold and emphatic statement "that the source of CWM's understanding of mission is contained in the Bible." In 1977, this mandate was derived from Matthew 28:18–20:

---

eds. F. Cooper and A.L. Stoler (Berkeley: University of California Press, 1997), 153.
[224] Escobar, *The New Global Mission*, 134.
[225] *Handbook of the Council for World Mission*, London: CWM, 1994.

And Jesus came and said to them, 'All authority in heaven and on earth has been given to me. Go therefore and make disciples of all nations, baptizing them in the name of the Father and of the Son and of the Holy Spirit, and teaching them to obey everything that I have commanded you. And remember, I am with you always, to the end of the age.'

In the 1991 edition of this handbook, this understanding was made more explicit through four exemplifying texts:

- The motivation for mission
  Acts 1:8: "But you will receive power when the Holy Spirit has come upon you; and you will be my witnesses in Jerusalem, in all Judea and Samaria, and to the ends of the earth."
- The pattern of mission following in the example of Jesus Christ
  John 20:21, 22: "Jesus said to them again, 'Peace be with you. As the Father has sent me, so I send you.' When he had said this, he breathed on them and said to them, 'Receive the Holy Spirit.'"
- The goal of mission to reconcile
  2 Corinthians 5:18, 19: "All this is from God, who reconciled us to himself through Christ, and has given us the ministry of reconciliation; that is, in Christ God was reconciling the world to himself, not counting their trespasses against them, and entrusting the message of reconciliation to us."
- Unity in mission
  John 17:21: "… that they may all be one. As you, Father, are in me and I am in you, may they also be in us, so that the world may believe that you have sent me."

It is clear from the above texts that a certain change in biblical emphasis for mission was made in CWM, since its inception in 1977. As Van der Water notes: "The missional paradigm shift that came with the change from London Missionary Society (LMS) to CWM was also reflected in a new understanding of the New Testament mission mandate as no longer only arising from Matthew 28:18–20 but also – and perhaps more so now - from Acts 1:8, John 20:21 and 2 Cor. 5:18–19." He goes further to assert that a new understanding of mission emerged from this focus on new texts. "The new emphasis in the CWM theological equation was therefore on the church being drawn into the *Missio Dei* and, as such, being at best only an agent and an instrument in the movement of the Trinity."[226]

If this paradigm shift is understood in terms of Kritzinger's continuum model, it would seem that the CWM was moving from right to left – from an evangelistic approach to a more liberationist one. If the motivation for mission was on sharing the 'good news,' the question is what is this good news? In the opening paragraph, the pastor understood this 'good news' to be guiding people to heaven – he understood 'good news' to mean conversion.

Notwithstanding the paradigm shift described above and the recent documents of the CWM, which promotes an understanding of the content and focus of mission being on 'social justice' issues such as the environment, violence and poverty, De Gruchy's analysis shows that this has not translated back into the work that the member churches undertake.[227] While there is a wide-ranging engagement in seemingly social justice issues, such as related to women and youth, his analysis nonetheless shows that there is still an overwhelming focus on evangelism in the mission work that the churches engage with and although there are general references made to women and youth, it is not clear whether they are the subjects or objects of mission. Thus concludes, "The one large area that requires future work lies in the tension between inter-faith dialogue and evangelism, and it may be the

---

[226] Van der Water, "Council for World Mission," 307.

[227] De Gruchy, "'Growing Up and Increasing and Yielding Thirty…': Change and Continuity in the Council for World Mission, 1977–2007," (chapter in this volume). De Gruchy puts forward an increasing statistic: "Evangelism, which is underplayed in most of the missiological statements of CWM, emerged as the major area in which churches engaged in mission, with 411 or 71.6% of the entries referring to evangelism or sharing Christian values."

greater attention needs to be given to this area of mission theology and practice."[228]

It seems that while there was a shift in focus since 1975, from conversion and church-related activities[229] to social justice, this new focus has had limited impact on the ways in which the member churches understand their mission. In fact, they are perhaps still singing the same notes to the tune of conversion, and possibly with even greater enthusiasm than before, given the current context of conservative Christianity sweeping across the world, which is illustrated below.

Mission Challenges in the Context of Globalization

I have argued elsewhere that:

> Through globalisation, neo-Pentecostalism has reproduced itself all over the world. Whether one is in a village in Europe or downtown Johannesburg, it is not unusual to tune into satellite beamed preachers churning out their versions of the gospel ... Because this phenomenon is so pervasive, it is important to assess its interpretive tradition. I understand 'neo-Pentecostal' to include some classical Pentecostal and charismatic theologies and beliefs but, for me, the term does not exclude mainline denominations. Research has demonstrated not only the phenomenal growth of Pentecostalism as a denomination, but also the 'Pentecostalization' or 'charismaticization' of traditional churches, particularly in Africa. In fact, Anderson and Tang have argued that in Africa it is difficult to separate

---

[228] De Gruchy, "'Growing Up and Increasing."
[229] De Gruchy notes that these were the phrases that defined the CWM's commitment to mission at the time:
Conversion – forgiveness – new life – eternal hope;
Reconciliation – peace –community;
Liberation – justice – humanisation;
Sacrificial caring – healing – wholeness; and
Preaching and teaching – baptism – church growth.
It is our belief that all these aspects of Christian mission are true to the New Testament and that none of them can be isolated from the others and made the one controlling emphasis for all missionary work (CWM, 1975. Para. 2.2).

The Bible In *and For Mission* 141

traditional churches as 'mainline' from Pentecostal churches as 'sects.'[230]

Given the current Pentecostalisation of churches across the globe, it is perhaps not stretching the bounds of credulity to suggest that this particular brand of globalised gospel has affected CWM member churches too. The reason for this return towards conservative forms of mission is precisely the globalised forms of religion described above. In fact, on the CWM web site, an article entitled 'What can mainline churches learn from the Pentecostal movement?'[231] is featured. The article lists six features of Pentecostal style mission that the author, Anderson, a doyen of Pentecostal studies, claims should 'challenge' other Christians.[232] These six features are described in detail because I believe that these are precisely the characteristics of mission that CWM would do well to evaluate cautiously. While they may well appear rather 'soft' statements about mission, a deeper analysis may suggest more disturbing motives, particularly with regard to issues of inter-faith dialogue and a critical reading of Scripture, the latter of which is most concerning.

The first feature listed is that Pentecostal mission is spirit-led. Anderson claims that "People called missionaries are doing that job because the Spirit directed them to do it, often through some spiritual revelation like a prophecy, a dream or a vision, and even through an audible voice perceived to be that of God." The second feature is termed *dynamic mission* and here it is maintained that "Pentecostals believe that the coming of the Spirit brings an ability to do signs and wonders ... [and] emphasise that these signs and wonders should accompany the

---

[230] S. Nadar, "Who's Afraid of Bible-believing Christians?," in *Lutherans Respond to Pentecostalism*, ed. K.L. Bloomquist (Minneapolis: Lutheran University Press and Lutheran World Federation, 2008), 68–81.
[231] A. Anderson, "What Can Mainline Churches Learn from the Pentecostal Movement?" (2007), http://www.cwmission.org.uk/features/what-can-mainline-churches-learn-from-the-pentecostal-movement.html (accessed 29 April 2009).
[232] Anderson is a contributor to CWM's magazine *Inside Out*. While his views do not reflect the stand of CWM on Pentecostalism, he does assert that CWM can learn lessons from Pentecostal styles and views of mission. While Pentecostalism and fundamentalism are not necessarily inter-changeable, the styles and views of mission described by Anderson certainly border on the fundamentalist.

preaching of the word in evangelism, and that divine healing in particular is an indispensable part of evangelism." The third feature of Pentecostal mission is termed *evangelistic priority* and here "aggressive forms of evangelism" are highlighted.

The fourth and fifth features focus on local leadership and mobilization, and the latter feature is heralded particularly for Pentecostalism's focus on the enabling of all people, whether trained or untrained clergy, to be involved in mission. "A theologically articulate clergy was not the priority, because cerebral and clerical Christianity had, in the minds of many people, already failed them." The final feature that is hailed as one of Pentecostalism's successful characteristics is its ability to contextualize missiology – the mainly oral and narrative worship styles. "These practices made Pentecostal worship easily assimilated into different contexts," Anderson claims. Although Anderson concludes that "all this does not say that Pentecostals provide all the right answers," he notes that "the enormous and unparalleled contribution made by Pentecostals independently has altered the face of world Christianity irrevocably and has enriched the universal church in its ongoing task of spreading the gospel of Christ by proclamation and demonstration."

It is Anderson's latter assertion that is the most concerning. My concern is not that I disagree with him – on the contrary, I think that his assertion is exactly right. It is true that Pentecostalism has altered the face of world Christianity irrevocably, but this has not always been for the good. It is the kind of "aggressive evangelism" style and the disdain for what Anderson calls "cerebral" Christianity that concerns me. When our mission ceases to be critical and 'cerebral' and relies only on our intuition to save people from hell, then the door is left wide open for the kind of abuse that the pastor in the opening paragraph hurled at the Hindu and Muslim mourners.

The pastor's interpretation of mission, like most Pentecostal understandings of mission, finds its most logical home in the right-hand side of the continuum indicated by an evangelistic approach, provided by Kritzinger – mission being defined solely as saving the lost. Moreover, studies on globalisation have demonstrated that there is a direct link

The Bible In and For Mission 143

between globalisation and religious fundamentalism and imperialism.[233] Brouwer, Gifford and Rose's helpful and in-depth book *Exporting the American Gospel*, based on case studies and extensive research for example, has demonstrated the ways that American forms of Christianity are reproducing disciples all over the world who relegate all who do not share in their beliefs regarding matters ranging from sexual orientation to abortion to eternal damnation.[234] In fact, they are incapable of identifying with the local culture, often describing what is essentially American enculturation euphemistically as 'kingdom culture.' This can be seen in the choice of many churches to jettison the reading of the bible in the vernacular and to take up English versions of the bible (mostly the King James Version, which is considered authoritative). Thus while the work of African theologians and biblical scholars, which can arguably be placed on the liberationist side of Kritzinger's continuum, have focused on *inculturation*,[235] the globalised forms of Pentecostalism that are sweeping across many parts of the Global South are entrenching a 'kingdom' (read American) *enculturation*, one which expresses disapproval of local cultures often naming such as demonic and heathen.

An example of this is the story of South African Indian Pentecostalism. Pillay notes that the Pentecostal pastor visiting the home of a potential convert would require that all Hindu cultural or religious symbols be destroyed, the convert being persuaded that these objects of veneration and devotion are agencies of the devil, "an understanding which does not allow for Hinduism or any other non-Christian

---

[233] See S. Nadar and G.S.D. Leonard, "Indentured Theology: White Souls/Black Skins? Decolonizing Pentecostals within the Indian Diaspora," in *Spirits of Globalization: The Growth of Pentecostalism and Spiritualities in a Global Age*, ed. S.J. Stålsett (London: SCM Canterbury Press, 2006). For a fuller description of the ways in which religious fundamentalism and globalisation are related see the collection of essays in this volume.

[234] S. Brouwer, P. Gifford, and S. Rose, *Exporting the American Gospel: Global Christian Fundamentalism* (New York: Routledge, 1996).

[235] View the collection of essays in *Inculturation and Postcolonial Discourse in African Theology*. Most of the essays in the volume argue that inculturation represents the decolonisation of Christianity in Africa and through inculturation Christianity in Africa can gain a true identity of its own rather than as a surrogate of the West. E.P. Antonio, *Inculturation and Postcolonial Discourse in African Theology* (New York: Peter Lang, 2006).

philosophy to be a possible *praeparatio evangelica*."[236] Pillay further notes that the reaction of the new convert was "often so strong that not only was the former religion rejected but so also were many purely cultural features"[237] resulting in such a destructive tension being created between the old and new that it "provided the mentality that stimulated innovations within Pentecostal thinking."[238] Such 'innovations' were abundantly clear in the opening paragraph of the pastor's zealous need for religious conversion at a funeral.

Using the Bible *In* Mission: Contextual Bible Study as a Method of Mission

Given the current situation of an increase in religious fundamentalism through the 'back to the bible' culture of globalised forms of Christianity, which espouses less than life-giving messages for the poor and the oppressed and which also encourages aggressive mission, a more holistic understanding of the ways the bible can be used in mission is required. This means that the bible is used not only as a mandate for mission, but also as a source of what our mission in church and society ought to be. In other words, to look beyond the traditional mission texts that act as motivators for mission to other texts that may provide us with clues to what the content of our mission could look like. But the content of the bible is as important as the method that we employ to study the bible. As was illustrated by the pastor's interpretation of Matthew 28, if we do not have the appropriate tools or lenses with which to read the bible, our interpretations can sometimes prove to be more harmful than helpful.

Kritzinger notes the importance of education in Protestant mission.[239] In the final part of this paper, the focus is on the liberationist Protestant mission model of education, and it is suggested that the

---

[236] G.J. Pillay, *Religion at the Limits? Pentecostalism Among Indian South Africans* (Pretoria: UNISA, 1994), 186.
[237] Pillay, *Religion at the Limits?*, 187.
[238] Pillay, *Religion at the Limits?*, 187.
[239] "Working as they did with limited resources among the poor and suffering, liberationists concentrated on adult education and organised workshops and community projects to conscientize the marginalised to stand up and work for justice." Kritzinger, "The Function of the Bible," 25.

CBS[240] method that scholars in Latin America and Africa have used as a basis for conscientisation, may be one way to engage with the bible in a more life-giving way than the ways in which it is increasingly being used for the opposite.

Methods to read the bible that are more liberating and critical is crucial because this bridges the gap between evangelistic and liberationist approaches to mission. As Boff has noted:

> In Pentecostalism there is a prophetic-political potential which is that of the Bible. If one can prove to them that the Bible talks about the struggle for justice, they will become the most revolutionary of all revolutionaries because such is the word of God. A chief of police complained to me about the fact that Pentecostals are too fanatical and he said that instead of abiding by the law they say 'it is written in the Bible.'[241]

An extension of Kritzinger's notion of a continuum between liberationist and evangelistic modes of mission to an intersectional model, in which the bible is a common denominator between the two, is proposed. Taking Boff's argument about the value and authority attached to the bible, CBS can prove to be a valuable tool for conscientisation within the church.

Nadar's Biblical Intersectional Typology of Mission

Taking the bible seriously in this way also helps to address the problem of what de Gruchy terms "the captivity of and by the Bible." He argues:

> It is clear to me ... [that] the Bible is imprisoned in a strange set of preconceived notions that blunts its radical message and leads in turn to it becoming a tool of control. For all the reverence for the Bible, there has been little recognition of the fundamental message of the Bible—grace. The Bible has become a rulebook, a code of law, that lays down the rights and wrongs of God

---

[240] See G. West, *Contextual Bible Study* (Pietermaritzburg: Cluster Publications, 1995).

[241] C. Boff, "The Search for Justice and Solidarity: Meeting the 'New Churches,'" http://www.sedos.org/english/boff_2.html (accessed 4 October 2009).

against the community and the internal critique of such a notion in the very Bible itself is not appreciated. There has been no sustained effort in our generation to break this imprisonment. A key task awaits us then to begin to distil the gains made by critical Biblical studies in the past generation—particularly in the area of sociological and feminist critiques of the texts.[242]

Contextual Bible Study (CBS) can be this sustained effort for which de Gruchy calls in making critical readings of the bible more accessible to communities of faith. The importance of this cannot be sufficiently stressed in our current conservative environment of Christianity, which uses the bible to promote oppression and injustice. Because the method is interactive and not instructive as in traditional bible studies or sermons, CBS has taken the power away from the person at the pulpit as the only person who can interpret the bible. This signals an important shift. A similar shift has happened structurally within CWM. The shift from colonial to postcolonial mission structures, in which power is now shared in partnership (rather than in top-down fashion), has been an important step in the life of CWM.

Is it possible to envisage a similar shift in the ways in which we interpret the bible for and in mission? The power dynamics of North taking the bible to the South is mirrored in the context of a preacher and the congregation. Contextual Bible Studies are a breakdown of that power dynamic. Contextual Bible Study provides a tool for experiencing the shift in the act of reading the bible, and thus truly allowing for new insights about the bible and mission to emerge. A more detailed description of the method using Mark 7:24–50 illustrates this below.[243]

Contextual Bible Study is a method of interactive study of particular texts in the bible, which brings the perspectives of both the context of the reader and the context of the bible into dialogue, for the

---

[242] S. de Gruchy, "Doing Theology in the Kalahari," *Journal of Theology for Southern Africa* 99 (Nov 1997): 60.

[243] The use of the text of the Mark 7:24–30 pericope is for illustrative purposes only, that is to elucidate the *method* of the CBS. The scope of this article does not permit a detailed exegetical study of this text.

purpose of transformation.[244] It is usually facilitated by someone with theological training. It uses a literary method; that is, it asks textual and narrative questions about character and plot, and allows socio-historical questions to develop out of this. The key feature of the CBS is that it is interactive and participatory in nature, so that everyone in the group is given a chance to speak. It is difficult to describe the process on paper, as it is something that one learns by doing – a key principle of the CWM's policy on education in mission. This is why I believe that the CBS can be a tool in helping churches find more holistic ways of interpreting the bible in Christian contexts that appear to be ever more conservative in their interpretation of the bible. It offers a method of using the bible *in* mission in ways that are positive. Using Mark 7:24–30 (NRSV), an example of the way this can be done follows:

> From there he set out and went away to the region of Tyre. He entered a house and did not want anyone to know that he was there. Yet he could not escape notice. But a woman whose little daughter had an unclean spirit immediately heard about him, and she came and bowed down at his feet. Now the woman was a Gentile, of Syrophoenician origin. She begged him to cast the demon out of her daughter. He said to her: 'Let the children be fed first, for it is not fair to take the children's food and throw it to the dogs.' But she answered him, 'Sir, even the dogs under the table eat the children's crumbs.' Then he said to her: 'For saying that, you may go – the demon has left your daughter.' So she went home, found the child lying on the bed, and the demon gone.

The bible study is constructed around five questions, three with their own sub-questions. These questions are answered in groups after the text has been read aloud in the plenary session.
- Tell the story in your own words; begin with 'once upon a time';
- What are the themes of this text?

---

[244] For a fuller description and example of the CBS see "Doing and Understanding Contextual Bible Study," http://www.ukzn.ac.za/sorat/ujamaa/esther.ppt.

- Main characters
  How does Jesus respond to the woman?
  How does the woman respond to Jesus?
  How do the disciples respond to the woman?
- Bringing the text home
  4.1 Do we have women like the Syrophoenician women in our contexts today? Who are they and how do they challenge our ideas of mission?
  4.2 Do we have people like the disciples in our contexts today – who are they and how do they challenge our ideas of mission?
  4.3 Who are our daughters who need saving today? And who are the demons they need saving from?
  4.4 Jesus responds in a particular way to this woman. Has his actions told you anything about God's mission (*Missio Dei*) in the world today?
- Action plan
  5.1 What will you do now in response to this bible study?
  5.2 Are there resources to do what you want to do?

As already stated it is difficult to sketch the nuances of an interactive bible study on paper, but some of the theological insights that can be drawn from this particular bible study on mission, may help clarify thoughts on the theological underpinnings of the work of the CWM.

a) Mission as Deliverance or Development – Healing or Bread?

Much has been said about the bible's role in development as a key characteristic of CWM's vocation.[245] In this text, Jesus equates the healing that the woman requires for her daughter with food or bread, which is a basic need. Bread provides security/nourishment, but its benefits go beyond the physical to the intellectual and the spiritual. Both healing and food is basic to human development. Unfortunately, in

---

[245] See for example Steve de Gruchy's article on bible and development focusing on development as social justice, http://www.cwmission.org.uk/features/bible-and-development-land-of-promise.html (accessed 4 May 2009). See also S. de Gruchy, "Integrating Mission and Development: Ten Theological Theses," *International Congregational Journal* 5, no. 1 (2005): 27–36.

mission, we have dichotomized the two. And this is the reason that Anderson argues that mainline churches need to learn from the Pentecostal movements.[246] In a sense, the Pentecostal churches focus far more on the deliverance (the healing through signs and wonders) than the development (such as education and food security). The thousands who throng to these deliverance meetings, particularly in Africa, attest to a need that conceivably needs to be met by mainline mission too. The challenge is to be able to meet this need in a way that does not smack of the charlatan nature of most of these mission outreaches. The wisdom of organisations such as African Religious Health Assets Program perhaps needs to be sought in this regard.[247]

b) 'Give Us This Day our Daily Crumbs': Mission as Survival or Abundant Life?

In the story of Mark 7, the Syrophoenician woman appears to take whatever she can get – she settles for the crumbs. I often ask bible study participants if they think that she is simply accepting her oppression, like a chicken that votes for KFC. After the laughter, this question begins a discussion about who gets the bread and who gets the crumbs. Why do some people get the bread and some people get the crumbs? But the discussion goes even further to whether there are times when crumbs are enough? A good example of this is the debate in the Anglican Church in 2008, about whether women priests can become bishops – the suggestion in one of the debates was that half a loaf was really better than none – after all, at least the women were already ordained as priests.

Rev. Lalchungnunga, the principal of Serampore College in India, laments in a feature article on the CWM web site, that women in the Presbyterian Church in India are still not ordained. "We allow women to do anything in the church except be ordained,"[248] he says. A significant statement he makes further on, points to the importance of

---

[246] Anderson, "What Can Mainline Churches Learn," http://www.cwmission.org.uk/features/what-can-mainline-churches-learn-from-the-pentecostal-movement.html (accessed 29 April 2009).
[247] See for example P. Germond and S. Molapo, "In Search of Bophelo in a Time of AIDS: Seeking a Coherence of Economies of Health and Economies of Salvation," *Journal of Theology for Southern Africa* 126 (2006): 27-47.
[248] "One Thing we Lack," http://www.cwmission.org/features/one-thing-we-lack (accessed 4 May 2009).

conducting bible study as mission *within* the church. He says: "Theologically trained people can understand but lay people do not accept that women should be ordained .... Paul's letters can be interpreted so that it seems his view on women is that they shouldn't teach or wear certain garments, but rather listen quietly. But that ignores the part of the Bible that says that there's no male or female in Christ."

In addition to the need for bible reading as mission within the church, we should also consider the ways in which the story challenges our throwing crumbs at people too. How do we move beyond valorizing the soup kitchens, for example, to a point where people can be empowered enough, to get a little more than soup? Is a theology of survival the only theology we can muster up in terms of mission? Is valorizing survival a way to ease our consciousness? These are questions that this text forces us to ask.

c) *'Who is at the Table?' – Mission as Exclusive?*

"We do not presume to come to this your table merciful Lord, trusting in our own righteousness, but in your manifold and great mercies. We are not worthy so much as to gather the crumbs under your table ..." The Anglican Eucharistic prayer that points to grace is in memory of this woman who fought for inclusion. Many churches use the prayer and yet women, people of differing sexual orientation, foreigners, people with disability are glaring in their absence from the table.

A survey of the CWM member churches on their views on the ordination of homosexual priests, on the United Reformed Churches web site,[249] speaks volumes about the church's inability to accommodate all at the table. The following are the comments of four churches regarding the issue:

- The Church of North India: "[We] live by the guideline that those who are called to office in the church are to lead a life in obedience to scripture and in conformity to the historic confessional standards of the church."
- The Congregational Union of New Zealand: Discussed at the 1991 Assembly and agreed that at the point of entry to the ministry a person living in a homosexual relationship should not be called to the pastoral ministry.

---

[249] "Sexuality Report – Appendix 10," http://www.urc.org.uk/what_we_do/general_assembly/human_sexuality/10_app endices (accessed 5 May 2009).

- Ekalesia Kelisiano Tuvalu: Does not allow homosexuals in the ordained ministry of their church. Their representative stated that "Our culture and traditions oppose the practice and we strongly stand on the biblical understanding that male and female were created for divine purpose of procreation."
- Presbyterian Church of India: Their representative states that the Presbyterian Church of India will never ordain people whose sexual orientation is homosexual. It will also be very difficult to recognize those people as ordinary members of the church.

The Syrophoenician woman's story invites us to consider the interconnectedness of oppressions – racism is sexism is classism is homophobia. The Syrophoenician woman is oppressed because of her sex, her ethnicity, her religion and a host of other factors. When we exclude her from the table, when we force her to accept crumbs on the basis of her sex, then we can also exclude people on the basis of their ethnicity and when we do that, we can also begin to exclude those who are of a differing sexual orientation, those with disabilities, perhaps even children. Where do we draw the line in our ecclesiological practices of exclusion?

Duraisingh, in an issue of *Inside Out*,[250] reflects on his tenure as General Secretary of CWM. He relates a pertinent story regarding the church as a round table: "During my term, I visited Singapore where we ate at round tables with a rotating tray on top. Each person would bring a dish, nobody knew who brought what but we would share as equals. Can CWM learn to throw away the rectangular table for the round table? It is constituted by what everybody brings to it; therefore, the vision of CWM is that we need to play our part in adding to this rich table. This means we also need to learn and challenge one another to value non-material resources such as cultural and social insights and personnel."[251]

Duraisingh's call for CWM to change the shape of the table is as important as asking who is at the table. Perhaps it is because we have not changed the shape of the table that some people are still excluded from it. But changing the table requires education. As Lalchungnunga said above about the Presbyterian Church of North India's refusal to ordain women: "Theologically trained people can understand but lay people do not

---

[250] *Inside Out* is CWM's quarterly journal.
[251] C. Duraisingh, "From Everywhere to Everywhere," *Inside Out* (2007).

accept that women should be ordained. They think that women should be subordinate." If these ideas originate from the church's interpretation of the bible, then we need to be offering new and more holistic interpretations. We cannot be satisfied with the shape of the table and then complain about the exclusion of people from the table, which is not designed to accommodate them.

d) *"For saying that...the demon has left your daughter": Mission as Critical*

Anderson downplays cerebral Christianity and a theologically articulate clergy.[252] This, to my mind, is probably the most dangerous part of the current mission enterprise in Christianity. The 'leave your brain at the door when you come to church' approach leads to an uncritical acceptance of injustice and oppression because Christians are simply told to do as their Bible says.

The difference between Matthew's and Mark's accounts of this story is that Matthew attributes the healing of this woman's daughter to her faith: "Then Jesus answered her, 'Woman, great is your faith! Let it be done for you as you wish.' And her daughter was healed instantly." (Matthew 15:28). In contrast, Mark 7:29 attributes the healing to what she said. "Then he said to her: 'For saying that, you may go – the demon has left your daughter.'" The 'that' referred to is the woman's challenge to him, when he tells her that he cannot take the children's food and throw it to the dogs. "But she answered him, 'Sir, even the dogs under the table eat the children's crumbs.'" The inference we draw from Mark is that the daughter is healed because of what the woman said – her refusal to accept the norm of her being an outcast, her ability to speak to a man in public – in summary, her courage.[253] Jesus changed his mind when challenged and confronted by radical truth presented to him by 'the

---

[252] Anderson, "What Can Mainline Churches Learn," http://www.cwmission.org.uk/features/what-can-mainline-churches-learn-from-the-pentecostal-movement.html (accessed 29 April 2009).

[253] Her status as an outsider as both a woman and a Greek highlights her courage. Downing points to Mark's exaggeration of her status as a woman and as an outsider: "She heard of him, a woman did, a woman with a daughter … and she came to him and furthermore she was a Greek woman, a Syrophoenicianess." (G.F. Downing, "The Woman from Syrophoenicia, and Her Doggedness: Mark 7:24–31 (Matthew 15:21–28)," in *Women in the Biblical Tradition*, ed. G.J. Brooke (Lewiston: Edwin Mellen, 1992), 133.

other.' He does not ask her to 'convert' before healing; rather it is he who is converted after his encounter with her.

Unfortunately, this critical consciousness is what is lacking in our mission encounters. The inability to listen to the other, to see truth in what people of other faiths, sex and ethnicities may offer, causes a certain amount of arrogance to build up within the church. We wish to rush to the answers before we have asked the right questions. The famous adage by Bishop Camara: "When I give bread to the poor, I'm called a saint. When I asked why they had no bread, they called me a communist" is what people who think critically within the church are continually confronted with. The critical questions are dealt with not in building more shelters or in helping with food parcels (albeit that these are important), but through education – raising critical consciousness. It was heartening to see on the CWM web site that the Church of Jesus Christ in Madagascar has run courses to educate women about the ways in which human rights can help them with problems such as domestic violence, being denied their inheritance or having their children taken away after a relationship break-up.[254] This is the kind of critical education that is needed as complementary to the shelters that we build for abused women.

e) *"Let the Children be Fed **First***"*: Hierarchies of Grace and Mission?*

Finally, the story of the Syrophoenician woman invites us to consider the ways in which we set up hierarchies of mission. Jesus' response to the woman: "I was sent only to the lost sheep of Israel" is reminiscent of the unwillingness of the church to work ecumenically sometimes. One of the four key texts that the CWM has focused on as part of its call to mission is its commitment to unity in mission – John 17:21: "that they may all be one. As you, Father, are in me and I am in you, may they also be in us, so that the world may believe that you have sent me."

The question is: Has the CWM lived up to this in its practices? Has it reached beyond the confines of its member churches?

---

[254] "Community of Women and Men in Mission," http://www.cwm-genderissues.org/news/index.php (accessed 5 May 2009).

Conclusion

In conclusion, it has been argued in this paper that in this increasingly globalised world that has returned us to conservative forms of mission and biblical interpretation, the task that lies ahead for organisations like the CWM is perhaps to look to the bible not only for motivation to do mission, but also to provide the content for what our mission should be. The narrative of the Syrophoenician woman challenges us to re-think mission. First, to think of mission holistically – not just as physical sustenance – but healing, physical and otherwise. Second, the story invites us to re-evaluate whether food/development is simply for survival or abundant life – it challenges us to be careful about valorising survival, the crumbs. Third, the story calls us to understand the inter-linking of oppressions – that ecclesiological practices of exclusion can be dangerous. Fourth, now more than ever the story challenges us to develop a critical consciousness around issues of mission and education. Finally, by extending the circle of healing beyond the lost sheep of Israel, the story challenges our understanding of mission – not just to reach out to other faiths, to "kick them into heaven," but to reach out ecumenically and more importantly to reach deep within ourselves to find the core of the gospel to do justice, to love kindness and to walk humbly with our God.

7

From Mountain to Valley:
An Ecumenical Evangelism in the Interfaith Context

Jooseop Keum[255]

Much research on the role of evangelism and mission in the global South reveals a link between evangelism and colonialism.[256] And yet, an eminent ecumenist, Philip Potter, the third general secretary of the World Council of Churches (WCC), claimed "Evangelism is the test of true ecumenism."[257] His successor, Emilio Castro went on further, "the only valid theological method for evangelism is conscious participation in the whole of human life and its problems... evangelism is a question not of apologetics but of life."[258] Both Potter and Castro were re-defining evangelism in a postcolonial context. As God does not give us partial salvation, we cannot limit evangelism only to the personal and spiritual realm. Rather, we must acknowledge that evangelism (*euangelion* in Greek) is the good news for every part of our life, society and creation.[259]

---

[255] Programme Executive on Mission and Evangelism (CWME). Editor of the *International Review of Mission* (IRM) World Council of Churches.

[256] See for example, T.O Beidelman, *Colonial Evangelism: A Socio-Historical Study of an East African Mission at the Grassroots* (Bloomington: Indiana University Press, 1982); John Comaroff and Jean Comaroff, *Of Revelation and Revolution: Christianity, Colonialism, and Consciousness in South Africa* Vol. 1 (Chicago: University of Chicago Press, 1991).

[257] Philip Potter's speech to the Roman Catholic Synod of Bishops (Rome, 1974). Quoted in the 1982 document *Mission and Evangelism: An Ecumenical Affirmation*, 2.

[258] Emilio Castro, "Evangelism," in *Dictionary of the Ecumenical Movement,* eds. Nicholas Lossky et al., (Geneva: WCC Publications, 1991), 400.

[259] Jooseop Keum, "Editorial," *International Review of Mission* 97 no. 386/387 (2008): 184.

If we agree that evangelism is more than converting non-believers or people of other faiths to the religion of Christianity, dealing with the issue of holistic salvation of humanity and creation, we can apply the same approach in our understanding of ecumenism. The ecumenical movement is wider than the visible unity of churches. Wesley Ariarajah noted that the institutionalized ecumenical movement began with church-centred initiatives in Europe, but questioned whether the time had not come for Christians to look for a "wider ecumenism that would more truly represent the whole inhabited earth?" [260]

Since evangelism has to deal with the issue of holistic salvation and ecumenism with the whole *oikoumene*, we cannot exclude people of other faiths in this mission of life-giving and saving work. Rather, we should be able to work together to give relief to the suffering humanity and creation. Therefore, this essay will attempt to develop the concept of a life-centred ecumenical evangelism within the context of the multi-religious world today.

The Story of the Afghan Hostages

In August 2007, I was travelling to Seoul to speak at a consultation organized as part of the centenary celebration of the 1907 Great Revival in Korea. I remember this visit as the most difficult homecoming since I had left Korea nearly ten years ago. After visiting the families of the Afghan hostages, I left Korea with much sadness. [261]

---

[260] S. Wesley Ariarajah, "Wider Ecumenism: A Threat or a Promise," *Ecumenical Review* 50 (1998): 321.

[261] "The 2007 South Korean hostage crisis in Afghanistan began on July 19, 2007, when 23 South Korean missionaries were captured and held hostage by members of the Taliban while passing through Ghazni Province of Afghanistan. Two male hostages were executed before the deal was reached between the Taliban and the South Korean government. The group, composed of sixteen women and seven men, was captured while traveling from Kandahar to Kabul by bus on a mission sponsored by the Saemmul Presbyterian Church. The crisis began when two local men, who the driver had allowed to board, started shooting to bring the bus to a halt. Over the next month, the hostages were kept in cellars and farmhouses and regularly moved in groups of three to four. Of the 23 hostages captured, two men, Bae Hyeong-gyu, a 42-year-old South Korean pastor of Saemmul Church, and Shim Seong-min, a 29-year-old South Korean man, were executed on July 25 and July 30, respectively. Later, with negotiations making progress, two women, Kim Gyeong-ja and Kim Ji-na, were released on August 13 and the remaining 19 hostages on August 29 and August

Although the WCC utilized various channels available to help secure the release of the hostages through the organization's interfaith and international affairs desks, my beloved classmate, Rev. Bae Hyeong-gyu had already become the first victim of the *Taliban*. On my flight back to London, I thought about the death of this innocent Presbyterian minister who wanted to help the Afghan people and the wrong image of the missionary movement in Afghanistan. What had made the Talibans extremely nervous was the rumour that they were holding a prayer meeting in a ruined mosque in Kabul. Whether it was true or not, it seemed to the Afghans that the Koreans had a clear evangelistic mandate, although the Korean churches claimed that they were development workers, not missionaries.

The Korean churches and mission agencies are sending the second largest number of missionaries—over 20,000, next to the United States - to the four corners of the world. Samuel Kobia considered this a remarkable achievement in mission history. "There is no other church in the global South which has completely transformed itself, becoming a 'missionizing' church from having been a 'missionized' church... The transformation of the Korean churches from a 'receiving' church to a 'sending' church, both in human and financial resources, is indeed a significant example for the churches in the global South."[262]

However, there are negative aspects of this transformation which demand a critical assessment, as we saw in the story of Afghan hostages. In most cases, the world missionary movement in Korea is heavily armed with aggressive evangelism, recalling the slogan of the London Missionary Society (LMS): "Spreading the knowledge of Jesus Christ to the heathen world." The mission paradigm of the Korean churches is similar to that of the western missionary movement during the 19th century.

---

30. The release of the hostages was secured with a South Korean promise to withdraw its 200 troops from Afghanistan by the end of 2007. Although the South Korean government offered no statement, a Taliban spokesman claimed that the militant group also received some US$20 million in exchange for the safety of the captured missionaries." See http://en.wikipedia.org/wiki/2007_South_Korean_hostage_crisis_in_Afghanistan

[262] Samuel Kobia, (Keynote Speech, General Assembly of the National Council of Churches in Korea, 17 January 2009, Seoul).

The modern missionary movement was shaped by the cultures, the social values and the worldview of Europe. Western missionaries, closely connected with the colonial powers, sought to "civilize" the people in the "darkness" by sending their missionaries to the "heathen world." This 'sending' paradigm of world mission has powerfully influenced and dominated the missionary movement over the past centuries. It led to a calculation of the success and failure of mission in terms of the numbers of missionaries sent "out there." Consequently, the sending agencies came to be regarded as the subject of mission. The values, cultures, religions and civilizations of the people "over there" were understood as pagan; and that these should be conquered or even eradicated by western Christian civilization. Unfortunately, this paradigm influences the understanding of mission among the churches and mission bodies in the global South, including Koreans, until today.

The CWM: A Journey Paralleled or Accompanied?

As we noted above, the modern Protestant missionary movement was born out of the evangelical awakening in Europe, in the context of western expansionism and against the background of the Enlightenment. With a sense of urgency, missionary societies were established because they believed that people were dying without the knowledge of the salvation wrought by Jesus Christ and that their souls were doomed for hell. Against this background, the LMS was formed in 1795 as the second oldest autonomous missionary society in Britain. Richard Lovett stated that the LMS was "a child of the evangelical revival of England originated by Whitefield and John Wesley."[263] Although the LMS was one of the largest and the most famous missionary societies during the 19th century, its mission understanding was not entirely free from colonialism. Moreover, there was a certain paternalism in the relationship with the churches in the South. After the Second World War, the decline of the modern missionary era began to show up clearly. A deep sense of guilt also overwhelmed LMS and resulted in missionaries' withdrawal.

As one era in missions declined, a new era of world mission emerged. The growing selfhood of the churches in the third world and

---

[263] Richard Lovett, *The History of the London Missionary Society, 1795-1895*, Vol. I (London: Oxford University Press, 1899), 3.

their desire to participate in mission, locally and globally, marked the significance of the new era. The development of the ecumenical movement played a significant role in bringing about a paradigm shift in the understanding, agenda and structure of world mission. World mission no longer meant western Christian missions to the rest of the world, but the participation of churches across the world with mission in all six continents being the mission field. In the midst of this transformation, LMS went through major structural changes in 1977. The old missionary society ceased to exist and a new community of churches in mission, Council for World Mission (CWM), was founded on the following principles:

- Mutuality: Mutual learning in mission
- Sharing: Sharing people, resources and skills
- Partnership: Equal power in decision making

All former associate churches of LMS became full constituent members with equal powers and voting rights, regardless of the size and financial contribution of churches. All assets and funds were held in common. The CWM paved the way for a multi-directional movement of missionaries, each church being both a sender and receiver. Each member church contributed its financial, personnel and spiritual resources to the common pool according to its ability and received according to its needs. Biblically, the paradigm of mission understanding was shifted from Mt 28 to Acts 2. John Brown said, "There is no doubt that the CWM has achieved a significant shift from a missionary organisation characterised by donor-recipient relationship to a partnership in mission among its member churches. There is real sharing of power…the CWM has achieved a significant degree of mutuality in mission."[264] We are proud of this achievement because it has been achieved not through a sudden invention, but through a long struggle within the whole CWM family.

Although the CWM model of mutuality, sharing and partnership has made a difference to the mission practice of member churches - through developing new patterns of sending and receiving missionaries, restructuring the church for mission, and contributing to the wider ecumenical movement - I cannot avoid the question of "equal partnership

---

[264] John Brown, "International Relationships in Mission: A Study Project," *International Review of Mission* LXXXVI, no. 342 (July 1997): 228.

for what"? It has been successful in building up our new identity as a global family in mission. But for what missions? How has our experience really transformed ourselves and our mission understandings? These questions need to be answered theologically and missiologically by all the CWM member churches.

When the CWM was founded in 1977, some effort to answer the above questions was made. It was the debate on the moratorium and the development of ecumenical missiology which stimulated the transformation from the LMS to the CWM. The formation of the CWM was particularly influenced by ecumenical missiological concepts, such as *"Missio Dei,"* "Mission as the Task of the Whole People of God," "Mission in Six Continents," the studies on "The Missionary Structure of the Congregation," developed by the International Missionary Council (IMC) and her successor, the WCC Commission on World Mission and Evangelism (CWME). Particularly, LMS was encouraged by the WCC World Mission Conference on "Salvation Today," Bangkok, 1972/3 to imagine more radical and fundamental changes both in terms of mission thinking and practice.[265] With internal challenges and external inputs, in its founding document, "Sharing in One World Mission," the CWM developed a new and holistic understanding of mission, called "five faces in mission."

> *conversion - forgiveness - new life - eternal hope*
> *reconciliation – peace – community*
> *liberation – justice – humanisation*
> *sacrificial caring – healing – wholeness*
> *preaching and teaching – baptism – church growth*[266]

Indeed it was a comprehensive articulation of most of all the aspects of Christian mission in the life and mission of Jesus Christ in the New Testament, and it successfully overcame the mission paradigm of LMS. However, the founding document lacked in-depth theological articulation. Clear missiological definitions of each face were missing. Furthermore, the document did not explain how each concept connects with the others to bring coherence in mission, i.e. *inter-relatedness and inter-dependency of each of the five faces towards an authentic holistic mission.* It may be misleading to the member churches' mission

---

[265] See, *Sharing in One World Mission: Proposals for the Council for World Mission*, (December 1975), § 2.1.
[266] *Sharing in One World Mission*, § 2.2.

understanding, that "everything is mission" and the CWM is a kind of mission department store that sells every item in the name of mission. I am not an advocate of Stephen Neill's dictum that "if everything is mission then nothing is mission."[267] Rather I agree with David Bosch's broad view, a view that encompasses the comprehensive saving work of Jesus Christ. However, if the CWM fails to develop a deeper theological reflection and missiological articulation on what is God's mission today and how the CWM family can participate in it, there is the danger of falling into a "cheap" holism in mission.

On the other hand, the Korean churches were not aware that the LMS had ceased to exist until the end of the 1980s. Most of the Korean churches, except a few, still have a strong nostalgia for the LMS days because it was a LMS missionary who was the first Protestant martyr (or simply a victim of a colonial conflict) in Korea.[268] Encouraged by the Presbyterian Church in Taiwan (PCT), the Presbyterian Church of Korea (PCK) has since joined the CWM in 1989, and there have been 20 years of journeying together as a community of churches in mission through the CWM.

Again coming back to the tragic story of the Afghan hostages, it is vital to raise the following questions about the 20 years' journey. What have the Korean churches (particularly PCK) learned through their journey within the CWM in terms of their mission thinking and policies? Has the CWM been successful in shaping and re-shaping their mission understanding and practice (particularly on evangelism and interfaith dialogue)? Has it been a journey paralleled or accompanied between the member churches in their deep longing for mission? What is the CWM's understanding of evangelism in the multi-religious context? Because I have been given the topic of the last question with limited scope, I will only examine it here with an introduction to a concept of ecumenical evangelism which has been developed within WCC Commission on World Mission and Evangelism (CWME).

---

[267] Stephen Neill, *Creative Tension: The Duff Lectures, 1959* (London: Edinburgh House Press, 1959), 81.

[268] It is quite controversial whether Rev Robert J. Thomas was a martyr or not. See, Koh, Moo-song, "Robert J. Thomas: A Historical Study of East-West Encounter through His Mission" (PhD Thesis, University of Birmingham, 1995).

A *Kenotic* Understanding of Evangelism

In ecumenical terms, "mission" carries a holistic understanding which includes evangelism as a particular task of mission: the proclamation and sharing of the good news of the gospel by word (*kerygma*), deed (*diakonia*), prayer and worship (*leiturgia*), and the everyday witness of the Christian life (*martyria*).[269] Evangelism is proclaiming the good news of the kingdom of God. It is sharing the news of salvation through the crucifixion and resurrection of Jesus Christ, without overwhelming others by our stories. Therefore, evangelism is witnessing to the sacrificial love of God. The nature of this love is the servanthood of Christ who was sent as the Lamb of God for the world. "The self-emptying of the servant who lived among the people, sharing in their hopes and sufferings, giving his life on the cross for all humanity – this was Christ's way of proclaiming the good news, and as disciples we are summoned to follow the same way."[270]

As the subject of mission is the Triune God, we are the servants of God, proclaiming the good news to all suffering humanity and creation who are longing for a new hope in their life. Ecumenical evangelism is not a matter of conquering or winning over/against others. Rather, it is an invitation from God to the "feast in the kingdom of God" (Luke 14:16). Our mission is to prepare a banquet and to go out to the streets and market places of the town to deliver invitations to all of God's peoples. We (the people of God) are not conquerors, but humble servants called to invite them (all of God's peoples) to God's banquet in the "garden of life."

This *kenotic* understanding of evangelism is not merely talking about our methods of evangelism, but it is the very nature and essence of our faith in Christ. Jesus became Christ not through power or money but through his *kenosis* (Phil. 2:7). We believe in God who "made himself nothing" (ἐκένωσε, *ekénōse*). Therefore, we, the disciples who have been sent by Christ to proclaim the good news, have to follow Christ's footsteps by witnessing to his humility. In the CWM, a comprehensive report from the theological roundtable titled "The People of God among All God's Peoples: Frontiers in Christian Mission," which is one of the

---

[269] *Mission and Evangelism in Unity Today* (Commission on World Mission and Evangelism, World Council of Churches, 2000), § 7, par 7.
[270] *Mission and Evangelism: An Ecumenical Affirmation* (World Council of Churches, 1982), § 4.

From Mountain to Valley 163

most articulate theological statements since "Sharing One World Mission" in my own view, reaffirmed this kenotic understanding.[271]

What then does this imply when we engage in dialogue with people of other faiths? As we empty ourselves, and place ourselves beneath them so as to serve all of God's peoples, is there anything left to proclaim or to share?

The Story of Sam Bo Il Bae

Some years ago, the Korean government announced a land reclamation plan in *Samangeum*, which is one of the largest mud flats in the world. A huge amount of arable land (in fact, an industrial area) will emerge on the western coast of the Korean peninsula if the plan is successfully carried out. One day, four religious leaders from Buddhism, an indigenous religion, Protestant Christianity and Roman Catholicism appeared in *Samangeum*. They silently distributed their written statement. Then they started to walk three steps and to bow once. It was not a half bowing but a full Buddhist bowing of kneeling, touching the earth with the head and stretching the arms out front. Then the four religious leaders marched for about four hundreds kilometres to the Parliament in Seoul always doing "three steps and one bowing." It took almost three months to reach Seoul. But, still they did not say a single word during the whole march! However, during these three months, all of Korean society was astir with the news. There was much controversy on issues of development and environment. Many people joined the march of *Sam Bo Il Bae* or Three Steps and One Bowing with tears for the asceticism of these four priests. In *Samangeum*, they were only four, but when they arrived in Seoul, an interreligious group of thousands had joined the march and was following the actions of the priests.

In the statement, the priests had said, "We hear the cries of numerous living creatures in *Samangeum* every night." "The people in this mud flat called us to stop the wind of death in the name of development." "Therefore, we, as priests of Korean religions, began Sam Bo Il Bae for the repentance of all human exploitation against nature." They declared, "The creatures living in this mud are alive and breathing and they are our neighbours!" This statement was a strong request for the

---

[271] See Philip L. Wickeri, ed., *The People of God Among All God's Peoples: Frontiers in Mission* (Hong Kong: CWM/CCA, 2000), 23-25.

repentance of modern humanity. It requires from us to change our way of life away from emphasizing only material richness. The message of the four priests underlines that all living creatures have the same nature and value of life from heaven. They affirmed, "The spirituality of co-existence in the web of life is the only way to heal the sin of our greed." These four priests read together the story of the Good Samaritan from an entirely different aspect. They enlarged the anthropocentric meaning of the text, saying that all creation is our neighbour as humans. In their protest, they chose not a struggle, but Sam Bo Il Bae, which is a traditional ascetic discipline for repentance in Korean Buddhism. They expressed their message as an act of asceticism like the suffering of the lives in the mud flat. As is the custom in Roman Catholic retreats, they did not speak out in spoken language during the march, but prayed as a whole body for three months. This created a soundless spiritual echo for all Koreans.

These four priests did not seek to proclaim their own religious message as an act of evangelism. Rather, they gave up some of their identity in order to open themselves and to accept the others. Finally, they were able to witness together to the cosmic value of life, joined by thousands of followers, which I would call cosmic evangelism. Is this kenotic action and life not the core of evangelism (sacrificial love of Jesus Christ) that we have to proclaim?

From Mountain to Valley[272]

Many of us are familiar with the analogy that God is like the top of a mountain and there are many paths which lead to the truth. However, are we really climbing the same mountain? The concept and belief in salvation is unique and exists only within Christianity. The Buddhist understanding of *nirvana* is totally different. According to Mark Heim, we are in fact climbing different mountains and the truths that could be found on the top are not all the same.[273] Those who believe

---

[272] Some part of this chapter was delivered by the author in his keynote address at Communitas Contextual Theology Conference (United Theological College, 18-21 April 2009, Sydney, Australia) with the title, "Mission as an Invitation to the Feast of Life: Re-visioning the Ecumenical Understanding and Practice of Mission in the 21st Century."

[273] See, S. Mark Heim, *Salvations: Truth and Difference in Religion* (New York: Orbis, 1995).

that we can only reach the top through one way can be considered as exclusivists, those who admit many ways as universalists, and those who assume many mountains as pluralists.

However, when we apply the kenotic understanding of evangelism, why do we imagine only *climbing up* the mountain as a true way of religious discipline to find the truth or truths? Would it not be possible to suggest a pilgrimage of *climbing down* from the *mountain* to the *valley* where people are living? As long as we are staying on the mountain (very few on the top), we cannot meet, listen, dialogue and work together *with* the people, including people of other faiths who are struggling to survive in their daily life because the mountain is too high for the ordinary people to climb, and too narrow for them to stay on the top. If we are different mountains as Heim claims, how could we listen to each other, meet face to face, and talk and eat together on the top of different mountains? It is too far away to listen, meet and talk. It is an impossible task to work on together while we are sitting on different and remote mountain tops. In fact, it is in the valley, not on the top of the mountain where we can meet people of other faiths. It is in the valley where we can *live in* a community and where we can *live out* the truth of what we believe in.

Indeed, to go down to the valley and to the villages was Jesus' answer to Peter when he insisted that Jesus and the three disciples live forever on the top of the Mountain of Transfiguration because "it was so good that they were there" (Luke 9:33). In many religious traditions from east or west, the mountain represents sacred space for spiritual discipline. But, no matter how "good" it is to receive the truth from heaven at Mount Sinai or listening to the heavenly voice at the Mount of Transfiguration, Jesus never allowed his disciples to stay there. Jesus said, "Stand up, do not be afraid" (Matthew 17:7) to go down to the valley where people were inheriting households and waiting for some good news. As soon as they came back to the community, the disciples were met by a father whose son was an epileptic, and their mission began (Matthew 17:15).

The proclamation of the good news is not climbing up to the mountain but rather going down to the valley. We believe in an incarnate God, the Son of Man who voluntarily gave up his heavenly position and became a servant to wash our feet. It is this God in whom we believe as Christians. An authentic evangelism in an interfaith context must follow this direction of God's missionary journey from heaven to earth - Jesus' journey from mountain to valley. It is not staying on our own top of the mountain and closing ourselves to the other faiths, but opening ourselves up to the others in view of a constant reshaping and reforming of our vision of the new heaven and earth.

Ecumenical Evangelism[274]
Proselytism and Evangelism

> We are living in a "highly competitive environment of the free market [which] is reinforcing many churches and para-church movements in their perception of mission as the effort to attract and recruit new "customers," while retaining the old ones... They evaluate the success of their mission in terms of growth, of numbers of converts or of newly planted churches. Unfortunately, very often their "new members" already belonged to other churches. Thus *proselytism* (as competition and "sheep-stealing") is one of the sharp contemporary issues facing the churches.[275]

While the word "proselyte" was "originally a positive term in early Christian times used to designate a person of another faith converting to Christianity," proselytism in later centuries took a negative connotation. Proselytism is now used to mean the encouragement of Christians who belong to a church to change their denominational allegiance. It brings about tensions, scandal and division, and is thus a destabilizing factor for the witness of the church in the world.[276]

Edinburgh 1910 has been long regarded as the historic landmark of world mission and the modern ecumenical movement in various ways.

---

[274] Some part of this chapter was taken from the present author's writing in Study Paper on Theme 8 of the Edinburgh 2010 Study Process, submitted by the Commission on World Mission and Evangelism, World Council of Churches, "Towards Common Witness to Christ Today: Mission and Visible Unity of the Church." For the full text, see, *International Review of Mission* 99. no. 390 (April 2010): 86-106.
[275] *Mission and Evangelism in Unity Today*, §27.
[276] Dietrich Werner, "Ecumenical Evangelism : Some Perspective for Panel Discussion," CWME and F&O Joint Consultation on Mission and Ecclesiology, Manuscript, 3-7 March 2009, Berekfürdö, Hungary, 3.

From Mountain to Valley

It is important to remember that one of the outcomes of Edinburgh 1910 was a desire to seek unity in mission. Particularly, the report of Commission VIII and the discussion emphasized the importance of practical measures between mission societies of different nationalities and denominations to find agreements in the "mission fields" in order to avoid competition, duplication and division of missionary efforts.[277] The Commission insisted on the importance of learning to know each other, of consultation, discussion and agreement as essential ways to avoid waste of time as well as human and financial resources. "The report still deplores too much unconcerted policy, mutual ignorance, overlapping and competition among actors in mission."[278]

But seeking unity in mission and evangelism is more than merely working together for an effectiveness to save our energy, resources and time through coordinated policy and actions. It is more than overcoming the scandal of disunity to attain more credibility in evangelism. It is a *notae ecclesia* or a distinct mark as a church to be called, identified by the Nicene Creed. It is an imperative from God to proclaim the good news of the unity of churches and of humanity.

Towards Common Witness

The churches are called to identify ways of witnessing in unity in evangelism. According to a study text of the Commission on World Mission and Evangelism of WCC, "Mission and Evangelism in Unity Today," in order to reach such a mutually enriching missionary ethos, the churches must:

- repent of past failures and reflect more self-critically on their ways of relating to one another and their methods of evangelizing;
- renounce all forms of denominational competition and rivalry and the temptation to proselytize members of other Christian traditions;

---

[277] See, *World Missionary Conference 1910 – Report of Commission VIII: Co-operation and the Promotion of Unity*, (Edinburgh/London: Oliphant, Anderson and Ferrier; New York/Chicago/Toronto: Fleming H. Revell Company, 1910).
[278] Samuel Kobia, "Cooperation and the Promotion of Unity: A World Council of Churches Perspective," (Lectures Reflecting on Edinburgh 1910 Commission 8, 27-28 April 2007, New College, Edinburgh, Manuscript), 1.

- avoid establishing parallel ecclesial structures, but rather stimulate, help and cooperate with the existing local churches in their evangelistic work;
- condemn any manipulation of humanitarian assistance to individual Christians or churches to induce people into changing their denominational allegiance or to further the missionary goals of one church at the expense of another...[279]

In order to overcome the scandal of proselytism, we are called to practice common witness as an act of ecumenical evangelism. *Common witness* is the "witness that the churches, even while separated, bear together, especially through joint efforts, by manifesting whatever divine gifts of truth and life they already share and experience in common."[280] In order to do so, churches in partnership in mission must commit themselves to:

- deepened understanding of what it means to be church in today's world, and acceptance and celebration of their interrelatedness in the on body of Christ (cf. 1 Cor. 12:12);
- deepened conviction that it is God's mission in which the churches share as God's co-workers, not their own;
- efforts to come to a greater common understanding and vision of their missionary role in contemporary society;
- reaching out together in Christ's way to new frontiers of mission – listening, accompanying, walking with, resourcing, receiving from one another;
- renewed determination to manifest together "the one hope of [their] calling" (Eph. 4:4) in order to

---

[279] *Mission and Evangelism in Unity Today*, §73.
[280] Thomas F. Best and Günther Gassmann, eds., *On the Way to Fuller Koinonia: Official Report of the Fifth World Conference on Faith and Order, Santiago de Compostela, 1993* (Geneva: WCC, 1994), 254.

- share more fully in the divine plan of salvation for the reconciliation and gathering up of all peoples and all things in Christ (cf. Eph. 1:9-10).[281]

Does ecumenical evangelism therefore mean overcoming proselytism and working together toward common witness only among the Christian churches? What are the implications when we extend the issue of proselytism and evangelism in the multi-religious context, keeping in mind the story of *Sam Bo Il Bae*?

In recent years, especially after September 11, 2001, there have been increasing inter-religious conflicts and some of them caused by unethical means of conversion. In response to this challenge, the WCC programme on Interfaith Dialogue and Cooperation, and the Pontifical Council for Inter-religious Dialogue in partnership with the World Evangelical Alliance (WEA) started a joint process on "Inter-religious Reflecting on Conversion: From Controversy to a Shared Code of Conduct (Code of Conduct)."[282] Although we have not yet reached a more concrete form of inter-religious cooperation and solidarity on the global issues, the Code of Conduct is an important ecumenical endeavour at least to avoid the tragic story in Afghanistan. Here are some working principles that are developing:

1. ***Imitating Jesus Christ****. As Christians in our witness we need to follow the example and teachings of Jesus Christ.*

---

[281] Best and Gassman, *On the Way*, 52-53.
[282] *The process of "Towards a code of conduct on conversion" is a joint effort by the Pontifical Council for Interreligious Dialogue, the WCC and World Evangelical Alliance (WEA). It affirms that "while everyone has a right to invite others to an understanding of their faith, it should not be exercised by violating other's rights and religious sensibilities... all should heal themselves from the obsession of converting others." With the goal of establishing a* **code of conduct on conversion**, *this activity will bring Christians from various denominations and theological traditions - the WCC constituency, the Roman Catholic Church, Evangelical and Pentecostal churches - together to discuss approaches and limitations on the conflictual issue of conversion and changes of affiliation in a religiously plural world. See,* http://www.oikoumene.org/gr/news/news-management/eng/a/article/1634/christian-code-of-conduct.html.

2. ***Mutual respect***. *We commit ourselves to working with those of other religions and people of goodwill in mutual respect, in harmony, and common action to build a better world.*
3. ***The rights of others***. *We acknowledge that followers of other religions have also the right and the freedom to profess, practice and propagate their religion.*
4. ***Christian virtues***. *We shall seek to conduct ourselves with charity and compassion, renouncing all forms of arrogance, boasting, superiority, condescension, and disparagement in our relationships with adherents of other religions.*
5. ***Incentives***. *We condemn all forms of allurements, including financial incentives and rewards, which are manipulative means for the conversion of others...*
6. ***Good in other religions***. *We recognize the responsibility to acknowledge, preserve, and promote what is good and true, in the beliefs and practices of other religions.*
7. ***Respect for culture***. *We shall strive to show respect for others through a desire to understand their language, history, traditions, and religion. We renounce the view that our own particular culture and expression of Christian life can be a universal norm.*
8. ***Rejection of violence and abuse of power***. *Following the example of Jesus Christ we reject all violence and the abuse of power in our witness.*
9. ***Solidarity with the persecuted***. *We recognise that in some countries, sometimes as a consequence of unethical missionary practices, our fellow believers are suffering discrimination and persecution...We shall do all we can to support them in their Christian witness and be a voice for the voiceless.*
10. ***Building inter-religious relationships.*** *Intentional relationship-building with people of different religions provides an opportunity for deeper mutual*

understanding and harmonious living in friendship and mutual respect...[283]

In fact already in 2000, the CWM developed more advanced approaches than the above principles. Chapter 5 of "The People of God among All God's Peoples" articulated well the CWM's missiological paradigms and strategies for mission, particularly with 12 affirmations and 12 rejections in participating in God's mission today.[284] For instance, with regards to evangelism, it affirmed, "Mission as proclaiming the gospel, which includes both the celebration of life in all its fullness as well as lamentation, grief and mourning." This concept of evangelism is more progressive and expanded, compared to the concept in its founding document which looked at evangelism merely as conversion and church growth. In terms of inter-religious dialogue, it affirmed, "Mission as understanding the many and distinct ways in which salvation is experienced in the lives of religious communities" and "Mission as the emergence of the Kingdom of God within history in which all religious traditions participate until the Reign of God is established." While the code of conduct focuses mainly on relational aspects, such as peace and respect regarding other faiths, the CWM seeks dialogue for life at least on a missiological level. If we read the 12 rejections, we can find similarities in the above "Code of Conduct" of 2009.

However, as we have seen in the case of the Korean churches, these affirmations and rejections have been almost a one-off theological declaration that mostly echoed in international ecumenical circles. It was neither discussed fully and accepted by the member churches, nor a constant process of missiological dialogue within the CWM family. Some parallel gaps between global missiological discourse and local practice in mission in the CWM can be noted. I do not think this is because the work of "The People of God..."[285] was irrelevant but because of the lack of intentional efforts and conversations for the reception of the text. Originally, the former unit of Mission Development would deal with this task. However, after the failure of some

---

[283] Draft, *Christian Witness in a Multi-Religious World: Recommendations for Code of Conduct* (Pontifical Council for Inter-Religious Dialogue and WCC Office on Inter-Religious Dialogue and Cooperation, 2009), 2-3.
[284] For details, see, Wickeri, *The People of God*, 43-46.
[285] I personally think that it was one of the most creative and well articulated missiological texts produced by CWM so far.

experiments, the unit changed to Mission Programme, putting more emphasis on missional activities and movements. Although some theological work was done under the general secretariat, during the last decade, I would have wished to see more emphasis on a constant missiological dialogue as a process or programme in the CWM. Based on my experience in the CWM in different capacities, I think that probably, since the early days of CWM, there has been a tendency to bring outsiders to help our missiological articulation. It seems that we have not wrestled enough to develop our own mission thinking; this may be the weakest area in the global CWM.

Ecumenical Evangelism as Proclamation of Life in Hope

Samuel Kobia claims that *oikoumene* is a movement for the affirmation of life – a movement to uphold the sanctity, integrity and dignity of all God's people. When God created human beings, God's final act was to breathe into Adam's nostrils "the breath of life" so that Adam became a living creature (Genesis 2:7). Therefore, all living creatures are alive with God's breath of life. Because of that, all lives on earth are sacred. All the efforts to save and to give life, spiritual as well as physical, partake in God's sacred mission, of which evangelism is a part.

Our faith is in a living, life-giving God. "The realization of life, in all its fullness, including the material basis of life, is the primary mediation of the approach to God,"[286] who is the creator, redeemer and sustainer of all life. For Jesus, God is a God of life and God's mission is one of giving life (John 10:10; 14:6). According to K. C. Abraham, God's messianic signs are signs of life in its fullness. "To believe in God is to affirm the supremacy of life over death."[287] "This also means any assault of life – hunger, destitution, squalor, oppression, and injustice – is an attack on God, on God's will for the life of humankind. A denial of life, therefore, is a rejection of the God of life."[288] Jürgen Moltmann states, "Where Jesus is, there is life. There is abundant life, vigorous life,

---

[286] Jon Sonrono, "The Epiphany of the God of Life in Jesus Nazareth," in *Idols of Death and the God of Life*, ed. Richard Pablo (New York: Orbis, 1983), 73.
[287] K. C. Abraham, "Mission as Celebration of Life," *CTC Bulletin* 24, no.1-2 (2008): 31.
[288] Gustavo Gutierrez, as quoted in Araya Vitorio, *God of the Poor* (New York: Orbis, 1987), 73.

loved life and eternal life."[289] Indeed, our mission is to follow this life-saving and life-giving mission of Christ, and evangelism is to witness to the abundant life in Christ in words and deeds.

We live in a world where this sacred God-given life is at stake. For instance, the current global economic crisis is a human-made disaster for humanity and creation. The global scale of economic dictatorship by the neo-liberal market is causing the "genocide" of creation and the environment. Neo-liberal economic globalization has a strong ideological dimension or a quasi-religious message, too, that suggests, "The global market system will save the world."[290] It is not only a threat to economic life but also to the spiritual life of people and demands an interfaith resistance to this idolatry.[291]

In the context of global economic crisis, how then can we reclaim evangelism as a life-affirming force over and against the free market evangelism? How can we celebrate life in the midst of news of wars, disasters and crises? Celebrating life in this situation means pointing to the eschatological hope on the horizon of history. Duncan B. Forrester states, "Hope is resistance to a hopeless situation...The hope is good news to the poor and all who suffer."[292] Therefore, evangelism in the context of the neo-liberal economic globalization means telling and sharing stories about finding, nurturing and growing seeds of new hope in the hopeless situation, in solidarity with people of other faiths. In this regard, the OIKOTREE movement, which is a joint collaboration between the CWM, WCC and WARC, is a remarkable example of proclaiming the gospel in the global market, although there is no interfaith dimension yet.[293]

Therefore, an urgent mission task today is, through stories and experiences such as the one of *Sam Bo Il Bae,* to find a wider ecumenical

---

[289] Jürgen Moltman, *The Passion for Life* (Philadelphia: Fortress, 1978), 22.

[290] The injustice of the global economy has been projected by neo-liberal economists, who believe that if they remove the intervention of state and ethical values from the market, the world economy will dramatically grow. They claim that this growth will bring the ultimate wellbeing and even salvation of humanity. F. A. Hayek, *Law, Legislation and Liberty*, vol. II: *The Mirage of Social Justice*, 2nd ed. (London: Routledge, 1982), 63-70.

[291] Keum, "Editorial,"183-184.

[292] Duncan B. Forrester, *Christian Justice and Public Policy* (Cambridge: Cambridge University Press, 1997), 246-7.

[293] For more information, see, www.oikotree.org.

interfaith solidarity for life, to nurture them as a new sign of hope in the midst of growing religious fundamentalism. It is vital to recover the affirmation of life as the heart of mission in all religions and to share their wisdoms for the abundant life of the whole creation.

Conclusion

Mission and evangelism means to participate in God's plan and work to save the whole *oikoumene*. We are called as co-workers for this glorious task as the people of God and disciples of Jesus Christ. Our missionary mandate is to be servants, preparing together the feast of life with all of God's peoples, regardless of religious background. It is urgent for the CWM and its member churches to re-introduce this life affirming and interfaith evangelical paradigm in re-visioning their partnership in mission in the 21st century. For this purpose, I have argued for an ecumenical evangelism as an invitation to the feast of life, focusing on humility, hope, celebration of life, and interfaith cooperation. Indeed, our evangelism is to follow the way of Jesus Christ who said, "I have come that they may have life, and may have it in all its fullness" (John 10:10).

Ecumenical evangelism does not mean unity at any price. It is about costly unity for the sake of our God-given life and the salvation of the world, seeking the holistic understanding of mission of which interfaith dialogue is an essential part. It is not a "cheap" holism justifying everything in the name of mission but "costly" frontiership in mission. It must therefore not only be open to dialogue but also actively seek cooperation with people of other faiths and with secular society. It is a mission imperative for the CWM family today if we want to be a genuine frontier in mission!

Lastly, I would like to suggest the following three key themes for possible further studies of the CWM's perspective and practice of evangelism in the years to come:

Evangelism as interfaith solidarity for peace and life
- Contextual understanding and practice of evangelism
  (e.g. The Asian understanding of evangelism which is distinctive from the American school of church growth)
- Authentic spirituality of evangelism

> (Different from aggressive militant spirituality such as 'spiritual warfare' as spiritual foundation of evangelism)

During the 200 years of LMS/CWM history, when it was most comfortable, there began a new crisis. And when there were troubled waters, a new vision would emerge. I recall the theme of the 200th anniversary of LMS/CWM at this particular juncture of time. It is indeed a time to "dare to dream," and not always about matters of governance and structure, but about mission thinking so that the "gales of change" can blow.

8

Economic and Ecological Justice: Challenging Mission in the 21st Century in the Work of the Council for World Mission and the Ecumenical Family

Rogate R. Mshana[294]

This essay is written in the context of the celebration of thirty years of the existence of the Council for World Mission (hereafter the CWM) and to highlight its contribution to what it terms as "postcolonial mission studies in the 21st century." The "partner principle" (which refers to a concept framed at the 2006 Assembly of the CWM in Ocho Rios, as a pattern and style of engagement that is personal, communal and pastoral and includes the understanding that the journey together is as important as the destination), challenges the CWM to identify fundamental subjects that need to inform the discussions on the "partner principle," in the next few years. This is crucial in trying to discover what transformative mission means for the CWM in the 21st century.

I will limit myself to the work done by the CWM and by the ecumenical family. The essay raises the following three fundamental questions: To what extent have churches seriously addressed economic and ecological justice as a matter of transformative mission? How can the CWM and the wider ecumenical family address this issue adequately? What are the areas that need attention and improvement as the churches engage themselves in transformative mission in the 21st

---

[294] Director for Justice, Diakonia and Responsibility for Creation, World Council of Churches.

century? These questions will hopefully trigger further studies in these areas of concern.

The essay hinges on the premise that the current context of economic and ecological injustice requires transformative mission that will open doors into a better understanding of the terms "economic and ecological justice." This formulation emerged out of reflections in the ecumenical movement. The mission work done by the CWM churches thus far, does not, sufficiently address this problem probably because, among other factors, the CWM carries within it some legacy of the traditional understandings of mission. Some churches still situate mission predominantly as a purely spiritual experience and as evangelism for conversion. This is the present reality even though the CWM handbook (1991) and various other documents theologically clarify and address justice and respect for the integrity of creation as important aspects of mission.

It is suggested that one of the major reasons why the CWM member churches do not address economic and ecological injustice as integral to mission may be due to the fact that the local agenda of the churches is not informed by global issues. To move to a holistic and transformative mission that promotes justice and integrity of creation might be enhanced by a new format for the CWM assemblies, which are themselves a new phenomenon for the CWM family. Assemblies could be a useful arena, if utilized well, to challenge the churches to address the current economic and ecological crises and to move to a transformative mission agenda. The past three assemblies have already begun the process of raising systemic challenges, in a coherent manner. This could be enhanced by ensuring that the Assemblies can be the place where local and contextual experiences are shared and exchanged, where common ground in transformative mission work for the churches is set, and where global issues are articulated and clarified.

The 2006 the CWM assembly for instance, issued a statement that indicated a shift from the past,[295] *"under the guidance of the Holy Spirit we sought wisdom and direction in positioning ourselves as the CWM to rise to the awesome challenge of the 21st century, of human suffering and destruction of nature and our environment."*[296] The

---

[295] Although this was already identified in the 1999 mission statement.
[296] *CWM Assembly Statement 2006* (Ocho Rios, Jamaica, 18-27 June 2006), 1.

statement outlined priorities whereby, . ". *We identified globalization and economic justice...gender justice, care for the environment and new ways of being church as priority areas.* "[297] In other words, these priorities, among others, were identified as part of the mission agenda. Commitments relevant to the topic of economic and ecological justice that were outlined for three years from this assembly included *"building capacity to respond to economic poverty and deprivation and giving urgent attention to ecological and environmental stewardship."*

In practice, however, we see a different picture regarding how the churches prioritize their work. A CWM survey conducted by Susannah Steele and Steve de Gruchy pointed out that churches put poverty and economic justice as the third area of priority covering 224 or 39% of the entries. Social justice and human rights were the second priority with 45.4%, while priority one was evangelism with 71.6% of the entries. Nature, ecology and food security, which form the axis for life, were accorded only 11% of the entries.[298] This survey certainly ought to have set the stage for the CWM to shift its agenda and focus on the study of economic and ecological justice in the context of transformative mission in the 21st century. Why did this shift not take place? Is it because the CWM is also, "a place where the dominant style of the engagement is personal and pastoral rather than pragmatic or goal oriented" as stated in the CWM paper on "The Postcolonial Mission Perspectives"?[299]

The CWM's commitment to ensuring that the agenda is set by the issues that emerge from the local context is appropriate. However, the role of the global fellowship is to ensure that the local agenda is shaped by an awareness of its global ramifications and our interconnectedness with each other. It is at the assemblies where the antithesis of globalization needs to be discussed so that its reductionism of people, communities and countries into entities of materialism, competition and consumerism can be addressed and clarified. It is essential that the local is also informed by the global in order to get the

---

[297] *CWM Assembly Statement 2006*, 2.
[298] See research by Susannah Steel and Steve de Gruchy in S. de Gruchy, "'Growing Up Increasing and Yielding Thirty...':Change and Continuity in the Council for World Mission, 1977-2007" which is a chapter in this book.
[299] "Post-Colonial Mission Perspectives" (New Note Colloquium, Devon Valley Hotel, Stellenbosch, South Africa, 19-21 May 2009), section 5.1.2.

complete picture. In this globalizing world, local areas are deeply affected by global issues such as climate change, trade, finance and energy use. Global policies articulated in Washington, London or Paris destroy the local base. Assemblies should be arenas to highlight these issues so as to sharpen and even re-orient the local work in mission.

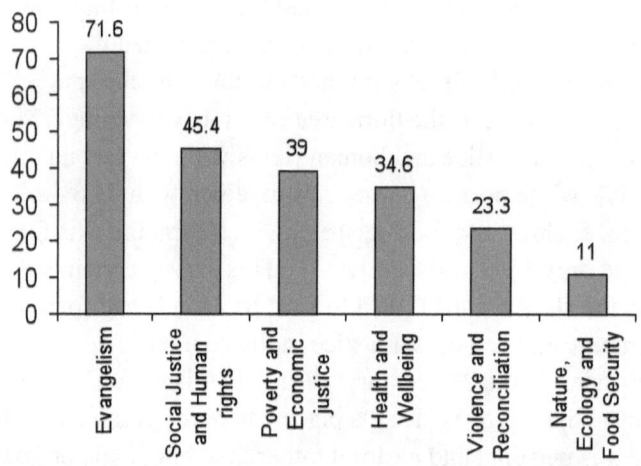

Source: CWM survey by Steel and de Gruchy in S. de Gruchy's article in this book (graph by R. Mshana, July, 2009.)

To go back to the CWM survey, it is clear that churches are mainly concerned with priority one where they see themselves as having an advantage in the area of skills and knowledge, based on traditional mission. Priorities two, three and four in the survey, call for special analytical skills. The survey by Steel and de Gruchy also indicates that nature, ecology and food security are given the least priority while issues that relate to a traditional understandings of diakonia and pastoral care (health issues such as HIV and Aids and violence) are given precedence. This is, therefore, one of the challenges the churches need to engage themselves in, to address economic and ecological justice. Before we go further to examine the extent to which churches are engaged in addressing economic and ecological justice, it is pertinent to explain the following terms: ***economic justice, social justice, ecological justice and environmental justice.***

Understanding Economic and Ecological Justice

The term *economic justice* is often used interchangeably with *social justice* - these terms stress different but complementary points. *Economic justice* is about how economic life is organized in terms of production, distribution and consumption of material goods and services. The manner in which these goods and services are produced, distributed and consumed could be done unjustly and hence lead to what can be termed **economic injustice**. John Calvin stated that, *"According to the Bible, hoarding is to be condemned, because no wealth could belong solely to one individual. Every benefit is really from the result of the collaboration of those who are linked together working on the same task, and more generally depends on the work of the whole society."*[300] He spoke of greater sharing and averting greed as the way forward. The main mistake that humanity faces is the increasing belief that the market alone can enhance economic justice. The market, when it is an uncontrolled mechanism, has failed to lead to economic justice; it has instead created more injustice and the gap between the rich and poor has only systematically increased.

Social justice is about just relationships and encompasses economic relationships and justice. Social justice is the virtue that guides us in creating those organized human interactions we call institutions. In turn, social institutions, when justly organized, provide us with access to what is good for the person, both individually and in our associations with others. Social justice also imposes on each individual a personal responsibility to work with others to design and continually perfect our institutions as tools for personal and social development. It involves addressing issues such as inequalities and exclusion at various levels of institutional organization in our societies. Institutions are set up mainly to monitor whether all human beings are treated with dignity and that all have the right to enjoy the fruits of their economic achievements. The language of rights is used to emphasize the need to implement "social justice" as "social rights" under the auspices of the United Nations declaration on Economic, Social and Cultural Rights. Social justice, as a term, is used more often by churches than by secular institutions because

---

[300] André Biéler, *Calvin's Economic and Social Thought, Translation* (Geneva: WCC Publications, 2005), 298.

in a faith context, justice goes beyond rights of each individual – it is based on God's justice founded in agape love that embraces the whole community and the earth.

The terms **ecological justice** and **environmental justice** surfaced in the last part of the 20th century, when it was recognized, largely based on the wisdom of indigenous communities all over the world, that the earth and its distress need to be heeded. Aruna Gnanadason speaks of recognizing that there is something to be learnt from the alternative cosmo-visions offered by those who live in prudent relationships with the earth.[301] Indigenous Peoples challenge Christian theologians, ethicists and economists to recognize that the earth has its own integrity and therefore requires respect. The ecumenical principle on which this is based is that both the poor and the earth cry out for justice. Nature can be seen as the new poor, "not the poor that crowds out the human poor, but the 'also' poor; and as such it demands our attention and care."[302] Abraham, writing on a theological response to ecological crisis, illuminated the meaning of eco-justice by quoting Moltmann who said, *"We shall not be able to achieve social justice without justice for the natural environment; we shall not be able to achieve justice for nature without social justice."*[303] Abraham points out that several dimensions of this eco-justice are coming to the fore through the experiences of the struggles of the marginalized.

Leonardo Boff, the eminent Latin American theologian of Liberation Theology, while speaking of different ecologies, portrayed social ecology as the way that social and economic systems interact with the natural ecosystem, and "since the human race is part of the environment, social injustice goes hand-in-hand with ecological injustice."[304] Larry Rasmussen defines the earth's distress as socio-

---

[301] Aruna Gnanadason, *Listen to the Women: Listen to the Earth* (Geneva: WCC Publications, 2005), 104. (The text in the next few paragraphs has been inspired by her book).
[302] Sallie McFague, *Super, Natural Christians: How We Should Love Nature* (Minneapolis: Fortress Press, 1997), 6.
[303] See K.C. Abraham, "A Theological Response to Ecological Crisis," in *Ecotheology: Voices from South and North*, ed. David Hallman (Geneva: WCC Publications, 1994), 68. Quoting from Jürgen Moltmann, *The Future of Creation* (Philadelphia: Fortress, 1979), 128.
[304] Leonardo Boff, *Ecology and Liberation: A New Paradigm* (Maryknoll, NY: Orbis Books, 2000), 88.

ecological. In other words, the rights attributed to the earth include the rights of all of humankind (not just some) to also live and survive. He underlines that it is not possible to see "'humanity' as some nebulous whole...but for varied human beings who presently occupy different strata in domestic and world social orders."[305] Many environmental, feminist and social movements have placed the demand for ecological justice at the centre, remembering that economy and ecology represent two interrelated and inseparable perspectives on God's household of life (*oikos*).[306]

David Hallman, who has contributed extensively to the WCC programme on Climate Change, has advised the ecumenical family to avoid reductionism as it refers to the natural world and the ecological crisis, by clarifying the commonly used terms such as **nature**, or **environment**. He chooses to use the more comprehensive term **Creation** and the **Earth** with a capital letter in order to grant to them respect. According to Hallman, the term **environment** has its drawbacks because it seems to speak of that which surrounds us, as if we are not part of it. It is also problematic when people refer to "*our* environment" revealing a mentality of ownership. **Nature** has been another option. It has the benefit of evoking images of beauty, but people would think of nature as trees, birds, and seas and would exclude human beings. The term nature, according to Hallman, can also be inadequate because it connotes either a hard scientific perspective or a soft romanticized sentimentality.

According to Hallman, **Creation** on the other hand, evokes a very comprehensive holistic perspective. It refers to the entire natural world, including the expanses of the universe. He argues that "We humans think ourselves as full part of creation. Furthermore creation is more than the physical reality of this world. It carries with it a spiritual sense that is important to recapture if we are to learn to respect and live in harmony with the rest of it...We need to integrate to the insights of science, the spirituality of religion, and the analysis of economics if we

---

[305] Larry L. Rasmussen, *Earth Community, Earth Ethics* (Geneva: WCC Publications, 1996), 74.
[306] *Alternative Globalization Addressing Peoples and Earth (AGAPE)* (Background Document, WCC, JPC, Reprint, Geneva: WCC, 2006), 40.

are to develop a more ecological way of life."[307] Churches and the ecumenical family are still giving lip service to taking seriously economics and creation as a theological issue and an issue of spirituality. It is therefore essential for churches in mission to highlight the theology of creation as fundamental in addressing the ecological crisis today.

Therefore, the term *ecological justice* or *eco-justice* - which is used to combine the concepts of ecological sustainability and social justice - is based on two principles. First, it is about addressing humanity's mutilation of the earth with impunity through production, distribution and consumption - the way humanity manages industries, agriculture, mining, transport and so on. Injustice happens when the earth and its atmosphere are destroyed in the name of generating economic growth. Secondly, it addresses the process by which those who are richer and stronger destroy the earth, further impoverishing the poor, making them even more vulnerable, and resulting in social injustice. These have very high **ecological foot prints**[308] and are therefore indebted to the earth. They have to pay an ecological debt[309] to the earth. Recently the WCC sent out a draft statement on "Eco-justice and Ecological Debt"

---

[307] David G. Hallman, *A Place in Creation: Ecological Visions In Science, Religion, and Economics* (Toronto: The United Church Publishing House, 1992), xii-xiii. Hallman has also developed these perspectives in *Ecotheology, Voices from South and North* (Geneva: WCC, 1994) and *Spirituality Values for Earth Community* (Geneva: WCC, 2000).

[308] **Ecological foot print** is a rough estimate of the amount of biologically productive land per person that would be needed in order for renewable resources to provide all goods and services (food and water, shelter, possessions, energy and other physical requirements, including the recycling of waste) needed to sustain a particular life style. Two extreme examples: Mozambique has a footprint of 0.5 acres while the U.S footprint is 24 acres. Much of the U.S foot print comes from energy use. At present the footprint of people in the North average 6.4 ha/person, which is substantially higher than the ecological footprints of people in the South which averages 0.8 ha/person.

[309] **Ecological debt** is a concept describing the imbalance between the perceived "fair share" of natural resources and one's actual usage of those resources. Overuse of natural resources through operations such as mining, deforestation and some industrial activities leads to the contamination of rivers, lakes and the sea, and the pollution of the earth. Unsustainable consumption and production patterns lead some to leave heavier ecological footprints – this has been identified as an ecological debt that is owed to the earth and to those who have little access to the so-called benefits of development.

to its member churches for their input. Another policy statement of the WCC stresses the fact that climate change is a matter of justice, particularly for those who are and will increasingly be affected - these are the impoverished and vulnerable communities, in particular in the global South, who are dependent on natural resources for their survival and who do not have the means to adapt to the changes that climate change provokes.[310]

It is essential to understand that poverty-stricken people are created by economic injustices done to them rather than by ecological destruction or climate change as it is now being contended. The people who are called environmental refugees become refugees because of economic and ecological injustice. Their movement in search of survival should therefore not to be attributed solely to climate change. Climate change, on the other hand, is the result of economic models that are not sustainable - models that therefore need to hold together for common action, economic, social and ecological injustice. The restoration of economic justice and ecological justice is, therefore, an obligation for all human beings. The statement of the WCC on Climate Change underlines that: "All humanity is made in the image and likeness of God and all nature bears the marks of God. This demands (requires) of us to adopt the guiding principle of equity. God's inheritance is for the communal body, a concept that includes all of nature."[311]

Mission in the 21st Century, therefore needs to encompass a reflection on how God acts to protect and promote justice in creation and in human society. Mission has to recognize that where there is **eco-injustice** there is "sin that deeply violates God's good will, God's steadfast love for life, for human beings and for the whole creation."[312]

---

[310] *Minute on Global Warming and Climate Change* (WCC Central Committee, Geneva, February 2008).
[311] WCC, "The Earth's Atmosphere : Responsible Caring and Equitable Sharing For A Global Commons: A Justice Statement regarding Climate Change from the World Council of Churches," (for the 6th Session of the Conference of Parties (COP6) to the UN Framework Convention on Climate Change ; The Hague, The Netherlands, November 2000) (unpublished), 2.
[312] *AGAPE*, 41.

Transformative Mission

If economic justice and ecological justice are to be brought centre-stage into the mission agenda, it becomes essential to speak of and define *transformative mission.* This is a process of living God's life-giving promise of transformation for a world where life can be celebrated and enjoyed by all people with integrity and dignity. It is about giving life to suffering humanity and creation as we continue to seek the Kingdom of God. Transformative mission is about promoting *economic justice and eco-justice.*

A brief look at ecumenical history will situate this discussion better. At the World Council of Churches Assembly in Uppsala in 1968, it is this understanding of transformative mission that had been stressed when reference was made to Christ's mission: "The Spirit of the Lord is upon me, because he has anointed me to preach good news to the poor. He has sent me to proclaim release to the captives and recovery of sight to the blind; to set at liberty those who are oppressed, to claim the acceptable year of the Lord..." (Luke 4:18f). Based on this text from Luke, the Assembly stated: "We heard the cry of those who long for peace; of the hungry and exploited who demand bread and justice; of the victims of discrimination who claim human justice; and the increasing millions who seek for the meaning of life."[313] Then again, in 1978, the then WCC Commission on Inter-Church Aid, Refugee and World Service (CICARWS) stated something that comes close to the understanding of transformative mission. It is such an understanding that is also at the heart of the WCC's AGAPE process, which is referred to and described in detail, later in this essay: "It is in the Eucharistic act where we find the imperative of service in the world. The Lord who we meet in the bread and wine is the same Lord whom we meet in the poor, the oppressed and the needy...Our Lord sends us to join him in bringing good news to the poor and the oppressed."[314] The CWM Assembly theme of 2009, "Living the Good News" provides the CWM churches with the opportunity to engage with the message in this text (Luke 4:18f) and related texts so as to address economic and ecological justice.

There is, therefore, no doubt that today, "good news to the poor" is a combination of economic justice, ecological justice and human

---

[313] World Council of Churches, *The Uppsala Report 1968: Official Report of the Fourth Assembly of the World Council of Churches* (Geneva :WCC, 1968), 5.
[314] "Service and Unity," *Midstream* 28 (1979): 174f.

dignity. These are the basic components of what could be defined as transformative mission. It marks a paradigm shift from mission as focused exclusively on converting souls from other religions to Christianity, or on small acts of charity. It calls for the rescuing of humanity and the earth from a resource consuming economy that has degraded an estimated 60% of the world's ecosystems, put whole communities and their jobs and livelihoods at risk, and has led to disintegration and fragmentation of societies.

David Bosch interprets the phrase, "to let the oppressed go free" as having a distinctly social profile in Judah, in a context where there was the exploitation of the poor by the rich. Even on a day of fasting, the rich pursue their own interests, make their employees work harder (v3) and wrangle with those who owe them money (v4).[315] At that time, in order to pay the taxes levied by the Persian King, as reflected in Nehemiah chapter five, the people had to mortgage their vineyards and homes and even sell their children into slavery to other rich Jews. The latter grasped the opportunity to capitalize on the predicament of the poor.

The same scenario is present in the world today - we read about those losing their homes due to foreclosures because of the effects of the sub-prime mortgage market effect; or of women in Asia who sell their kidneys to pay their debts, or sell their children into prostitution; or of those who lose their lands to mining companies without compensation; or of farmers in Africa who lose their livelihoods because subsidized products from the US and Europe are dumped on African markets; or of workers in Europe who lose their jobs due to companies outsourcing their jobs to places with cheap labour in the South; or of women working 18 hours in sweat shops like slaves – the list is endless.

Clearly, transformative mission is about promoting transformative justice - of creating just relationships and righting these wrongs, and in the process addressing those with power and wealth. "Woe to them that devise iniquity, and work evil upon their beds! When the morning is light they practice it, because it is in the power of their hand. And they covet fields, and take them by violence; and houses, and take them away," warns the prophet Micah (Micah 2:1-2).

---

[315] David J. Bosch, *Transforming Mission: Paradigm Shifts in Theology of Mission* (Maryknoll, New York: Orbis Books, 1992), 100.

Transformative mission is about freeing people who are enslaved by unfettered markets which are surreptitiously stealing resources from the poor and giving it to the rich, widening the gap between the rich and the poor.

Transformative Mission is about Economic and Ecological Justice

The aforementioned understanding of economic and ecological justice in the context of transformative mission could be the prism through which we assess whether the CWM churches and the ecumenical family in general have implemented a new mission agenda. About 71% of the CWM member churches are also members of the World Council of Churches (WCC) and a small portion of them are members of the World Alliance of Reformed Churches (WARC). In theory, this should mean that the issues on economic and ecological justice in the context of mission raised by the assemblies of the WCC and WARC and those of the CWM should actually be part of the mission work of these churches. The assemblies of the WCC and of WARC had produced radical statements that were to be discussed by the churches and followed up on.

During the VIII Assembly of the World Council of Churches (1998) in Harare, Zimbabwe, the question was raised, "How do we live our faith in the context of globalization?" In response to this, the AGAPE (Alternative Globalization Addressing People and Earth) background document was produced. This led to a seven year process of study and analysis of economic globalization which was done jointly by the WCC, WARC and the Lutheran World Federation in conjunction with the churches, including those that are members of the CWM. At the WCC General assembly in Porto Alegre in 2006, an AGAPE call was issued, encouraging churches to engage themselves in promoting economic justice by addressing eight issues: these are poverty eradication; just trade; just finance; sustainable use of land and natural resources, advocacy against privatization of public goods and services: promotion of life-giving agriculture; advocacy for decent jobs, emancipated work and people's livelihoods. The eighth issue focuses on the churches and the empire, encouraging the churches to question power and empire from a biblical and theological perspective, and to take a firm faith stance against hegemonic powers. This would manifest the churches' belief that all power is accountable to God, and no human empire should have the ability to control the lives of the people.[316]

In a similar vein, responding to the first challenge issued in Kitwe (October, 1995),[317] a Confession on Covenanting for Justice in the Economy and the Earth was adopted by the delegates of the World Alliance of Reformed Churches (WARC) at its 24th General Council in Accra, Ghana (2004). The ACCRA Confession is based on the theological conviction that economic and ecological injustice requires the Reformed family to respond to these issues as a matter of faith in the gospel of Jesus Christ. The Accra Confession called upon *"Reformed Christians around the world to engage injustices in the world as and integral part of their churches' witness and mission."*[318] One of the first roles of WARC was *"to covenant for justice in the economy and the earth: programmes include mobilizing churches to address economic and ecological justice issues and advocating for just models for trade, agriculture and economics."*[319] A number of WARC members organized workshops on how to live out the Accra confession. The discussion continues to clarify terms, including whether the term "empire" should be used or not.

---

[316] *Alternative Globalization Addressing Peoples and Earth (AGAPE) A Background Document*, Revised New Edition (Geneva: WCC Publications, 2006), 63-64.

[317] "Reformed Faith and Economic Justice," (World Alliance of Reformed Churches and Southern Africa Alliance of Reformed Churches Consultation, Kitwe, Zambia, October 1995) (unpublished). www.warc.ch/pc/rfej/07. The WARC-SAARC consultation on Reformed faith and economic justice, held in Kitwe, Zambia, in October 1995, "painfully" concluded that the African experience of global economic forces can no longer be seen as merely an ethical problem. It has become a theological problem, causing strained loyalties: either God or mammon. "The gospel to the poor is at stake in the very mechanism of the global economy today." Simultaneously, the Kitwe consultation requested WARC's executive to make allowance for an encounter, in a limited pre-conference at Debrecen, of churches from the South to consider the challenge of faith raised by the sacrifice of humanity on the altar of the global economy.

[318] *The Accra Confession: Covenanting for Justice in the Economy and the Earth* (Accra, Ghana, 2004, published in World Alliance of Reformed Churches, 24th General Council Proceedings, WARC, Switzerland, 2005). www.warc.ch.

[319] *The Accra Confession.*

The production of the AGAPE and Covenanting for Justice Statements was based on various studies, reflections and consultations organized separately and jointly by the WCC and WARC between 1997 and 2004. Some churches took the statements and used them to produce their own reflections and documents, something which is commendable, while others took the effort to organize workshops on the issues so as to determine how to implement the various recommendations. Some theological colleges discussed them from a faith perspective. This is encouraging. However, many churches did very little concerning these statements.

Having recognized that the discussions are far from over, the three ecumenical organizations, namely, the WARC, WCC and the CWM, initiated a new process to respond to the unfinished agenda of AGAPE and Covenanting for Justice, through a coordinated ecumenical journey. *Oikotree: Putting Justice at the Heart of Faith* was initiated as a follow-up to the 2006 CWM/WARC Kuala Lumpur consultation on *Living out the Accra Confession: Implications for our Spirituality and Mission.* The vision for Oikotree was inspired by the possibilities to connect theology with people's struggles to build a 'covenanting for justice' movement in partnership with social movements. Oikotree followed on the AGAPE and Covenanting for Justice Processes, both of which explore the problems with neo-liberal economic globalization and its impact on the earth and its peoples. This process of putting justice at the heart of faith is a new opportunity for the CWM members to raise issues of economic and ecological justice at various levels, and in conjunction with other ecumenical bodies. As has been noted, there has been a very rudimentary approach to address this task as part of CWM mission. While there are several theology statements issued by the CWM's theological working groups, and also those issued by the assemblies, in reality one sees very little in terms of advocacy work on these issues at various levels. However, in the process of building a partnership within the CWM based on mutual trust and sharing of resources, it has demonstrated a model that is exemplary to the secular and ecclesial world. The secular world is based on unequal sharing of resources and no model is yet created to ensure there is equity in the world. The ecclesial relationships in reality are also not based on sharing resources as mentioned in the WCC El Escorial Consultation on Sharing life in held in 1987,[320] where guidelines on sharing resources were outlined. CWM took a bold step further on this issue by demonstrating a new way of sharing in mission. This move needs now to be a stepping stone to challenging the world, by addressing the current inequity in the world where the rich become richer and the poor become poorer, and where resources flow from the poor to the rich. Within the Oikotree process, the CWM could share many ideas and actions on how to address socio-economic and ecological inequality.

An informal WCC/CWM/WARC group met several times following the Kuala Lumpur meeting and agreed to sponsor Oikotree as a joint covenanting for justice movement, as proposed in Kuala Lumpur. In February 2007, the CWM convened a meeting in Chiang Mai with representatives of all three bodies to prepare a concept paper for the way forward. From this, a facilitating group was established to develop a covenanting for justice movement based on the outcomes of the Chiang Mai meeting. The Chiang Mai meeting had highlighted six core areas of work, building on the Kuala Lumpur statement: Theology; Spirituality; Mission; Economy; Ecology and Empire.

Two workshops have been organized on re-reading the bible from the perspective of economic, ecological issue, the meaning and implications of empire, and another on spirituality. The results of these workshops can be found on the newly established Oikotree website www.oikotree.org. This website invites individuals, groups and organizations to share experiences and resource materials articulating how we can put justice at the heart of faith.

Oikotree is now integrated into the CWM programmes and informs programme plans of both the WCC and WARC. An important learning through this process is that the work of mission that addresses economic and ecological justice can not be done by the churches alone, without cooperating with other social movements that are campaigning for alternatives. This is a challenge to most churches, particularly to those who are members of the CWM, as they are used to seeing mission work only within their own confines such as through their own roundtables. The CWM's commitment to work at the local level should challenge congregations to relate, on this subject, to social movements

---

[320] *El Escorial Consultation Report, Sharing Life, Official Report of the WCC Consultation on Koinonia : Sharing Life in a World Community*, edited by Hubbert van Beek (Geneva: WCC Publications, 1989).

working at the grass roots. At the regional and global levels, there is need to connect with other global initiatives working on alternatives. The World Social Forum and its regional and national branches is one such arena to connect with other networks that build their alternative visions on the understanding that "another world is possible." At the 2007 World Social Forum in Nairobi, fifty thousand participants attended and 50% of these were from churches working in poverty-stricken areas. The churches opened their doors for the opening worship and other events of the World Social Forum.[321] This link should be continued and strengthened.

Studies done by the ecumenical family need to be available at the local context as well. This raises a fundamental question: How can ecumenical studies be made available in local languages? Part of this could include initiatives carried out within the context of mission work. There has been a constant critique that issues discussed at the global ecumenical level do not reach churches at the local areas. While this criticism is well-founded, the tendency should not be to neglect the issues at the global level and only work at the local level, but rather to see how such invaluable information can be discussed in local contexts.

While working together at all levels of the ecumenical movement is significant, it is also necessary to underline what individual churches could work on. There are churches that are well- resourced with information, technology and financial resources. Churches in rich countries are equipped with academies and research institutions that analyze and bring issues to the attention of policy makers, while churches in the South have inadequate financial resources and infrastructure but have rich local expertise. The partner principle is about solidarity in sharing knowledge and resources within the ecumenical family. The following are some suggestions of how we could integrate ecological and economic justice into the work of transformative mission based on the "partner principle."

---

[321] See the World Social Forum in Nairobi 2007, www.forumsocialmundial.org.br.

Addressing Economic Ecological Justice as Transformative Mission in the Frame of the "Partner Principle"

If economic and ecological justice as transformative mission work is to be done in genuine partnership, then the churches in the north and in the south need to be fully involved in it, together. The next section of this essay will address this. Work in economic and ecological injustice is normally divided into two parts. The first task is to analyze present realities and to develop **an alternative economic system** that will provide life for both people and the earth. The second task is to engage in comprehensive **advocacy work** that will show a way forward in promoting the alternatives.

Based on an all-encompassing definition of transformative mission, the work of mission includes giving the world the sense of hope that there are sustainable alternatives to prevailing economic systems that have been engineered by so-called "free market capitalism." Some would claim that critiquing free market capitalism is advocating for failed communism! No, today we should simply work for just systems that are good for the people and the earth. Today there are financial, labor, food and climate crises because capitalism has designed economic systems that cause these crises to happen. They create social injustice. Cutting edge research has indicated that rich people and nations become richer and poor people and nations become poorer.[322] This inequality cannot be resolved by advocating for more growth. Free market capitalism rewards greed and punishes cooperation and sharing. Globally, we have allowed just a few big companies to dominate, particularly in the public sector.

Due to their social location, churches in the North happen to be at the centre of power, where economic and monetary theories and practices that shaped the current devastating economic model first emerged. Therefore, the journey to the search for alternatives cannot be done by the churches in their mission work alone. They must involve social movements that are working on the alternatives. Change is difficult because the churches are operating at the centre of capitalism. No one is able to find a way to change the existing industrial-complex

---

[322] UNDP, *Human Development Report* (1999). The report mentions that 20% of the richest share 86 % of Global GDP while the middle 60% shares 13 %. The poorest 20% share only 1% of global GDP. This scenario has not changed over years. The system can be reversed by Equity, Ethics, Inclusion, Human security, sustainability and development.

based economy – an economy that has developed over the centuries and is dependent on exploiting people and the earth. Together with churches in the South, they need to address how to change this model.

Churches in the South, on the other hand, struggle to overcome poverty by promoting projects to help poor people, though they recognize that the problem is systemic in nature. Diakonia in the South focuses on helping the destitute with projects addressing clean water, agriculture and also health institutions and schools – all dependent on funds from the North. In order to deal with poverty, others have devised small loan schemes; income generating projects or other financial incentives for people in poverty. These initiatives are helpful in the short run but they are still just drops in the sea of poverty. They also face threats of dying out as aid from churches, mission-related organizations and government development agencies are running out!

Some churches in the North have worked on alternatives: ethical investment of pension funds, fair trade shops, debt cancellation campaigns, clean cloth campaigns and economy of communion to mention a few.[323] However, a review of these initiatives indicates that they are mainly done to help the South rather than to critically look at capitalism as a problem to both North and South. Addressing the gap between the rich and the poor is not only an issue between nations, but is a concern within the North itself. Hence the need is for a complete change.

In other words, the plethora of partnerships so far developed by churches in the Southern congregations and those in the North will need to improve in content, by raising the issue of alternative models of economy that are sustainable. So far, partnerships have been reduced to donations of gifts from the North to the South, creating sympathies or empathy about the poverty in the South without really addressing its root causes – it has also led to a feeling of dependence by the churches in the South. The churches in the North and in the South need to go beyond these short term answers and pose a fundamental question as to whether there are alternatives to free market capitalism itself – a system that has brought about these problems in the first place.

---

[323] See Luigino Bruni, ed., *Toward a Multi-Dimensional Economic Culture: The Economy of Communion* (Roma: New City Press, 2002).

Working on Alternative Models – Some Examples From Various Parts of the World and Various Communities

A search for such alternative life-sustaining economic models is the work of mission that CWM and the wider ecumenical family should focus on. This search should no longer be left to economists; it should incorporate all disciplines, including theology and spirituality, because economics is a matter of faith.[324]

Therefore the first element in the partner principle for economic and ecological justice, is to identify alternatives to the current capitalist systems of economy, and to explore how we can together care for mother earth. Alternative models of economy and care for the earth are needed so as to transform mission relationships. The mission of the churches in the North should be to address the question as to why there is less and less funds for real development. They will need to place the issues of wealth creation and its related industrial production systems on their agenda. Studies on Christianity, poverty and wealth, such as the one done by the churches in Germany, should continue to challenge societies to change their lifestyles - which are presently dependent on intensive energy use.[325]

Mission in the field of economic justice involves working for alternative finance systems that are connected to real life. It involves campaigns against money laundering and speculation, and stopping capital flights through tax evasion from poor regions to rich ones. Promotion of savings and credit societies and starting church community banks, like the one by the Evangelical Lutheran Church in Tanzania - Uchumi Bank - and its related savings and credit societies (SACCOS),[326]

---

[324] See *Christian Faith and the World Economy Today: A Study Document of the World Council of Churches* (Geneva: WCC Publications, 1992). Drafted by economists, theologians, ethicists and Church leaders, the text identifies « signposts » for judging how economy works and exposing the hidden values behind economic decisions, and offers suggestions about how these insights can lead to Christian action for greater economic justice.

[325] See also Michael Taylor, *Christianity Poverty and Wealth* (Geneva: WCC Publications, 2003) and Rogate Mshana, *Wealth, Poverty and Ecology and their Links* (Geneva: WCC Publications, 2008). The ecological footprints of peoples in the developed world have to be challenged. At present the footprint of people in the North average 6.4 ha/person, which is substantially higher than the ecological footprints of people in the South which average 0.8 ha/person.

[326] See www.africasustainable.ning.com on how such a bank started.

are concrete examples of alternative finance. The illegitimate foreign debt cancellation campaign should continue to be a mission challenge for the churches. Relating to social movements such as the Jubilee South will be an asset.[327] The church must be a living example in fighting corruption and speculation, but most of all it should be in the forefront of working for an alternative financial system that is just.

The mission work of the churches in the North should call for the building of new institutions that are not based on a consumer culture. Initiatives such as "Sustainable Germany,"[328] though they do not go deep enough to suggest alternatives to the free market capitalism, should be supported and encouraged as the first step. In the South, efforts such as life-giving agriculture, which is free of toxins, is something to be supported. Promoting food sovereignty should be the focus of mission. The Churches in South Korea have begun to implement organic agriculture and chemical free villages – this is a worthy effort to support.[329] Within the partnership principle of CWM, it should be possible for members to work out joint programs for the creation of just, sustainable and participatory communities, where issues of economy and ecology are linked. The Oikotree process could be a forum where sustainable models can evolve.

There are now initiatives suggesting other ways of measuring economy - such as a **growth happiness index**. This differs from the **growth in domestic product index** that is normally used, measuring increases in material assets alone. A happiness index focuses less on emphasizing the promotion of corporations, but rather on people's cooperatives. Some communities like those in Brazil are beginning to create their own currencies that link finance to real economy, encouraging the development of an economy of solidarity. "Solidarity socio-economy is directed to producing and to ensuring a fair share of all sufficient material wealth to generate sustainable conditions for self-managed human development by all members of society, all peoples and the planet."[330] Churches in Latin America are also supporting the

---

[327] See www.jubileesouth.org.
[328] http://www.zukunftsfaehiges-deutschland.de/en/sustainable_germany/the_project/.
[329] See *Life –Giving Agriculture Global Forum Report* (8-12 April 2005, Wonju , Korea).
[330] Visit http://aloe.socioeco.org.

creation of the Bank of the South. They have started cooperating with countries that are seeking alternative economic models that are people-centered called *Alternativa Bolivariana para America Latina y Caribe (ALBA)*.[331] Solidarity economy is distinguished from social economy. It involves social enterprises, cooperatives, just trade, mutual credit, community enterprises, voluntary organizations, trade union support agencies, time banks and barter groups with social money, home based production units, remittances from emigrants in rich countries, and all that is known as a self-help economy.

Transforming mission must invite people of other faiths to bring to the table their alternatives as well. In Indonesia, during a discussion on alternative finance at a WARC/CWM organized seminar May 2006 on *Living out the Accra Confession: Implications for our spirituality and mission*, participants heard about Islamic Sharia Banks and the fight against usury as an alternative to the so called normal banks. This attempt to learn from the wisdom of other faiths is very important for the work in mission.

Feminist economists are also suggesting alternatives based on women's experiences. They have developed the concept of an economy of care or a caring economy.[332] A caring economy goes beyond equity and justice. It connotes among others being present and attentive, opening one's eyes to needs of others, and worrying about others. It ensures the provision of basic needs for all women and men. It recognizes social reproduction. Efficiency is defined in light of social costs and benefits. In this economy, caring and care work are made visible, (revalued), (re)affirmed, (re)produced and (re)distributed equitably by both men and women. It is a way of organizing life as a whole and comprises all activities that keep daily life functioning. It is about communities experiencing life together, of relationships, mutuality and reciprocity and not about individual satisfaction and competition. It moves away from values of accumulation and profit to values of redistribution and reparation. In caring economy power is not linked to markets but it includes moving from free trade to just and responsible trade and above all caring for the earth for future generations. There are

---

[331] www.alternativabolivariana.org/modules.php?name .
[332] Athena K. Peralta, *A Caring Economy: A Feminist Contribution to Alternatives to Globalization Addressing People and Earth (AGAPE)* (Geneva: WCC, 2005), 50.

many studies done by women on alternative models. Reference is made here to Aruna Gnanadason's book *Listen to Women: Listen to the Earth* where she outlines concrete examples of Indigenous Peoples, and especially women, to preserve traditions of prudent care for the earth in opposition to the models pushed by multinational and financial institutions and governments.[333]

Comprehensive Advocacy

The second task of churches in transformative mission is to promote economic justice and ecological justice through comprehensive advocacy. Advocacy in the context of transformative mission goes deeper than its reductionist form – or "one issue campaigns" as practiced by the Ecumenical Advocacy Alliance's (EAA) among others. According to EAA, advocacy is a specific form of witness on political, economic, cultural and social issues by churches and their members, church-related agencies, and other organizations. It aims to influence policies and practices of governments, international institutions, corporations and our own communities in order to bring about a more just, peaceful and sustainable world.[334] Although CWM is one of the partner agencies that journey with this programme and share resources, the programme can go beyond a one-issue campaign approach to addressing systemic issues. Advocacy in the context of transformative mission needs to go deeper into critically analyzing the current unsustainable economic paradigm, in order to come up with an alternative system that will guarantee fullness of life for the people and the earth while promoting economic and ecologically sustainable life.

Theology Undergirding Advocacy

The term advocacy, in the understanding of the WCC, is rooted in the Gospel. "The term advocate is used in some English versions of the Bible to translate the Greek Parakletos in John 14:15&26; 15:26; 16:7 and I John 2:1. The word is also translated as comforter, helper and one who pleads for us. Parakletos means the one who is summoned or called to one's side; called to one's aid. Particularly in I John 2, Jesus is seen as the one who pleads people's cause with God. In the gospel of St.

---

[333] Aruna Gnanadason, *Listen to the Women! Listen to the Earth* (Geneva: WCC Publications, 2005).

[334] Definition by the Ecumenical Advocacy Alliance to which WCC and related Agencies are participants.

John, the Parakletos can be understood as the Holy Spirit. "Advocacy also comes from Latin "ad-vocare," literally to call/speak towards. "Vocare" is the verb from which "vocation" comes from, but also provoke (pro-vocare), convocation (con-vocare) and others."[335]

Advocacy has a very important theological meaning: standing before God and the world with, and on behalf of, suffering people and the suffering creation. The crucified and risen Christ identifies with the suffering people, and speaks through them. Advocacy that takes place above the heads of the people it concerns is illegitimate. Advocacy is a form of accompaniment, rooted in faith and is people-centered. It does not start in the corridors of power but with people at the local level and with their struggles for life.

Advocacy is a necessary and important dimension of our witness, where we give account of the hope that is in us (1 Peter 3:15) and speak truth to power (1 Kings 22:16 and John 18:37). Mahatma Gandhi, the Indian political leader, during his South African struggle said, "God is truth." Towards the end of his life he said, "Truth is God, Love is God, Compassion is God." Compassion and truth should therefore be manifested not only within ourselves and among members of our communities but also outwardly, as the Holy Spirit leads us into the whole world, in our work for transformation and change. Advocacy must be rooted in the vision of power derived from the gospel, a vision of power based on humility, on non-violence, on prayer and spiritual discernment. Spiritual discernment directs our attention to people's lives, to questioning trendy interpretations of economics and societies, to searching for the deeper reality that gives our advocacy depth and passion and the strength of our convictions.[336] So churches are called to see advocacy work on economic and ecological justice as part of mission.

---

[335] Rogate Mshana, "WCC - Ecumenical Advocacy" (paper presented at the APRODEV-PAG meeting in Brussels- 14-15 March 2007). Ideas collected from WCC colleagues who are theologians, namely Dr. Guillermo Gerber-Mas (Climate Change); Simon Oxley (Educationist); Tom Best (Faith and Order network) and Martin Robra (Ecumenism in the 21st Century).

[336] Sam Kobia, "The Ecumenical Movement : Responding to the Challenges of Today's World" (address at the Act Development Assembly, Nairobi, Kenya, 6-7 February 2007).

There are stages that are basic in preparing advocacy work for a church. **The first phase is the ability to identify the problem**. Here insights could come from people at the local context who identify what is at stake, but also informed by global institutions that raise global concerns in the form of studies and statements such as the UN, and also global ecumenical bodies.

The second stage is analysis - understanding the root causes of the problem. This work is followed by the third stage of working out the **details of the campaign and lobby work** based on the analysis, followed by mobilizing the congregations and the people. Activities that follow from the process might include the production of resource materials to help equip all institutions of the church - including Sunday schools and theological colleges – and preparation of worship and homiletic resources to harness the power of the pulpit.

For example, advocacy work on the right to food could entail analyzing why food is abundant yet not available to all people - only to a few. It could provoke the following questions: Is the production of more food, at the expense of the ecology, a panacea? Is an increase in food availability a matter of working out good distributive measures? How can such issues be developed into resource material for awareness building? Doing such things means actually implementing part of transformative mission. If mission is devoid of such life-related issues then it lacks substantial content.

Resolving Economic and Ecological Crisis

Issues of economic and ecological crisis must be part of the mission agenda because they are about life and death. Ecological issues have moral and ethical dimensions. Often they involve the depletion or degradation of the basic conditions for survival of all living beings on earth, including the human race. These include air, water, food, and so on. Moreover, while major ecological problems such as climate change and the loss of biodiversity pose threats to all people in the long-run, it is the most vulnerable - including people in poverty, women, indigenous communities and people living in low coastal areas - who are disproportionately affected, especially in the short and medium term. People living in the economic margins are highly dependent on pastures, fishing grounds and forests for their livelihoods, food, medicine, and fuel, making them acutely vulnerable to the degradation, depletion and appropriation of natural resources. In other words, ecological destruction, when super-imposed on existing structural disparities of class, gender and race, tends to aggravate inequalities and deepen poverty. At the core, therefore, struggles for ecological justice are essentially struggles for life and human dignity.

Second, analyses of ecological problems cannot be de-linked from the economic and political systems of our times. There are dynamic linkages between the present-day dominance of neo-liberal economic ideologies (free market capitalism) and ongoing processes of economic globalization on the one hand, and worsening ecological degradation on the other. Free market policies have increasingly eroded and transferred government decision-making power to unaccountable, profit-oriented corporations at the expense of environmental protection. In the relentless pursuit of economic growth, international financial institutions have financed massive development projects (e.g. mega-dams) and imposed structural adjustment programmes on indebted countries, with tremendous ecological and social consequences. Moreover, the globalizing of economic models based on ever-expanding production and consumption has further undermined ecological sustainability. Thus, it becomes even more apparent that efforts to protect the environment must be situated in the broader context of transforming the economy.

Third, creating a new mission for sustainable communities requires not only a deep-seated critique of our economic and political systems, institutions and policies, but also, and just as crucially, of peoples' values and lifestyles. Models of human domination of the earth – whether for economic growth, profit or material consumption – have been deeply entrenched in economic theory and practice for many centuries, and have further intensified and proliferated in the current era of economic globalization. Yet there are continuing pockets of resistance and sources of hope. Mission should highlight these.

Conclusion

This essay has clarified the terms economic and ecological justice, and has underlined that their achievement will depend on churches implementing transformative mission. This transformative mission should aim at addressing so-called "free market capitalism" or neo-liberal economic model of development. Churches are encouraged to go beyond their current diaconal work and current alternatives to that of critically addressing capitalism. This transformative journey demands a new spirituality, "a *different model of desires and aspirations for life and life in abundance in which there is no confusion between the quality of life and the quantity of consumption...This new spirituality must contribute to a change in objectives of economic policies that day by day replicate the standards of consumerism found in the West."*[337] Embedded in transformative mission is, therefore, an embrace of a kind of spirituality as described by Konrad Raiser, former General Secretary of the WCC, as, *"the praxis of affirming and caring for life as sacred gift from the Creator, which is being sustained only as it is being shared in community. By the same token, spirituality as the energy for life in all its fullness implies the commitment to resist all forces, power and systems which reduce, deny or destroy life."*[338] This form of resistance is essential even for those churches that are caught in the midst of free market capitalism.

This spirituality that is critical to countering the global powers of political and economic domination is called spirituality of resistance. Since the mission adopted by CWM and churches that participate in covenanting for justice and the AGAPE process is to address those powers responsible for the current economic and ecological injustice, they need to enhance a spirituality of resistance against such powers now termed the **empire.**

Empire has to do with massive concentrations of power that permeate all aspects of life, that cannot be controlled by any one actor alone. "Empire *displays strong tendencies to domesticate Christ and anything else that poses a challenge to its powers. Christ becomes part of the system to such a degree that little or nor room exist for the pursuit of alternative realities of Christ."*[339] At present, the pressures of empire manifest themselves, for instance, in sanctions against nations that refuse to comply with norms established by the powers that be, in economic

---

[337] See Gustavo Driau, "Neoliberal Rationale Versus Diaconal Reasoning," in *Life in All Fullness: Latin American Churches Facing Neoliberal Globalization*, ed. René Krüger (Buenos Aires: ISEDET, 2007), 199.
[338] See Konrad Raiser, *Spirituality of Resistance* in *Passion for Another World: Building Just and Participatory Communities*, ed. Rogate R. Mshana (Geneva: WCC Publications, 2004), 10.
[339] Joerg Rieger, *Christ and Empire: From Paul to Postcolonial Times* (Minneapolis: Fortress Press, 2007), 3.

arrangements that exploit the labour power, land or other assets of less powerful nations, and the stimulus of a seductive consumer culture that permeates more and more spaces around the globe through the media and the market. All these pressures are directly transmitted to the people. The elements of the empire today are vested with those who wield political, cultural, military and corporate power. As it has been described, *"Empire seeks to extend its control as far as possible; not only geographically, politically, and economically but also intellectually, emotionally, psychologically, spiritually, culturally and religiously."*[340] This is the reason why it is so difficult for the churches to critique it or even to acknowledge that it exists. The questions that need to be raised by the churches in the 21st century are: how can churches through transformative mission address the empire or the powers that push free market capitalism which destroy the people and the earth? How can churches move from single-issue based advocacy to challenging these powers at all levels of their manifestations, including within the churches and among churches?

    This essay has attempted to define how we as churches would make the partnership principle come alive - from being a concept to becoming a lived experience. For this, it is imperative for the churches to review their present work in mission and begin to propagate an Oikotree ecumenical movement, as mentioned in this essay. The Oikotree ecumenical movement is about putting justice at the heart of faith; it is driven by a spirituality of love and resistance to the empire. To be part of this movement is to be like Christ, who refused to be part of the empire of his times. The churches today need to be ready for the costly discipleship of Christ, as part of transformative mission. Such a *metanoia* and transformative mission is needed for economic and ecological justice to become real in the world.

---

[340] Michael Hardt and Antonio Negri, *Empire* (Cambridge, Mass.: Harvard University Press, 2000), 23.

9

Contexualization, Worldviews and Plurality in the Work of the Council for World Mission: A Caribbean Womanist Reflection

Marjorie Lewis[341]

When one charts significant historical milestones in the work of the Council for World Mission (CWM), changes and developments in the perspectives of the mission body with respect to the identifiable and intersecting issues of contextualization, worldviews and plurality become evident. This paper will offer working definitions of the three concepts, outline dominant trends within the three broad areas as reflected in select publications of the CWM, and offer a Caribbean womanist reflection on the identified trends. An important strand that is evident throughout the history of CWM and that links the issues of contextualization, worldviews and plurality, is the influence of postcolonial theory. Many scholars, including Franz Fanon,[342] Edward Said[343] and Gayatri Chakravorty Spivak[344] have identified the oppressive nature of the western colonial enterprise, not only in terms of the political and geographical aspect of colonialism, but also at the ideological level of devaluing and silencing the voices of those on the margins of society,

---

[341] Marjorie Lewis is president of the United Theological College of the West Indies.
[342] See for example, Frantz Fanon, *Black Skin, White Masks*, transl. Charles Lam Markmann (1967 translation of the 1952 book, New York: Grove Press).
[343] See for example, Edward Said, *Orientalism* (New York: Vintage Book Edition, 1979).
[344] See for example, Gayatri Chakravorty Spivak, "Can the Subaltern Speak?" in *Marxism and the Interpretation of Culture,* eds. Cary Nelson and Lawrence Grossberg (London: Macmillan, 1988).

sometimes referred to as the subaltern voices. Within CWM, the transition from the London Missionary Society (LMS) to the CWM involved deep discussions, tensions and a subsequent consensus to overturn the colonial structure, theology, and mission strategies of the LMS and embrace a *de facto* postcolonial model embodied in CWM. This paper will trace some aspects of the postcolonial project within the history of CWM – the negotiation of power, privilege and identity in the context of a mutating and persistent Western hegemony.

The CWM had evolved from the London Missionary Society, founded "to send the glorious Gospel of the Blessed God in to the heathen,"[345] to become the CWM—an organization whose objective was 'sharing in one world mission.' Along the journey of the institution, significant milestones were experienced, notably, in 1975 at the conference in Singapore, the two hundredth anniversary of the founding of the LMS in 1995, and the six yearly Assemblies of the CWM with themes that signified important developments in the mission understanding of CWM. These developments were undergirded with a postcolonial perspective, as noted by Steve de Gruchy:

> The ...CWM is the successor body to the ...LMS. In 1977 the Council took a bold decision to end the almost 200 years of European missionary hegemony, and to develop a new way of doing mission. It is now a global community of 31 churches with an equal share in common work and witness...[346]

The Reformed tradition of Christianity has been dominant in the work of the CWM over the years, and consistent with this tradition emphasis has been placed on the perspective of the church being reformed and always reforming, as well as on the Bible as a source for theology. *Ecclesia reformata, semper reformanda* as a guide for mission has been implied and stated within the work of CWM, including the engagement with postcolonial analyses. Consistent with the Reformed

---

[345] D. Preman Niles, "The Mission Thinking and Partnership Journey of CWC: A Review," *Missiological and Theological Statements and Position Papers: 1975-2006*, (1995), 1.

[346] Steve de Gruchy, "'*Growing Up and Increasing and Yielding Thirty...*': Change and Continuity in the Council for World Mission, 1977 – 2007," (chapter in this book), 1.

tradition, CWM has exhibited intentionality in seeking to journey towards a more authentic faith based on the biblical roots of the Christian heritage, and to guard against oppression and corruption in its work. The desire to guard against triumphalism, to hold in tension the ancient principles and the need for innovation, to listen to the stories of the poor and marginalized and express solidarity with these groups in faithfulness to the triune God, are all reflections of the perspective of a church reformed and always reforming.

Being reformed and always reforming has also been engaged within CWM by way of postcolonial perspectives on biblical interpretation. Christopher Duraisingh[347] identified some of the key texts from the bible which informed the CWM's work. It was noted that the Matthew 28:19 text was not given prominence within CWM's work. With respect to the basis of mission, Acts 1: 8 was identified as offering the significant insights that mission is of the Spirit, that it is God's mission and the Church is a function of the on-going mission of God. The Church, therefore, cannot 'domesticate' mission. The pattern of mission had, as its point of departure, reflection on John 20: 21, "As the Father sent me, so do I send you." This was not understood as a type of 'prescription,' but an invitation to reflect on what it means to engage in mission in Christ's way, and to reflect on the understanding of 'incarnation.' II Corinthians 15:8 was a key text in seeking to understand the goal of mission, and from this text the importance of reconciliation as part of the Church's mission was identified. How then should CWM and its member churches be "signs, witnesses and instruments of God's reconciling love manifested in Christ's self-offering on the cross"? The realities of contexts of conflict, of people's struggles all over the world, the prophetic role of the Church, the goal of one new humanity and one new creation in Christ were aspects of the reflections on the II Corinthians text. A third significant text, John 17: 21, was identified in relation to the recognition that mission and unity are inseparable correlates. Reflections on Christian unity and joint activities with other Christians are to be seen throughout the work of CWM. In all the reflections and actions on the above-mentioned text and others, the interpretations from Africa, Asia, the Pacific, the Caribbean were now to

---

[347] Christopher Duraisingh, "Some Key Missiological Motifs," in *Mission in Partnership: A CWM Experience, Missionary Training Module 4* (London: Council for World Mission, 1999).

be heard through the crucible of experiences in the respective contexts, and not only the voices of Europe and North America.

Along the journey of just over thirty years, the postcolonial intent of CWM has been expressed in the out-workings of the impulse of the Church, reformed and reforming, in readings of the biblical text from the perspectives of persons from the global South, and in the Council's grappling with the issues of contextualization, worldviews and plurality.

Contextualization

Contextualization is used within this paper to refer to location as both a sense of the geographical location of missionary endeavours, and a point of departure for the different companions in the CWM journey. It includes the approach of indigenizing the gospel, taking the local culture into consideration. Within the concept of contextualization is the debate about Christ and culture and the rejection of the imposition of imperial or colonial cultures and value systems from other geographical locations. It raises the issue of discerning that which is revealed of God within the existing culture, coupled with the need to discern prophetic challenges to aspects of local culture that are death-dealing rather than life-affirming. The CWM evolved out of the London Missionary Society established in 1795 by the Anglicans, Presbyterians and independent churches. It received its name, the London Missionary Society, in 1818. It experienced additions to membership up to the watershed moment of 1973 when the re-defined and re-structured Council for World Mission (CWM) was named.

In the understanding of the LMS, the British context and other areas in the global North were not seen as mission fields. The context of the North was the repository of Knowledge, Truth and Salvation, while the context that needed the gospel was the global South. While some laud the founding principle of the LMS "to spread the knowledge of Christ throughout the world,"[348] and note that ecumenism was a priority at the very inception of the LMS, others noted the limitations of categorizing people from the South as "heathens"[349] and "unenlightened." Missionaries were sent from England to countries in the global South, the implication being that these outsiders were the experts

---

[348] Desmond van der Water, *From Ayr to Ocho Rios – CWM's Mission Journey from 2003-2006* (CWM, 2006), 20.
[349] Niles, *Mission Thinking*, 1.

in assessing the needs in the respective contexts, as well as experts in developing and implementing programmes to train local leaders and spread the Gospel in these lands.

In 1975 at Singapore, African and Asian churches offered another evaluation of the impact of previous missionary activity in their respective continents. They objected to the negative effects of former missionary endeavours in their countries, and some called for a moratorium on the sending of British missionaries to Africa. The consensus of the churches from the South was summarized by the former CWM General Secretary, Preman Niles in this way: "Give us the space to be obedient to God's calling in our own context in our own way."[350]

In view of the critique of the missionary strategies of the nineteenth and twentieth centuries, the CWM, through dialogue in various fora, re-envisioned the issue of contextualization. Greater emphasis was placed on the understanding that the primary focus of mission of any church is its own geographical location. This implied that the countries in the North had an imperative to see their countries as contexts for mission, and the churches in the South had the possibility of doing mission in their own context without the direction of missionaries from the North. The CWM consultations also noted that the centre of gravity of Christianity had shifted from the North to the South, as the majority of Christians and CWM members were in the global South. The South was recognized as the location of a vibrant spirituality and rapidly growing congregations and denominations, while church membership had dwindled significantly in the North. Secularism and other forces in the North were identified as factors contributing to the decline in church membership. The need to encounter the gospel was as much an imperative in Great Britain as it was in Ghana.

Questions were raised on the issue of power – were those churches from contexts with the most money (the North) to have the dominant influence within the CWM, or would all the gifts of all the member churches be valued and power be shared? An important shift took place away from the mission perspective of the LMS as indicated by the title of the founding document of the CWM. All its members were now "Sharing in One World Mission.'

---

[350] Niles, *Mission Thinking*, 2.

The contexts where CWM Assemblies were held seemed to offer special opportunities for the Holy Spirit to blow a fresh wind of energy into the work. Preman Niles opined that having the Assembly in Singapore in the 1970s was probably a key factor in the reflections that lead to changes in the LMS. Subsequent Assemblies in Ayr, Ocho Rios and other parts of the world embodied the importance of contextualization and the diversity of contexts across the world. The discussions were thereby enriched.

The 2006 report of the CWM General Secretary, Rev. Dr. Desmond van der Water, among other things, signaled the areas in which the discussion on contextualization had developed between 2003 and 2006. A challenge emerged, for example, in reflecting on the advantages and limitations of registration in the British Charity law, resulting in CWM having to make adjustment to its legal registration. Some may argue that this is a minor administrative matter and not worthy of theological reflection. It could be argued, on the other hand, that the administrative structures and systems are an important locus of contextualization, with an implicit theological base. At the outset, one of the important changes in the CWM structure was the democratization of the structure so that two representatives from each participating church were involved in decision-making. In addition, money was placed in a common pool and expenditure decided on by a representative executive group. The 2003 action by the CWM to become a company limited by guarantee, in addition to retaining its status as a UK Charity, continued the trend of seeking an organizational and legal framework that would be consistent with the democratic values of the CWM, as well as facilitate the accompanying programmes. New wineskins needed to be provided for the new wine! Van der Water explained the rationale in this way:

> The new constitution that was adopted removed the need for custodian trustees, simplifying the administration of the charity and making CWM an internationally recognized establishment, with limited liability companies being common to most countries around the world.[351]

---

[351] Van der Water, *From Ayr to Ocho Rios*, 13.

Apart from an administrative change generated by external circumstances, the CWM continued to deepen its reflection and praxis on the issue of contextualization. This continuing theme in CWM's work was summarized by the theme of the 2006 Assembly, "Take Home the Good News." This was not simply a slogan, however, as examples of practical steps to engage in mission at home were shared. One interesting example is that of the United Reformed Church (URC) in Britain. It has sought to respond to the growing ineffectiveness of the 'Christendom' model of the church, coupled with a growing spiritual hunger in Europe, by exploring innovative ways of being church. Out of this reflection came the "Catch the Vision" Process. In this initiative, URC congregations were challenged to involve the whole people of God in Bible Studies, the telling of personal stories, and reflection on the implications of the biblical text and contemporary stories in relation to the church's mission priorities.

Within the global South, churches were continuing their reflection on the necessity for context to shape mission. Many, notably the youth, interrogated the links between indigenous culture, tradition and customs, and the Christian faith. As churches established by missionaries from the North, there was intentionality in the quest to 'incarnate' the gospel in the local context.[352] Whether the context was the global North or the global South, CWM conversations on contextualization became part of a wind of renewal and change. Churches sought to be faithful to the call to engage others, in their respective contexts, with the gospel. The CWM structure also evolved to accommodate regional structures within the CWM. This development has occasioned both cautious optimism at the positive results that were soon identifiable, and in other quarters, concern that the regional structures had the potential to undermine the global unity of the CWM.

The call to take the gospel home, is not, therefore, without potential pitfalls. Des van der Water warned[353] of the need to avoid parochialism; to heed the possibility that, like Jesus, it is possible to face rejection from those at home with whom the attempt is made to share the gospel. He warns that 'home' - whether family, church, community, country - can be places of conflict and alienation. Further, it may be

---

[352] Van der Water, *From Ayr to Ocho Rios*, 14.
[353] Van der Water, *From Ayr to Ocho Rios*, 18.

necessary to work hard to unlock the potential for love, peace, harmony and service that is blocked in the context of 'home.'

A three-pronged reading of the biblical concept of the household of God by van der Water has inherent in it the seeds of fruitful reflection and praxis. He points out that the Greek word *oikos* is the root of three significant terms – ecology, economics and ecumenism. In so doing, the link between the global overarching issues and the challenges of the local/home context are identified, thus calling CWM to a deeper analysis of the scope of the work in taking the good news home. For van der Water, taking the good news home implied grappling with at least five strands:

- The definitive nature of local context in shaping the church, ministry and mission;
- The necessity of equipping local churches, parishes and congregations as the primary agent and the first base of mission activity
- The important role that home and family life play in the building of healthy local churches and communities and the recognition of the home and family as a primary place of affirmation, growth and formation;
- The emphasis on the inter-connectedness between healing and reconciliation;
- The interpretation of the major global (macro) challenges, such as globalisation and economic justice, into local (micro) relevance and implementation.[354]

CWM has engaged in a process of giving prominence to the stories from contexts in the global South and allowing these experiences to become integral to the reflection and praxis of CWM. The respective contexts from which missionaries have come reflect distinctive worldviews and have in turn shaped the worldview of the missionaries. The postcolonial interrogation of power, privilege and identity has also been brought to bear on the CWM's engagement with a diversity of worldviews.

---

[354] Van der Water, *From Ayr to Ocho Rios*, 20.

Worldviews

The term 'worldview' has its inspiration from the German *weltanschauung*, and can be understood as encompassing a framework of knowledge, ideas, beliefs which have achieved a degree of consistency. This understanding of worldview includes elements such as language and explanations of the broad existential questions with which humanity has grappled over the ages.

In one sense, the transition from LMS to CWM could be seen as the relinquishing of notions of a normative Euro-American worldview, moving to engagement in dialogue with a number of equally valid perspectives. The LMS was formed at a time when the British Empire was in its heyday. At that time, many countries that are now part of the global South were not recognized as countries in their own right, but were part of the Empire of one or other European countries. Many Africans in the Americas had been forcefully transported there into chattel slavery. 1795 was a time when the lines between the norms of European culture and the requirements of Christian discipleship were blurred, and many good European Christians justified the enslavement of Africans. The worldview of Europe was seen as the superior worldview which should become universally normative. The authority to interpret scripture was seen to be vested in Europeans. The worldviews of many in the South were deemed to be 'heathen' and 'unenlightened' at best, and down right demonic at worst.

Within the context of the LMS, the control of funding, ideas and power within the organization was exercised in such a way that established the dominance of the British worldview. In the analysis of the CWM in the 1970s, notably at the Singapore meeting, the evolution of a type of donor/recipient relationship was criticized and rejected by assertive voices from the global South.

There was the demand for a transformation of the structure of the organization, and the acknowledgment of and opportunity to share the resources of those who did not have money. New concepts became dominant within the discourse of the CWM. There was now talk of "mutuality," "partnership," "mutual accountability," "sharing" and "journeying." Not only were there new 'buzz words,' but the people from the global South were exercising agency in expressing other theological perspectives. One such voice was Maitland Evans from

Jamaica who read the letter to Philemon from the perspective of the enslaved Onesimus and identified key motifs in the story that continue to be relevant in the CWM journey of involvement in God's mission.[355] Onesimus is identified as a 'victim,' or one trapped by oppressive systems, who decides to take the way out of injustice that is available to him. The encounter with Paul and subsequent conversion experience provides the opportunity for Paul to call Philemon to accountability to the 'plumbline' of God's justice. This includes a *koinonia* of caring and sharing beyond the strictures of civil law, in which Paul, Philemon and Onesimus are equal. The issue of power in areas such as gender relations, the sharing of resources, the distribution of funds received through the sale of property in Hong Kong referred to as the 'gift of grace,' and decision making has remained an important theme throughout the life of CWM.

CWM members engaged in vigorous theological reflections, for example, exemplified by Evans' exegesis of the letter to Philemon, and concerning the tension between dimensions of plurality and unity. The biblical metaphor of the body and the doctrine of the Trinity became important points of reference in the conversation. In addition, Jesus' prayer for unity recorded in John 17, was interrogated and it was acknowledged that unity was important for mission. CWM was therefore called upon to struggle with the unity/plurality tension within while recognizing that the CWM and the wider ecumenical movement could assist the world in understanding that a diverse church can live in harmony, as can a diverse world.

The notion of mission as the whole people of God to the whole world[356] and not just from the 'Christians' to the 'heathens' resulted in a change of how the 'other' was viewed. One consequence of this was that countries in the North were now also recipients of missionaries and not only contexts from which missionaries were sent. It was the opinion of Preman Niles that the far-reaching changes that ushered in CWM resulted from the movement of the Holy Spirit. One implication of this is the acknowledgement of the power of the Holy Spirit in challenging

---

[355] Maitland Evans, "The Council for World Mission's Partnership in Mission Model: Experiences and Insights," *International Review of Mission* LXXVI, no. 304 (October 1987): 458 – 472.
[356] Niles, *Mission Thinking*, 3.

embedded missionary theology and making way for new, liberating relationships in the *missio Dei*.

In succeeding years, CWM continued to explore the dimensions and implications of contending worldviews in the church and the world, for faithful participation in God's mission. One important area of significance was CWM's self understanding. While accepting the validity of the LMS and CWM shared objective of working for the time when "the earth will be filled with the knowledge of the Lord as the waters cover the sea" (Isaiah 11:19), van der Water notes an important change in the rhetoric of the two organizations. While LMS expressed their objective "to spread the knowledge of Christ throughout the world," the CWM seeks to "share experiences of Christ across all boundaries."[357]

Within this context, systems of domination were subjected to explicit and/or implicit postcolonial critiques. Recognizing the evils of colonialism and neo-colonialism, the CWMs work sought to take a stand against oppression, to privilege the perspective of the oppressed when designing programmes and when reading and interpreting the Bible. Systems of domination extant in the old LMS mode of mission were not only those critiqued. It included the lingering and evolving systems of domination based on social class/caste, race/ethnicity gender and the global neo-liberal economic model. The particular resource of the Reformed heritage - its commitment to always be in the process of reforming - has also been an important aspect of the evolution from the LMS to the CWM worldview. These reflections led to a new articulation of CWM's self-understanding as well as concrete programmes organized or facilitated by CWM and its member churches.

With respect to the CWM worldview expressed in its self-understanding, van der Water described a multi-faceted identity in this way:

- An international, regional and local ecumenical space for engagement, encounter and innovation in Christian mission thinking and acting;
- A mission movement that journeys with and accompanies other mission organizations on the basis of partnership and solidarity, not paternalism and charity, and in which the

---

[357] Van der Water, *From Ayr to Ocho Rios*, 20.

- partnership ethos is not merely a matter of expediency or functionalism but of principle, ecclesiology and missiology;
- A small but worldwide family of churches in which the quality of relationships in mission matter more than the rightness of each member's theology, where hospitality rather than hostility prevails, and where all members of the family are accepted, affirmed, and treated with respect;
- A place where the dominant style of the engagement is personal and pastoral rather than pragmatic or goal-oriented and where the journey of our being together is as important as our mission destinations;
- A global community of churches together, whose very being and modus operandi represents an antithesis of globalization with its reductionism of people, communities and countries into entities of materialism, competition and consumerism;
- A community of churches in mission together whose unity is enriched and not polarized by multi-national, multicultural and multiethnic diversity.[358]

Pivotal to the stance of always being in the process of reforming is the commitment to read and interpret the signs of the time. Van der Water notes that while the gospel is the same, Christians are called to interpret and share the gospel in their particular time and place. He identified, in the first decade of the twenty-first century, rapid and far reaching changes. Notably, extremely wealthy minorities are juxtaposed with over a billion people living in abject poverty. There are more frequent and devastating natural disasters, conflicts and wars within and between countries. These, van der Water identifies, are some of the realities of the current age within which CWM's membership is called to be faithfully partnering in God's mission.

---

[358] Van der Water, *From Ayr to Ocho Rios*, 21.

The CWM worldview, which gives priority to the marginalized and those whose voices are muted, is also expressed in the programmes. These programmes included Face to Face, New Face, Training in Mission, Training of Leaders, Women in Mission, Youth in Mission, Mission with Children, Short Term Global Exchange, Scholarships and Theological Education consultations and programmes. Concretely, this has meant that young Christians have been given the opportunity to experience new contexts, and to work and study with other young Christians from across the world. For women, workshops have been held to provide training in areas such as leadership development, gender awareness and socio-economic issues. Community development workshops were organized dealing with environmental issues. The relative merits of different delivery modes and curriculum content for theological education are assessed. Collaborating with the World Alliance of Reformed Churches (WARC) and the World Council of Churches (WCC), the 'Oikotree' alliance seeks justice in the economy and for the creation. The development of these new programmes has also meant the review and improvement of training and preparation of missionaries before their placement. Missionaries have assisted host churches with implementing more than a conversion/proselytizing agenda; grappling with a wide range of contextual issues, including racism and relationships with people of other faiths.

It is important to note that there is not unanimity among all member churches of the CWM on matters of theology. This is but one of the aspects of plurality with which the CWM continues to journey.

Plurality

Plurality can be understood as a description of the nature of the global community, as well as a rejection of a point of view that excludes all but a narrow range of perspectives as acceptable. Someone embracing plurality is open to engaging with perspectives other than those that are familiar or make one comfortable.

Within the context of the CWM, the very composition of the organization is an expression of plurality. The CWM members are drawn from many regions throughout the world. Under the LMS structure, the plurality was based on a hierarchy, with those from the global North perceiving those from the South in a negative light or from a paternalistic perspective. There were differences between the constituent bodies and the associated churches before the Singapore meeting, with the former dominant and in control of funds, theology and the sending of missionaries. The changes in the structure of the CWM from that of LMS resulted in a wider range of persons being involved in the decision-making processes, influencing changes, being hired as staff members, working as missionaries and participating in the other CWM programmes. It should be noted that the full implementation of the new structures took a long time and led to dissatisfaction among some members from the global South. Niles, in addition, pointed out[359] that the very concept of mission was understood as multi-faceted in nature and not restricted to conversion strategies. The early years of the CWM also emphasized deeper engagement with the wider ecumenical movement, though the dominant focus was still on relationships within the Reformed family of churches. Over the years, the CWM has not simply been passive or reactive in the engagement with plurality, but has faced the opportunities and misgivings involved in such an engagement. Notably, these include the response of the churches in the North to the CWM's postcolonial stance, issues of multi-faith relationships and mission with immigrant churches.

Plurality is understood to be expressed in the diversity of creation, and the theological insight that God loves the world and not just the church. The embracing of plurality, while bringing more voices to the CWM conversation, also resulted in a challenge for the constituency that had previously been hegemonic. How were churches in Britain, for example, to understand their identity as church, and cope with new understandings of mission, when they had previously engaged in the LMS approach with zeal and conviction? The LMS in its day had been seen as quite radical, and had even begun to review and re-assess its approach, encouraging "self-support, self-government, and self-propagation"[360] as the way forward for indigenous churches that emerged from missionary activities. The reaction of British churches to the 1977 development was described by John Smith in this way:

---

[359] Niles, *Mission Thinking*, 3.
[360] John Smith, "CWM: Rewriting the Drama of Mission – A European Testimony" in *Mission in Partnership: A CWM Experience Missionary Training Module 4* (London: Council for World Mission, 1999).

> When I was growing up in the 1950s 'the missionary
> hero/heroine' was still the aid to participating in mission.
> Lantern slides had been replaced by 35mm film and the
> 'hut boxes' – in the shape of African kraals – were
> giving way to contemporary receptacles (in theory at
> least, for one can still find them in use in some less
> progressive places!). But the concept of mission was
> that a number of self-sacrificial people were raised in our
> congregations, trained and sent forth, supported by the
> prayers and the money of British Christians. These
> missionaries cared for, taught, and evangelised the poor,
> benighted heathens so that God's children could sing
> their song far round the world. The portrayal had the
> undoubted advantage of being adventurous and
> exciting.[361]

The worldview outlined in Smith's story presented a challenge for the postcolonial direction of the CWM. A plurality of perspectives now shaped the understanding of mission and the perspectives from the global South presented serious challenges to those who had previously exercised hegemony. Smith, who became the World Mission Secretary of his denomination in 1978, noted that at that time, members of congregations still spoke with nostalgia and regret at not seeing missionaries visit to tell thrilling tales any more. He offered a critique of the old missionary model and the way his decision to return to pastoral ministry in 1986 revealed insights about changes that had taken place within the context of British congregations:

> The term 'missionary' had to do with crossing cultural
> and geographical frontiers to exercise leadership. The
> men and women in British pews identified with and
> acted vicariously through these people.
> The result was that concentration on the 'overseas'
> worker was negative. It blinded us to the daily work of
> the indigenous church. It highlighted one institution for
> us – where a known missionary served – while a similar
> centre of work 10 miles down the road – with similar

---

[361] Smith, "CWM: Rewriting the Drama of Mission," 1.

needs – was ignored because it was staffed by local
Christians. It gave missionaries considerable
fundraising potential, usually applied with no reference
to the priorities or strategies of the wider church. Within
the indigenous church, the missionary often held on to
positions of leadership longer than was appropriate –
admittedly on some occasions at the polite insistence of
the local people...
In 1986 I chose to return to the local ministry... But I
was conscious of the significant ways in which the role
of the congregation had changed – a rediscovery of the
sharp edge, a willingness to operate at the frontiers...
British CWM member churches may have taken some
pride in 1997 at their willingness to 'give up their
control' over world affairs. The truth of the matter,
though, is that they have discovered in the adjustment
strengths and encouragement. And that is making all the
difference![362]

Adjusting to plurality within the theology, leadership and structure of the CWM had in fact brought unexpected benefits to the British church. Within the CWM, there was also a recognition that the Church, called to participate in God's mission, has to address the implications of plurality not only in terms of relationships within the CWM family, but also with people of other faiths.

Within the CWM, increasing emphasis was placed on engagement with people of different faiths. This was especially through the testimonies and theological reflection of Asian Christians who lived as minorities in multi-religious context, and churches in contexts experiencing increasing immigration of people of other faiths into their communities. Van der Water noted that in the twenty first century there is an imperative to go beyond inter-faith dialogue to encounter and engagement with people of living faiths. This stance poses practical challenges and challenges to the understanding of mission. In van der Water's opinion, some elements of the response of Christians in multi-faith contexts are: faithfully witnessing to the gospel message of God's love, mercy and care for humanity and the creation, reflecting on the

---

[362] Smith, "CWM: Rewriting the Drama of Mission," 3-4.

nature of Christian identity within these contexts, and working creatively and cooperatively with persons of other faiths.

Of significance is the phenomenon of "immigrant" or "migrant" churches. The CWM member churches grapple with the ethics of the 'us and them' mentality, with the pros and cons regarding immigrants who worship in their mother tongue and not the official language of the host country. They debate the relative merits of multi-cultural congregations and they seek to listen to the dilemmas of generations born in a country to immigrant parents as they negotiate hybrid identities. The literature of the CWM does not provide pat answers to these issues, but rather prioritizes the telling of, and listening to stories, as well as commitment to relationships based on mutual respect, honouring commitments and integrity.[363] In grappling with the challenges and opportunities of plurality, the concepts of hospitality and creativity, described by van der Water are also applicable here.[364] Van der Water speaks of hospitality in the context of the CWM's approach of being open to, respectful of and welcoming to members who have differing views without trying to coerce persons into a predetermined mold, but rather providing opportunities for self-expression. It would seem that this principle of hospitality and openness to creativity could also enrich encounters with those who previously exercised hegemony, as well as persons of other faiths and those in migrant churches.

The CWM has been engaged in an explicit and implicit project of postcolonial analysis, notably as it has engaged with issues of contextualization, worldviews and plurality in its work. As one who served as a CWM missionary from the United Church in Jamaica and the Cayman Islands (UCJCI) to the United Reformed church (URC) in Britain, I offer the following reflection on contextualization, worldviews and plurality in CWM's work.

A Caribbean Womanist Reflection
Contextualization From the Perspective of Nannyish T'eology

The perspective from which I reflect on the CWM journey of contextualization, contending worldviews and plurality is that of a

---

[363] Van der Water, *From Ayr to Ocho Rios*, 21.
[364] Desmond van der Water, *Work in Progress or Mission Accomplishes? An Appraisal of 30 Years of CWM's Partnership in Mission* (London: Council for World Mission, 2007), 16.

contextualized Caribbean womanist theology called Nannyish t'eology.[365] This project can be viewed as part of the wider trend in countries in the South and among marginalized communities of the North to engage in a process of contextualization of theology, often articulated as a theology of liberation, by those who are poor, marginalized and oppressed. Black theology in the United States of America and South Africa as well as African American womanist theology are two examples of this trend. The phrase, Nannyish t'eology, is couched in the Jamaican language and describes the local consensus around a shared diasporic African cultural worldview, postcolonial reality and an attitude of hospitality to plurality. Nannyish t'eology has as its focus the iconic figure of Nanny of the Maroons, ancestor and national heroine, honoured as one who shared in the leadership of the struggle against enslavement and colonialism. Nanny of the Maroons was a freedom fighter who shared leadership of a guerilla movement with her brothers. They led Africans in Jamaica who had fled to the hills after the capture of the island from the Spanish by the British in the seventeenth century and who, through their superior military tactics, frustrated British efforts to capture the Maroons. The war ended with the signing of a peace treaty between the British and the Maroons. Some of the qualities that are attributed to Nanny and prized within the Jamaican culture are: a concept of mothering which is not simply biological, but includes the nurture of the entire community; equality with men in the struggle for liberation and the protection of the community; an integration of roles and functions, including warrior, priestess, healer, and farmer.

Nannyish t'eology, in my view, is manifested in the Jamaican context in the prizing of these aforementioned qualities within women by a wide cross-section of Jamaican women and men. Nanny is extolled in poetry, art and music, in academia and by national commemorative activities and memorials held on an annual basis. Stories of her exploits are told from generation to generation.

Within Nannyish t'eology, the complexity of the historical legacy in Jamaica and the wider Caribbean is implicit. While there is the pride in the legacy of Nanny and her associates, and the many named and un-named who struggled with courage and resilience to throw off chattel

---

[365] Marjorie Lewis, "Diaspora Dialogue: Womanist Theology in Engagement with Some Aspects of the Black British and Jamaican Experience," *Black Theology International* 2, no. 1 (January 2004) : 85-109.

slavery, the reality is that the Christianity to which the ancestors were introduced came in the context of human degradation. The change in objectives and structure of the LMS to the CWM to a certain extent parallels the journey from the theology and social order which supported chattel slavery to emancipation from enslavement in the nineteenth century and then to political independence in the twentieth century Caribbean. Historians such as Mary Turner, Brian Moore and Michelle Johnson indicate that often, missionaries who supported the abolition of the enslavement of Africans also had the notion that the focus of mission activity was the salvation of the souls of the enslaved. Good behaviour, lived out as faithful and loyal servants, would in time or in the hereafter be rewarded by God. In stark contrast to the exegesis of the Onesimus story in the context of CWM by Maitland Evans of Jamaica, the same text was used by Wesleyan missionaries as the basis of the following catechism:

> "Was [Onesimus] a good and dutiful slave?
> No, he was a very bad one, for he was a thief and a runaway.
> And how did the slave behave himself after his repentance and conversion to Jesus Christ?
> He behaved himself well and was profitable to his master.
> Does religion produce the same effect now on slaves that have it?
> Yes, they neither rob nor run away, but are good servants."[366]

A further dimension of complexity was added after 1865 in Jamaica when white missionaries re-doubled their efforts to train local leaders for the churches, carefully selecting from the black and brown population those to whom they could pass the torch of preaching and teaching a Christianity clothed in Victorian England's culture.[367] The issue of the co-option of people from the South - usually those given a

---

[366] Mary Turner, *Slaves and Missionaries: The Disintegration of Jamaican Slave Society, 1787 – 1834* (University of Illinois Press, 1982), 77.

[367] Brian L. Moore and Michele A. Johnson, *Neither Led nor Driven: Contesting British Cultural Imperialism in Jamaica, 1865 – 1920* (Kingston: University of the West Indies Press, 2004), 173.

little more privilege than others via education and other means to continue the implementation of a colonial agenda - is an issue that merits further reflection within the context of the CWM. The postcolonial project, therefore, needs to include strategies for unearthing internalized oppression, heeding the exhortation by the late Robert 'Bob' Marley's "Redemption Song": "Emancipate yourselves from mental slavery/None but ourselves can free our minds."

The collusion of theology and the norms of the dominant society are illustrated by the catechism and the co-option of sections of the oppressed group that internalize the oppressors' values. This contrasts with the hermeneutic of a descendant of enslaved Africans some two centuries later, demonstrating the way in which a person's location affects the insights that they bring to the table.

It is also instructive that two centuries divide these interpretations of the Epistle to Philemon. In some of the CWM literature, there are expressions of impatience and regret that some structural changes agreed upon and documented did not become reality until twenty years later. One could argue that changing two centuries of domination within an organization in twenty years is an ambitious undertaking. Within the context of the Caribbean, it is clear that even with the replacement of missionaries and expatriate clergy in the leadership of the church with local leaders, the colonial patterns of domination still linger, much as the 'smell' of Britain seems to linger within the CWM. In the zeal to faithfully participate in God's mission, care needs to be taken that in the process, leaders do not in fact 'heal the wounds of the people lightly.' The quest for holistic mission within CWM should also include attention to the healing of the wounds of history and patterns of dysfunctional internalization of the oppressive leadership patterns of the Christendom model of mission – even when it manifests among persons in the global South. The persistence of the practice of using skin bleaching compounds to render black skin nearer to the desired white aesthetic, in the Jamaican context, is but one visible indicator of the complexity of the task of mission into the future.

Taking the gospel home, from the perspective of Nannyish t'eology requires a deepening of the discussion about the extent to which the local church is open to be shaped by the context. It implies intentionality in tackling the fracturing of families caused by migration of custodial parents, and establishing partnerships with churches and communities in the countries in the North to which these Jamaican breadwinners migrate. Three Jamaican women scholars in reflecting on the mixed blessing of migration noted:

> While migration of parents from the Caribbean should not be assumed to have negative consequences, the potential trauma it poses for children has been generally overlooked. Health providers and caretakers of children need to recognize and acknowledge that the separation arising from migration and even the experience of later reuniting can negatively impact on the well-being of both child and parent. Caretakers of children therefore need to be more alert to identifying this population and assessing its needs to determine whether mental health intervention is necessary.[368]

With Jamaica now ranking fourth in the world on measures of the highest debt burden per capita, and a situation where debt servicing and civil servants' salaries consume nearly eighty percent of the national budget[369], it is imperative that mission initiatives in that context grapple with the interplay between the injustice of the neo-liberal economic model and its impact on the local context – a dynamic that has been identified in the CWM's work.

Within the complexities of the Jamaican and wider Caribbean context, Nannyish t'eology offers an unapologetic embrace of a diasporic African worldview as one important location of the encounter with the liberating gospel of Jesus Christ. It affirms the agency of women and men in their respective contexts: their right to speak on their own behalf, and to have their perspective respected and themselves recognized as *imago Dei*.

---

[368] Audrey M. Pottinger, Angela Gordon-Stair and Sharon Williams-Brown, "Migration of Parents from the Caribbean: Implications for Counseling Children and Families in the Receiving and Sending Countries," in *Freedom and Constraint in Caribbean Migration and Diaspora,* ed. Elizabeth Thomas-Hope (Kingston: Ian Randle Publishers, 2009), 181-191.

[369] Minh H. Pham, "Why Jamaica Needs a 'Kingstonclub' – How to Break the National Debt Squeeze," http://www.jamaica-gleaner.com/gleaner/20090405/focus/focus4.html (accessed 21 September 2010).

The Worldview of Nannyish T'eology

In addition to the issue of contextualization, an identified worldview with the attendant theological and ideological perspectives is included in Nannyish t'eology. Nanyish t'eology gives pride of place to worldviews anchored in the African religio-cultural heritage of the majority of Jamaicans. This African worldview has been described in various ways - despised and outlawed by the colonial leaders on the one hand, and acclaimed as a source of inspiration for resistance to oppression in Jamaica and the wider Caribbean on the other.

For the colonial Church in Jamaica, African worldviews expressed through religious and cultural ceremonies were, in the main, viewed as evil, satanic witchcraft. There were instances of prohibitions of ceremonies associated with African derived religions, and even today some publications associated with 'Obeah' are banned from Jamaica.[370] Other perspectives, for example that of Rev. Dr. Hyacinth Boothe, Jamaican Methodist Minister, highlight the positive aspects of African worldviews expressed in the rituals of the Revivalist Churches, held in sacred spaces in the homes of the leaders, called the 'balm-yard.' Dr. Boothe noted that the balm-yard is an intergenerational, egalitarian space in which women and men are restored to physical, emotional, psychological and spiritual well-being in the face of the 'soul-destroying trauma' of the daily experience of the marginalized in Jamaican society.[371] For the CWM members in Jamaica and the wider Caribbean context, there are implications for the response to emerging trends in ecclesiology. Some of the 'new ways of being church' in the Caribbean include the uncritical adoption of United States mega church strategies undergirded by the prosperity gospel. While membership in the churches started by missionary endeavours of the eighteenth and nineteenth centuries are declining in numbers, the African based Revivalism faith communities continue to thrive and the Seventh Day Adventist church is now the largest single denomination in the country with approximately ten percent of those recorded as Christians in the census figures.

Some writers have also noted that the African worldview has provided inspiration not only for survival in difficult times, but also for militant social action, for example, in the ritual that inaugurated the

---

[370] Moore and Johnson, "What is Obeah?"
[371] Hyacinth Boothe, "Caribbean Theology in Context," *Caribbean Journal of Religious Studies* 20, no. 1 (April 1999): 7–10.

Haitian Revolution. There is a challenge to bring the African heritage into the dialogue regarding new ways of being church in Jamaica, and to continue reflection on exactly what constitutes the survival and continuities of African culture in the diasporic context. George Mulrain, a Caribbean Methodist minister, identified seven attributes of the African spiritual worldview that survives in the Caribbean. These are:

- The concept of the spirit filled universe
- Death as a transition period
- Communication with the spirit world via dreams and visions
- The extended family structure alongside the spirit of polygamy
- Evil as a real and potent force in the universe
- Time awareness that centres around kairos
- Worship as an occasion for celebration made more enjoyable by the representatives of the spirit world[372]

This perspective of grounding theological reflection in the worldview of one's culture resonates with comments by van der Water, who commented on the CWM idea of the journey in this way:

> Born and bred within an African context, my own intuitive understanding of the fundamental nature of journeying is deeply influenced by an African worldview which holds that the journey of life, living and being is not linear and as such not moving in a straight line from one plateau to the next, or from one state of existence o another, but that it is circular – very much like he pattern of the seasons. CWM also experiences the passage of seasons in regard to its life and witness. The present season, in my viewpoint, can be characterised as spring-time of opportunity both to consolidate and to innovate, in tune with the movement and guidance of the Holy Spirit. But whatever season

---

[372] Quoted in Valentina Alexander, "Afrocentric and Black Christian Consciousness: Towards an Honest Intersection," *Black Theology in Britain: A Journal of Contextual Praxis* 1(1998).

we may be journeying through, we need to remind ourselves that there is never an ideal time or season, so we have to seize the moment and the opportunity for service as a partner in God's mission.[373]

The openness to the African worldview within the context of Nannyish t'eology embraced both nurturing/healing and militant aspects. For Nanny of the Maroons and her colleagues, their worldview led them to fight for the political liberation of their people. While the Jamaican context has passed through the fight for emancipation from enslaved Africans in the nineteenth century, and the struggle to end colonialism in the mid twentieth century, mutating forms of political marginalization are still the reality for many. At the level of institutions, including the church, the highest echelons of power are still dominated by men. Within the wider society, 'democracy' is mainly limited to voting once or twice every five years with limited opportunities to influence the workings of government once the elections are over. Globalization and the structure of the neo-liberal economic model has resulted in a new 'enslavement' and colonization of the country through the mechanism of debt. Women, in this context, have sought to establish their own organizations for capacity building and empowerment. The Young Women's Christian Association (YWCA) and the St. Andrew Business and Professional Women's Club joined forces to establish the Jamaica Women's Political Caucus in 1992[374] to support and train women who wanted to offer themselves as candidates for representational politics and as campaign managers/fund raisers. The organizations were led by Christian lay women who later invited women ministers in to assist with ritual functions. The involvement of Christians in politics is an area in which the CWM concern about the right use of power is applicable.

Developments in women's empowerment within the Jamaican context also include attempts by women pastors and theologians to create spaces for solidarity and peer critique of scholarly work. The Caribbean Women Theologians for Transformation (CWTT) is the latest attempt of

---

[373] Van der Water, *From Ayr to Ocho Rios*, 24.
[374] Marguerite Curtin, Evelyn Smart, Joan Browne, and Hermione McKenzie, *Pioneers in Politics: Jamaica Women's Political Caucus (JWPC) 10th Anniversary Report 1992 – 2002* (Kingston: Jamaica Women's Political Caucus, 2003).

this nature. Of significance is the fact that the impetus for the CWTT was derived from a visit of Prof. Musa Dube, member of the Circle of Concerned Women Theologians, to Jamaica in 2007. These stories of women's empowerment in Jamaica beg the question as to whether or not the CWM has yet achieved equitable power sharing with women, within the organizations' structures and within the life and witness of the constituent churches. Part of the postcolonial analysis is, after all, the need to dismantle patriarchy which continues in overt and subtle ways to marginalize and dis-empower women.

A look at the CWM website[375] in September, 2009 revealed brief descriptions of fifty-four missionaries who were listed there. Of the 54 missionaries listed, twenty-four were women without reference to spouses or children while only two men were listed without mention of families. What does this mean for those women who are single, in a world which still projects marriage as an ideal for young women? What discussions are there about sexuality and the unmarried missionary, or is it assumed that such a topic has been covered elsewhere?

It was interesting also that among the missionaries on the website, ten couples were identified by the narrative as partners in mission, and in two, the wives were described in a 'helping' role to their husband's 'missionary' role. What is the understanding of 'partnership in mission' when some couples seem to work equally, while in other cases one spouse is identified as the dominant 'missionary,' and in still others there is no indication of a role for the spouse in the missionary venture? Some years ago, in the late 1990s, I attended n Assembly of the URC during which an old white woman who had been the wife of a missionary addressed the gathering. She told us that in days gone by the Missionary, usually a man, was listed by name in the official documents and if he was married an asterisk would be placed beside his name. The wife was not named at all. She spoke of all the work both she and her husband had accomplished on the mission field and concluded that she had decided that she was not an asterisk, but a star!

How do spouses of missionaries express and negotiate their choices and others' expectations? Some years ago, Carol Gregory, the wife a Jamaican minister, noted that clergy spouses had to face five challenges: the lack of adequate spiritual/faith development and

---

[375] http://www.cwmission.org.uk.

enrichment, the lack of freedom to create and maintain one's own identity and independence, loneliness, the need to live up to the Church's expectations, and the lack of privacy.[376] She made a plea for ministers' spouses to be true to themselves, for the Christian community to be realistic in their expectations of the minister and the minister's spouse and to give adequate space for individual and family pursuits in order to prevent burn out, bitterness and resentment. Are these concerns also concerns that are relevant to the experiences of the spouses of CWM missionaries?

Nowadays, spouses of missionaries are named and not just indicated by a generic 'asterisk'; but perhaps there is need to develop different models of 'missionary' to reflect variety in family circumstance, while at the same time fostering true partnership in mission. Somehow, Biblical models that have been put forward[377] such as Abraham (Genesis 12: 1- 20), the Suffering Servant (Isaiah 42: 1 – 9), Jonah, in the book of Jonah, Esther, in the book of the same name and Paul, the 'servant ambassador,' while offering valuable insights, are still in my view, limited options, not least because only one woman is mentioned as a model missionary! I would like to see models explored such as the un-named servant girl, wife and servants of Naaman the Syrian who all contributed to Naaman's encounter with Elisha, Naaman's healing and subsequent allegiance to God (II Kings 5: 1 - 19; also that of the women who were the first to hear the news of the resurrection and sent to tell the apostles (Luke 24: 1 – 12); and the couple, Priscilla and Aquilla who worked together as tentmakers and together witnessed to Gospel and nurtured others like Apollos to a deeper understanding of the faith (Acts 18: 1 – 4, 24 – 26; Romans 16: 3 – 4; I Corinthians 16: 19; II Timothy 4:19). These examples speak of the God who uses the least and the lowly to bear good news to those who were sick, marginalized, fearful and without hope; a God who entrusted mission to both women and men.

Along with these models, I think more attention should be paid to the needs of the families of missionaries, and the knowledge, skills

---

[376] Carol F. E. Gregory, "Clergy Spouses and the Realities of the Manse," *Caribbean Journal of Religious Studies* 10, no. 1 (April 1989).
[377] Andrew Prasad, ed. *Missionary Training Module1 Being A Missionary A Biblical Perspective*
(London: Council for World Mission, 1996), 6-18.

and attitudes that these family members will need in their new context and on returning home. It is significant however that the worldview that seeks a sharing of power and authority among different genders, ethnicities and social classes, includes engagement not only with the identity of those wielding power, but also with the ideology embraced by the new power brokers.

How do people in the global South, women and other marginalized groups exercise power and authority? The biblical story of Deborah, told in the book of Judges chapters four and five, is in Nannyish t'eology simultaneously a reference point for reflecting on women's empowerment and a cautionary tale. While Deborah exhibits many qualities similar to Nanny of the Maroons, the description of the murder of Sisera by Jael, suggests that Sisera who had hoped to rape women as he claimed the spoils of victory is instead 'raped' by the hammering of a tent peg through his mouth. As women and others who were previously powerless become empowered, will they offer new paradigms of leadership or simply mimic the categories of their former oppressors?

The explicit reference to the influence of African worldviews on the theology of the CWM partners in Africa and the African diaspora indicates the richness and breath brought to the CWM journey by the embracing of plurality and the providing of opportunity for many different voices to be heard.

Plurality in Nannyish t'eology

Starting with one's specific context is an act of affirmation of the agency that is the birthright of human beings as imago Dei. Each context has its specific history, and worldview(s) that must contend with the existence of diversity in local and global contexts. In the logic of Nannyish t'eology, the opportunity of plurality, an openness to embrace the rich gifts of diversity, and growth through the challenges of seeming chaos and conflict should also be embraced.

In the Jamaican context, Nannyish t'eology seeks to identify the common values of people of all faiths and ideologies within the context as the starting point for praxis. In the case of Nanny of the Maroons, her virtues are acclaimed within cultural expressions, in national recognition, and specifically in the writings of women scholars and women of different faiths. Two significant examples are Rastafari feminist Imani

Tafari-Ama, who identifies Nanny as the inspiration for militant Rastafari women, and Muslim Sultana Afroz, who hails Nanny as exemplifying the militant tradition of Muslim women who are equals with the men in the struggle for justice. In the Jamaican context, in my view, plurality should be predicated on the shared values and aspirations which make it possible to see the 'other' as a valuable human being with whom one can dialogue, even if there is not agreement on all issues. It echoes the CWM movement away from 'spreading' the gospel to 'sharing' the gospel, all the while conscious that we are partners in God's mission.

This is not always an easy task, as experienced in two debates in Jamaica towards the end of the first decade of the twenty first century. One debate centered on the issue of pastoral care to the gay community. The other concerned proposed changes to the legislation on abortion. Since 2004, the United Theological College of the West Indies (UTCWI) has had a programme to train all final year students as specialist HIV/AIDS counsellors, in response to the high prevalence of HIV infection in the Caribbean. The Caribbean, in fact, has the second highest prevalence of HIV infection behind sub Saharan Africa. A storm of controversy was raised when the Practical Theology Department of UTCWI suggested that the College partner with local gay rights and HIV/AIDS (anti-stigma and discrimination) organizations and the Metropolitan Community Church to have a consultation on the nature of pastoral care to the gay community. Further, they proposed to offer, as a College, a Certificate of Participation for those who attended. After discussions at the Faculty meeting and the Board of Governors of the institution, three faculty members who were trainers of HIV/AIDS counsellors participated in the conference in their own right.

How should a theological college, and the church by extension, cope with the reality of persons in Jamaica, who claim to be gay and Christian, and who had invited a church from North America to minister to their pastoral needs? How could the church dialogue with gay persons, and engage with those who held diverse views about the nature of homosexual orientation and the ethics of homosexual practice? To a large extent the churches in the Reformed tradition have a consensus about the biblical basis for equality of persons across gender and ethnic/cultural lines. But can plurality for us include openness to diversity in sexual orientation and ethics. In the context of Jamaica, the debate continues, without any sign that a consensus on the matter will be achieved in the near future. Perhaps, like the principles of CWM, commitment to engagement with persons of divergent standpoints - without resorting to manipulation or abandoning respect - may serve us well in Jamaica.

In a similar vein, national and denominational controversy ensued when the General Secretary of the United Church in Jamaica and the Cayman Islands (UCJCI) decided to publicly support proposed legislation for decriminalizing the termination of pregnancy in the specific instances of incest, rape and threat to the life of the mother or child. The UCJCI General Secretary became the only church leader to make a submission to the Parliament supporting this legislation. He was supported by some members of the clergy and feminist lobby groups, and opposed by other church leaders and Christian organizations of doctors and lawyers. Within the denomination there was also vocal opposition to the stance, with one other member of the UCJCI clergy making a counter-proposal to the Parliament. In these types of issues, the protocols of engagement within the CWM are helpful, even as church leaders are called to have the courage of conviction in prophetic stances that go against the tide. The UCJCI is also representative of the family of united and uniting churches existing within the CWM family. These churches offer distinctive insights on the issue of plurality as they have had to negotiate and reconcile doctrinal issues such as baptism and Eucharist, integrate administrative structures and personnel, and journey with the on-going challenge of living with plurality. Perhaps the implications of plurality within the context of united and uniting churches, as they seek to engage in mission in context, could contribute to the wider reflections within the CWM. Related to the examination of contextualization, worldviews and plurality in the quest for faithful participation in God's mission, it is important to identify insights that may be gleaned from the bible in pursuing theology and praxis.

While recognizing the merits of key texts that have been exegeted within the context of the CWM, such as Galatians 6:1-5 with respect to partnership, and others mentioned above, I would propose that a model of mission which can help the CWM member churches face the challenges of contextualization, worldviews and plurality can be found in Luke's gospel. I am grateful to African American womanist theologian Linda Thomas for the insights about the Lukan model of mission.

Thomas notes that the 'Great commission' of Matthew 8:18-20, has been linked with the theological justification for colonialism. It is a model that assumed that a superior Western European Christianity had the right to justify the enslavement, indentureship and colonization of the people of the South. It is a model that despised the insights of African worldviews as antithetical to the Christian gospel. It is a model of religious arrogance. This challenge to the 'Great Commission' model was also articulated within the CWM conferences. Models from Acts 1:8, John 20:20 and II Corinthians 5:18-19 were proposed instead.

The Lukan model in which Jesus sends out the twelve (Luke 9:1-9) is offered as a model of mission from the standpoint of vulnerability and openness to the insights of those to whom the 'missionary' goes. Thomas states it in this way:

> [The disciples] go out as beggars; they have nothing to give. They are not teachers, nor proselytizers. They go out to encounter God's kingdom in ways quite unorthodox. The disciples can only hope that someone in the street or in a house will receive them in mercy and with grace. The disciples had to rely on others. The disciples did not bring god to others; no introduction was necessary. God's image greeted them at the door.[378]

With respect to the work of the Council for World Mission, what does the insight from the Lukan model of mission have to offer? How could 'the Church reformed and always reforming' principle be understood in light of this model of mission? I invite us to a process of dialogue that affirms the agency of all to speak of their experience of God, that opens itself to peer, local and global critique and accountability regarding our worldviews and that, in love, engages with the 'other' in participating in mission.

A Jamaican 'Sign'

In closing I want to share an example of bearing witness through ritual, combining the concerns of contextualization, worldviews and plurality. On March 25, 2007 an ancestors funeral rites Ceremony was

---

[378] Linda Thomas, "Anthropology, Mission and the African Woman: A Womanist Approach," *Black Theology: An International Journal*, 5, no.1 (2007): 18.

held "to give the ancestors a proper burial; to keep in the public eye the real history of the African holocaust, even as the UK celebrated Wilberforce and the Parliamentary campaign for the abolition of the trade in enslaved Africans. It was an interfaith ceremony, preceded by a dancing, singing procession from St. William Grant Park, led by Revivalist groups. The ceremony was held on the docks of Kingston where enslaved Africans had been off-loaded and the blowing of the Abeng by the maroons signalled the start of the ceremony. The ritual included prayers, scriptures and invocations by Ethiopian Orthodox, protestant, Anglican and Evangelical Christians; by Muslims; by Rastafari, Revivalist, Jewish, Hindu religious leaders as well as libation by a Traditional Africa Religion priest flown in by the government of Ghana. The names of 1,000 ancestors were read by members of the National schools' Council and simultaneously displayed by the unrolling of scroll on which the names were written. A coast guard boat took religious leaders out to sea to perform rites in the water, and local politicians, the Minister of culture of Ghana and the leadership of the bicentenary committee made interventions. The preacher was a minister of the United Church in Jamaica and the Cayman islands who was also a founder of the local Interfaith Council, and the liturgist was a woman.

10

Mission as Praxis for Peace-Building, Healing, and Reconciliation: Critical Appraisal of the Praxis of CWM

Paul John Isaak[379]

1. Introduction

This essay offers reflections on mission as praxis for peace-building, healing and reconciliation from an ecumenical mission point of view. It is shared as a critical appraisal of the praxis of Council of World Mission (CWM) with special reference to postcolonial situation. First, in our reflections on the *missional Church* and its *missionary action or praxis*,[380] we need to discern the actions of the Triune God, or what God in Jesus Christ together with the Holy Spirit is doing in the world to bring about peace, healing, reconciliation, wholeness, liberation and salvation. We shall maintain in this paper that innovative, creative, and more effective forms of evangelism and dialogue must be explored. We do this, however, not as "judges or lawyers, but as witnesses; not as soldiers, but as envoys of peace; not as high-pressure sales persons, but as ambassadors of the Servant Lord."[381]

Second, it should be stated at the outset that the issue of peace-building is high on the agenda of the CWM. At the Scotland CWM

---

[379] Professor of Missiology at the Ecumenical Institute of Bossey, Geneva, Switzerland

[380] The term, *missional Church,* is used here to denote mission as pertaining to the *being* of the Church, while *"missionary"* is reserved to describe the mission as the *action or praxis* of the Church. Thus in this paper the *missional Church* is called into the *missionary praxis of peacemaking, reconciliation, and healing.*

[381] David Bosch, *Transforming Mission: Paradigm Shifts in Theology of Mission* (Maryknoll: Orbis Books, 1991), 489.

Assembly held in Ayr from 15 to 25 June, 2003, the family of the CWM churches agreed to "encourage member churches to incorporate modules into their theological education programmes that will equip both ordained and lay people training for ministry in such areas as resolution of conflict and peace-building."[382] Encouraged by such statements of the CWM, we shall pay closer attention to the issue of peace-building in our broken world.

Third, we shall ask the question: what does it mean to be healing and reconciling communities in postcolonial era? This question particularly concerns the former mission societies that have been restructured in an attempt to enable rather than hinder equal relations, sharing of power and money, sharing of personnel, and *koinonia* (communion) among Christians from global South and North. In the view of the CWM, the ministries of healing and reconciliation are two sides of the same coin.[383] But unfortunately, according to Steve de Gruchy,

> ...in the heyday of the great Protestant mission societies the provision of health care through hospitals and dispensaries, and by doctors and nurses was seen as a crucial part of sharing the gospel. Yet, the same movement of missionaries from the North brought European ways of understanding the world. This has an important impact upon the relationship between mission and health, because in the North there was a growing separation between religion and medicine. Preaching, evangelism and Bible translation was the task of the ordained clergy, and medical work was the task of doctors and nurses...now medical work became scientific, driven by clinical evidence, taken from the

---

[382] "CWM Assembly Statement" (26 July 2003). http://www.cwmission.org/features/cwm-assembly-statement/print.html (accessed 11 June 2009).
[383] Desmond van der Water, *From Ayr to Ocho Rios: CWM's Mission Journey from 2003-2006* (CWM, 2006), 19.

church and given to a new professional person: the doctor.[384]

Fortunately, since the late 1980s, mission has been increasingly connected with healing and reconciliation. Today it is crucial to see such a connection, because mission is about participation in the liberating, transforming, reconciling work of God; it must involve healing and enjoyment of abundant life (John 10.10). The language of healing and reconciliation has come to the fore in many different contexts and catches the imagination of people inside and outside the churches. It is, further, a very timely subject as 2009 was proclaimed International Year of Reconciliation according to the resolution calendar of the United Nations (UN).[385] This is certainly also an invitation to the Christian Church to promote in this broken world the concepts of peace-building, healing and reconciliation in word and deeds.

Therefore, I now focus on these critical issues and challenges facing the CWM and its member churches as well as the Church worldwide. We do so in the spirit of *ecclesia simper reformande est*. Such a spirit stresses the Church's need for continual renewal and that, in a dynamic world, informed by God's enlivening word and presence, the Church is never static. In this process of the continual renewal of the missional Church in living out the praxis of peacemaking, reconciliation and healing is seen as one of the core missional Church's functions. I now turn to this aspect of the Church's self-understanding of being a missional Church, and how such a Church is living out fully its missionary praxis.

2. The Missional Church and Its Praxis in Postcolonial Era

The shift of Christianity's center of gravity to the global South will accelerate the process under way in African and Asian churches of clarifying how far these churches have been, and still are, dependent on western interpretations of Christianity. It will take these churches some time to rid themselves of their unnecessary excess of western baggage. At the same time, churches from the global South and North should

---

[384] "To Save or to Heal?" (8 May 2007). http://www.cwmission.org/features/to-save-or-to-heal/print.html (accessed 12 June 2009).
[385] On 20 November 2006, the General Assembly of the United Nations decided to proclaim 2009 as the International Year of Reconciliation (resolution 61/17).

embark together on a common search for a genuinely fresh apostolic understanding applicable in every local context of a globalised world. Only such an understanding can be instrumental in bringing new life to the suffering people of our time.[386]

However, according to Konrad Raiser, the former General Secretary of the WCC, the touchiest issue of Christianity's center of gravity shift to the global South, is the question of money and the power that goes with it. As Raiser said: "In the long run there can be no real partnership in regard of a lasting worldwide inequality in power, e.g. between the rich and poor, donors and receivers. Material dependency destroys human relationships elsewhere, too, however, hard one may try to achieve partnership."[387] In other words, questions of power still remain in the postcolonial Churches - Europe still has hegemony, as do males, whites, educated, English or German speakers, and so on. So the tensions elicit the search to find ways of being partners in a postcolonial way of relating that takes seriously questions of power. And of course these are difficult issues to resolve, so we live with constant sense of ambiguity and uncertainty.

Therefore, the following postcolonial reflections will concentrate on the missional Church in the context of the postcolonial era. The postcolonial era poses major challenges for Christian mission in a world increasingly torn apart by economic, political, cultural and religious diversities. It may be easy in such diverse contexts to develop new theological ideas, but their ultimate value lies in their practicality in the life and mission of the Churches. One should avoid creating an impression as if there is a universal theology and one united Church. Today in the postcolonial era, one should accept diverse theologies that do not necessary exclude each other; they form a multicoloured mosaic of complementary and mutual enriching as well as mutually challenging frames of reference.[388] This fact is affirmed by the WCC in the book,

---

[386] Risto A. Ahonen, *Mission in the New Millennium* (Helsinki: The Finnish Evangelical Lutheran Mission, 2006), 22-23.
[387] Kai Michael Funkscmidt, "Partnership Between Unequals - Mission Impossible?" *International Review of Mission* XCI, no. 362 (July 2002): 395-396.
[388] Bosch, *Transforming Mission*, 8.

Mission as Praxis for Peace-Building 241

Dictionary of the Ecumenical Movement.[389] In this volume, seventeen theologies are identified, such as African theology, Asian theology, Black theology, Feminist theology, including Womanist theology, Liberation theology, and Minjung theology. All these theologies are attempts to critically reflect on praxis in the light of the Word of God. At this critical point, doing theologies in the life of the Churches most disturbs classical theology - also known as "academic theology"[390] - because the partner and addressee of theological reflection became much less the non-believing and secular person than the person who is involved in the struggle for human dignity. In other words, studying and doing theologies in the life of the Churches tells us the good news - that in a very real yet mysterious sense, the poor are "proxies for Christ."[391] To put it differently, loving God and loving our neighbour is a single, not a sequential act. We should remember that the new thing about Jesus was that he put the two commandments in Deuteronomy 6.5 and Leviticus 19.18 in the same breath and gave them equal weight. In other words, Jesus makes the two commandments virtually one, such that there is no sense in which we can love God at the expense of our neighbour or vice versa.

    I am now in the position to turn to the practical implications of such a missionary theology. At the outset, I wish to state that missional Churches, especially in light of the postcolonial experiences, are called into the missionary praxis of peacemaking, reconciliation, and healing. In other words, for the missional Church, mission is not only what the Church does (missionary activities), but also the Church at work in specific contextual praxis. Word empowered and Spirit led, the Church knows that mission flows from its nature as a witnessing, peacemaking, reconciling and healing community.[392] In short, the Triune God creates the Church and sustains it through the gifts of Word and Sacrament by

---

[389] Nicholas Lossky et al., *Dictionary of the Ecumenical Movement - Second Edition* (Geneva: World Council of Churches Publications, 2002), 1099-1133.
[390] Lossky et al., *Dictionary*, 1119-1120.
[391] Andrew Walls and Cathy Ross, eds. *Mission in the 21st Century: Exploring the Five Marks of Global Mission* (Maryknoll: Orbis, 2008), 52.
[392] For further insights on the missional Church and the missionary praxis of the Church see the outstanding study on the understanding and practice of mission by the Lutheran World Federation's document, *Mission in Context: Transformation, Reconciliation, Empowerment.* (Geneva: Lutheran World Federation, 2004).

the power of the Spirit. It could also be said that the *being-ness* (the missional Church) and *sent-ness* (the missionary praxis) of the Church are inextricably linked and that, for example, the Christian community is an expression of God's intention for bringing reconciliation and healing to everyone, everywhere.

Such a missional Church understands its participation in God's mission (*missio Dei*) as contextual, faithfully addressing the challenges of ever-changing and complex contexts, in a comprehensive and holistic way. Mission is holistic and contextual with regard to its aim, practice, and location. Its aim encompasses the whole of creation (ecological concerns), the whole of life (spiritual, social, political, economic, and cultural), and the whole human being (i.e., soul and body). Its practice calls for the participation of the whole Church, women and men, young and old. Being holistic, mission flows from the being of the Church, as peacemaking, reconciling, and healing communities. As such a community, the Church seeks and works for peace, reconciliation, and healing.[393] That is the being-ness and the sent-ness of the Church.

For the missional Church to be engaged in such missionary activities and praxis, it needs to follow mission as a prophetic practice in faith, courage, bold humility, and prophetic dialogue and proclamation. Such mission as *action* of the Church is based on Micah 6.8, "do justice, love kindness, and walk humbly with God." These words are echoed in the Letter of James 2. 14-17: "What good it is, sisters and brothers, if you say you have faith but do not have works? Can faith save you? If a sister or brother is naked and lacks daily food, and one of you says to them, 'Go in peace; keep warm and eat your fill,' and yet you do not supply their bodily needs, what is the good of that? So faith by itself, if it does not works, is dead." This is the biblical and prophetic mission as well as the vision which the Church ought to follow in faith and good works. Put differently, Micah's and James' theological-ethics gravitates among the theological principles of *orthodoxy* (correct teachings and doctrines of the Church), *orthokardia* (right heartedness) or spirituality, and *orthopraxis* (right social action and involvement): it insists that spirituality and faith inspired by God's Word, must express itself in social action. This does not mean that works negate faith, but that justification always issues in social justice.

---

[393] LWF, *Mission in Context*, 36.

Orthokardia and *orthodoxy* are generally understood to mean experiencing God and the transformation of life as outcomes of that experience. In other words, spirituality and faith refer to a lived experience of God (thirst for God), and the life of prayer and action or *orthopraxis* which results from this. At the same time, these three theo-ethical aspects cannot be conceived apart from each other. All of them are essential, so that the divine human encounter might acquire greater depth and meaning. Therefore, a true understanding of the nature of spirituality and faith will effect personal, societal and structural transformation, and help to bring about more united, peaceful, reconciling and healing communities. In contrast to former views of spirituality, which considered it to be separated from earthly concerns, contemporary and postcolonial spirituality of the missional Church understands its participation in God's mission as contextual—addressing faithfully and passionately the challenges of contemporary praxis.

Perhaps an example from the Orthodox Churches on the relationship between spirituality and social activism will be useful at this stage. In the discussion of the consultation organized by Commission on World Mission and Evangelism (CWME) Desk for Orthodox Studies and relations in Etchmiadzine, Armenia, 16-21 September 1975,[394] on the topic "Confessing Christ through the liturgical life of the Church," the question was raised: What is the relationship between the *liturgical spirituality*, the personal experience gained by a meaningful participation in the Liturgy, and the witness to the Gospel in the world, witness which belongs to the very nature of the Church?

The consultation spoke of the *indispensable continuation* of the liturgical celebration and stated very clearly that "the liturgy has to be continued in the life of the faithful in all dimensions of life." Bishop Anastasios Yannoulatos, then professor at the University of Athens, asserted: "The Liturgy is not an escape from life, but a continuous transformation of life according to the prototype Jesus Christ, through the power of the Spirit... In the liturgy we participate in the great event of liberation from sin and of koinonia with Christ through the real presence of the Holy Spirit, then this event of our personal incorporation

---

[394] "Report of an Inter-Orthodox Consultation – Confessing Christ through the Liturgical Life of the Church Today," in *Orthodox Visions of Ecumenism*, compiled by Gennadios Limouris, Statements, Messages and Reports on the Ecumenical Movement 1902-1992, (Geneva: WCC, 1994), 55-59.

into the body of Christ... must be evident and be proclaimed in actual life. The Liturgy has to be continued in personal everyday situations."[395] Each of the faithful is called upon to continue their personal *liturgy* on the secret altar of his or her own heart, to realize a living proclamation of the good news for the sake of the whole world.

Without this continuation, the Liturgy remains incomplete. Since the liturgy is the participation in the great event of liberation from demonic powers, the continuation of Liturgy in life means a continuous liberation from the powers of evil that are working inside a person. It entails a continual reorientation and openness to insights and efforts aimed at liberating human persons from all demonic structures of injustice, exploitation, agony, and loneliness. It creates real communion with persons in love. To put it differently, there is a double movement in the Liturgy: The dismissal of the faithful at the end of the Liturgy with the words *"go forth in peace"* does not mean that the Liturgy is over, but that it is transposed into another form in which it continues, in a life immersed in the daily secular life. The liturgy after the Liturgy is linked to religious and moral experience, diaconal services, spirituality, and renewal. Such dynamics of liturgy may be helpful to correct the tendency to intellectualism in the *sola scriptura* (preaching) tradition and the tendency to ritualism in the sacramental (*ex opera operato*) tradition.[396]

Within such richness of Christian tradition, African theologian François Kabasele Lumbala from the Democratic Republic of Congo reflects on the relationship between *orthodoxy, orthokardia*, and *orthopraxis* from postcolonial experience.[397] Kabasele Lumbala's model of an African Christ intends to bridge the division between the human and the sacred, and suggests the vindication of the human as the place where God acts in the world and where the African Christ is likely to appear more meaningful. Kabasele Lumbala's work centers on his own tradition, and he examines the possibility of an African perception of the human in the sacred by way of the celebration of the sacraments.

Kabasele Lumbala has maintained that it is in the African liturgy and through the worship of localized African communities that

---

[395] Ion Bria, "The Liturgy after the Liturgy" in *Martyria Mission, The Witness of the Orthodox Churches Today*, ed. Ion Bria (Geneva: WCC, 1980), 66-67.
[396] Lossky et al., *Dictionary*, 705-706.
[397] Mario Aguilar, *Theology, Liberation and Genocide: A Theology of the Periphery* (London: SCM Press, 2009), 86-89.

indigenous African cultural elements can and must be incorporated. The centrality of such liturgical practice assumes that the theology of inculturation reflects a way of doing theology that comes out of postcolonial experience, an African experience of the spiritual and material worlds. Such experience is manifested and expressed through the body. It is subsequently lived and written by faith communities that reflect kinship and symbolic networks within a particular social history.

However, other African theologians have challenged the centrality of the liturgy suggested by Kabasele Lumbala. For example, Jean-Marc Ela has noted critically that "while people wallow in misery, we are centring our reflection on religious rites and customs!"[398] Thus, addressing Ela's concerns, one could say that it is through processes of liberation and their liturgical celebration that God becomes part of an African cultural experience. The concern for inculturation in the liturgy does not exclude. Instead, it includes processes of Christian liberation through cultural freedom and the use of contextualized theological paradigms.

In light of the above postcolonial African theology and liberation, one is in a position to formulate a thesis, namely that mission today must be lived out in "bold humility." According to Des van der Water, the General Secretary of the CWM, the ministry of healing and reconciliation should be done "with a spirit of repentance and an attitude of humility."[399] This involves discovering the living power of the Gospel in the worship and testimony of the people, that is, the life-changing Word speaking to Christians. It is argued that people are saved entirely by the gracious God who then directs us to be a gracious neighbour or Christ to others, thereby, landing in the arms of God and fellow humans. The nature of Gospel itself is not congruent with notions "of arrogance, self-importance or superiority and those who witness to the Good News, and who proclaim God's love, healing and forgiveness to others can only truly do so on the basis of themselves being under God's grace."[400]

However, it is still important to briefly mention the criticisms that have been raised against classical theology's relationship between *orthodoxy* and *orthopraxis*. This includes charges that it is escapist

---

[398] Aguilar, *Theology, Liberation and Genocide*, 87.

[399] See van der Water, *From Ayr to Ocho Rios*, 19. Compare also Bosch, *Transforming Mission*, 489.

[400] Van der Water, *From Ayr to Ocho Rios*, 19.

theology, and is insensitive to structural and social problems. Other criticisms point out its dualistic conception of life in which the world is viewed negatively; the legalism and fundamentalism that denies its members evangelical freedom; and the neo-Pentecostal theology of prosperity that gives false hope to the poor and the spiritualisation of the Gospel.[401]

But as Martin Luther has observed, "he or she who wants to be a true Christian ... must be truly a believer. But he or she does not truly believe if works of love do not follow his/her faith."[402] To put it differently, having been made righteous by Christ, we become "a Christ" toward the neighbour by enabling the poor to have their daily bread. According to Luther, "love your neighbour as yourself" has nothing to do with "childish toys" such as "walking around with a sour face and a downcast head" or "wearing dirty clothes."[403] Such religiosity and moral posturing is basically done out of self-interest. Against such a motive, God sets God's Word of justification by faith alone, which makes us righteous before God. At the same time, all human deeds and good works are redirected to earth, where we ought to be engaged in love seeking justice, reconciliation, healing and peace.

However, the cooperation between God and human beings is not merely a matter of opening the sluices and allowing the surging waters of praxis to gush over the thirsty land. Therefore, Karl Barth declares that "from the belief in God's righteousness there follows logically a very definite political problem and task."[404] Barth is highly specific on the nature and theological orientation of such a task, as can be appreciated when he states that "God always takes His stand unconditionally and

---

[401] Rafael Malpica-Padila, "Re-counter and Reconciliation: The Task for Latin America," in *Mission at the Dawn of the 21st Century: A Vision for the Church*, ed. Paul Varo Martinson (Minneapolis: Kirk House, 1999), 154.

[402] Martin Luther, "Lectures on Galatians—1535," in *Luther's Works*, Vol. 27, ed. Jaroslav Pelikan (Saint Louis: Concordia Publishing House, 1964), 30.

[403] Luther, "Lectures on Galatians," 367.

[404] As cited in Paul John Isaak, *The Influences of Missionary Work in Namibia* (Windhoek: MacMillan Namibia, 2007), 32.

passionately on this side and this side alone: against the lofty and on behalf of the lowly."⁴⁰⁵

To rephrase the statement of Karl Barth, I wish to state that Jesus Christ is the Saviour, Victor and Liberator, and we humans are minor liberators engaged in securing provisional and relative, yet joyful victories over such sins as economic exploitation, racism, gender inequalities, sexism and political oppression. To put it differently, one must ask how God is concretely dealing with humanity. Ulrich Duchrow notes that Matthew 25:31-46 answers Dietrich Bonhoeffer's important question, "Who and where is Jesus Christ for us today?"⁴⁰⁶ Jesus comes to Christians in those who are hungry, homeless, sick and imprisoned. Basic human needs are listed here--food, clothing, shelter, health care and, by implication, the basic political need for human dignity and integrity.

This is an indication of the concrete political tendency of the biblical message. It is not possible for this message to be heard and believed without it awakening a sense of social and spiritual responsibility to follow in that direction today. It awakens in us the responsibility to provide structures and processes for the reconstruction of a fractured society to one that is truthful and just, and to rebuild shattered lives. According to Des van der Water, "this is a vision which should surely also challenge and inspire the CWM at this time to press on in faith and fidelity to God, into whose mission partnership the CWM has been called."⁴⁰⁷

Put plainly, a Christian's zeal for God's honour and dignity must show itself in corresponding action that is directed toward the neighbour. Such an understanding of Christian ministry means that God breaks into our world and invites us to be involved in the creative and liberating dynamics of God's love in history. Moreover, while human efforts cannot remove sin from the world, God's creativity involves us in these dynamics, so that we engage in seeking partial, provisional and relative victories today.

---

⁴⁰⁵ Isaak, *Influences of Missionary Work in Namibia*, 32.
²⁸ Charles Villa-Vicencio and John W. de Gruchy, *Doing Ethics in Context: South African Perspectives* (Cape Town: David Philip, 1994), 200.

⁴⁰⁷ van der Water, *From Ayr to Ocho Rios*, 23.

3. Mission as Peace-Building: Postcolonial Experiences and Power Relations

At the outset let me ask a straight forward question: What is postcolonialism and how is it related to power? To begin with, the concept of postcolonialism is notoriously difficult to define. "Postcolonial" is used as a temporal marker referring to the period after official decolonization.[408] However, over time, the postcolonialism has moved beyond the confines of history (as a temporal marker) to become a "general" theory about what Ania Loomba et al. call "the shifting and often interrelated forms of dominance and resistance; about the constitution of the colonial archive; about the interdependent play of race and class; about the significance of gender and sexuality; about the complex forms in which subjectivities are experienced and collectivities mobilized; about representation itself; and about the ethnographic translation of cultures."[409]

The current understanding of postcolonialism, which has given rise to an entire field of studies known as "postcolonial studies," has its distant roots in the work of French philosopher Michel Foucault. Two insights from Foucault have particularly served as cornerstones for postcolonial studies. The first, insight concerns his assertion that knowledge, whether theoretical or practical, is essentially contextual. The second insight concerns Foucault's other assertion that no knowledge is for knowledge sake. Knowledge always involves a play of power. A discourse of knowledge is a discourse of power, for knowledge is an effort not only at ordering facts, social events and human activities, but also of ordering human beings according to a given center.[410]

To put it differently, the term "postcolonial" addresses all aspects of the colonial process from the beginning of colonial contact up to and including its present effects in both colonizing and colonized nations and people. The work of postcolonial interpretation is both that

---

[408] Susan Abraham, "What Does Mumbai Have to Do with Rome? Postcolonial Perspectives on Globalisation and Theology," *Theological Studies* 69 (June 2008): 376-393.
[409] As cited in Mabiala Justin-Robert Kenzo,"What is Postcolonialism and Why Does It Matter: An African Perspective." http://www.amahoro-africa.org/files/what-is-postcolonialism (accessed 10 April 2010).
[410] Kenzo, "What is Postcolonialism." http://www.amahoro-africa.org/files/what-is-postcolonialism

of analysis and that of resistance and reconstruction, as scholars examine the many contradictions between the colonial and neo-colonial rhetoric, and the continuing cultural, political, economic and religious oppression experienced by colonized people. Those who write this theory are committed to documenting the contradictions in their many fields, and to a future in which "post-" applies not only to the centuries after colonial contact and struggles for independence, but also to a time after which colonialism and imperialism are ended. In short, usually in Christian theology, colonialism begins with a discussion of the ways that the four Cs, Christianity, Commerce, Civilization, and Conquest or the unholy alliance of God, Mammon, Westernization, and Militarism were linked in the colonial white Euro-American expansion into countries of the Southern hemisphere.

Doing theological reflections from such a postcolonial experience is to go beyond, and reject, the colonial understanding of mission in service of the four Cs. Instead, from a postcolonial perspective, I shall make an attempt to capture an all-embracing dynamic of mission using a one-line definition; one can say that mission is proclamation, serving, dialogue and witnessing to God's reign of peacemaking, reconciliation, healing as well as justice and ultimately salvation. In other words, the *starting point and end point* for mission, Church, and, of course, human life in a holistic sense, is always God. Properly understood, mission *is* God's job description, capturing both who God *is* and what God *does*. Although the Church certainly never denied this, there has been a dangerous tendency over time, to overemphasise the goals of the institutional Church or individual missionary societies, or missionaries themselves, and to forget who God *is* and what God *does*. God is always bigger than our image of God and God always does bigger things for us. According to African American ex-slave Sojourner Truth, "Oh, God, I did not know you were so big."[411] Jesus is God's mission, and we Christians need to participate in *missio Dei* because people today search and yearn for God's love and compassion, justice and salvation. These are central in building reconciled and healing communities.

---

[411] Roger Schroeder, *What is the Mission of the Church? A Guide for Catholics* (Maryknoll: Orbis Books, 2008), 13.

The former General Secretary of the CWM, Dr. D. Preman Niles, makes interesting and helpful remarks by defining peace from a postcolonial experience. At the outset, he states what peace does not mean in some of the Asian languages. For example, the English word *peace* has its roots in *pax Romana,* leading to *pax Britannica,* and now to *pax Americana.* In this sense, to keep the peace is to impose the will of the Emperor or Pharaoh. Such a definition and understanding comes from the ruling and powerful elite.[412] Instead, according to Niles, in Tamil (India and Sri Lanka) language, there are two words, *amaidhi* and *samadhanam.*[413] *Amaidhi* literally means "rest" or "quiet." It is the absence of turbulence. It is the cessation of desiring after things that cause unrest. It is stillness. On the other hand, *samadhanam,* refers to the concentration of the mind as in meditation. From this understanding arises steadiness, composure, and the bringing together, or reconciling, of two groups. Furthermore, he states, "the ideogram *heiwa* or *ping-he* in the Chinese family of languages is made up of two characters: One denotes harmony and the other has mouth and grain. When all are fed, there is peace."[414]

But today not all are fed. There are the deep hurts and painful experiences that people across all the continents - and particularly the global South - have experienced. In positive terms, all people have the right to life, safety, and the free development of personality in so far as they do not injure the rights of others. No one has the right physically or psychically to capture, imprison, oppress, torture, and kill, any other human being. And no people, no state, no ethnic group, no religion has the right to hate, to discriminate against, to 'cleanse,' to exile, or to liquidate a minority group which is different in behaviour or holds different beliefs. In short, the peace-building message is: you shall not kill! Or in positive terms: Have respect for life![415]

At the same time, Christians must not deceive themselves: There is no survival for humanity without global peace. According to Hans Küng, "we must never be ruthless and brutal. Every people, every race,

---

[412] D. Preman Niles, *From East and West: Rethinking Christian Mission* (St. Louis, Missouri: Chalice Press, 2004), 170-171.
[413] Niles, *From East and West,* 170.
[414] Niles, *From East and West,* 171.
[415] Hans Küng, *A Global Ethic: The Declaration of the Parliament of the World's Religions* (New York: Continuum, 1993), 24-26.

every religion must show tolerance and respect - indeed high appreciation - for every other....We are **all intertwined together** in this cosmos and we are all dependent on each other. Each one of us depends on the welfare of all."[416]

Today, we are painfully aware that ethnic hatred and xenophobia are great hindrances to the Church's mission to live the life and love of Christ. Its major source is the problem of "otherness," which regards those unlike "us" as less human or unworthy. This "othering" extends to differences such as gender, class, ethnicity, and even religion. Difference should not be divisive but should be occasion to celebrate our diversity. The Church should reflect on this concept of otherness and foster what Miroslav Volf calls a "theology of embrace." He observes, "The future of the whole world depends on how we deal with ethnic, religious and gender otherness."[417] Volf considers the inability to relate the core theological beliefs about peace and reconciliation, to the shape of the Church's social responsibility.

Such a culture of respect for life invites the Church to mediate peace, reconciliation and healing. It calls for an ecumenical mission and vision that entails partnership in suffering by accompanying our members who are suffering. This includes, for example, ill health through HIV and AIDS, ethnic and civil conflicts, gender violence, child and woman abuse or any other form of violation of human dignity. We should not, as people of God, fail our moral duty to stand up for justice and speak out where it is violated. Today, the Church, including the CWM, should see its mission as bringing wholeness to people as Jesus Christ did. Jesus' ministry was grounded in the Hebrew "shalom"—a concept of peace that is inclusive of harmony and wellbeing.

Shalom entails justice, healed relations between individuals in society, between God and humanity and between humanity and the rest of creation. It has been said time and again in the famous slogan, "If you want peace, work for justice."[418] Furthermore, the same root is properly

---

[416] Küng, *A Global Ethic*, 26.
[417] Moroslav Volf cited in Anne-Marie Kool, "The Church in Hungary, Central and Eastern Trends and Challenges," *The Princeton Seminary Bulletin* 28, no. 2 (2007): 149.
[418] S.B.Bevans and R.B. Schroeder, *Constants in Context: a Theology of Mission for Today* (Maryknoll NY: Orbis, 2004), 369.

translated as liberation and salvation.[419] In other words, this shalom is fulfilled in the person and work of Jesus Christ—called "the good news" by the apostles. "Peace on earth" was promised by the angels in Luke 2.14. That the inauguration of God's reign is at hand was promised by John, as it was of Jesus. In light of this beginning, the seventh beatitude calls peace-makers "children of God" (Matthew 5.9).[420]

To put it differently, the peace-making function of the Church as community is undergirded theologically by the confession of Christ's lordship, which refuses to let the rulers of the present world sacralise their oppressive and divisive structures. Therefore, the Church's mission of justice is intrinsically linked to its mission of cultivating and preserving peace among the peoples and nations in the world. For this reason, the Church can promote peace to help peoples of the world to make "conscious choices" and help them to develop "deliberate policies" for peace, justice, and building of reconciled and healing communities. This peace, or shalom, was the dream of the Bible and it is still our dream (Is. 2.2-5, 9.5-6, Ez. 37.26, Rev. 21).[421]

Finally, since tension within and between religions is the source of so much violence in the world (such as Northern Ireland, India, Sri Lanka, Indonesia, Nigeria, Israel, Palestine, and Sudan), the Church's commitment to interreligious dialogue can be a way to foster better understanding and reduce suspicion among people of different religious beliefs. Such a challenge can only be met if the Church offers its prophetic voice to the world in a spirit of authentic dialogue, in order to lead the communities to post-conflict healing and reconciliation. Such dialogue is the spice of peace. The following statement is quoted by CWM concerning an interfaith workshop on peace building in India's troubled north-east. "[W]e need to build communities of peace irrespective of faith, language, race and culture...Today we blow up our little differences so much that we fail to see the common humanity that unites us...The challenge before us is to see everyone as children of God."[422]

---

[419] Lossky et al., *Dictionary*, 893.
[420] Lossky et al., *Dictionary*, 893.
[421] Bevans and Schroeder, 374.
[422] "How Indian Churches Can Do More to Build Peace" of 14 May 2008. http://www.cwmmission.org/features/how-indian-churches-can-do-more-to-build-peace/print.html (accessed 12/06/2009).

At this point, let us explore how peace-building may lead to justice and reconciliation. In the postcolonial society and church, one of the greatest challenges is the task of reconstruction. This is where confession, forgiveness, reconciliation and healing are necessary. This healing and reconciliation should not be a hasty process but one that respects and restores human dignity. It should be seen as a process that leads victims and perpetrators to discover God's mercy welling up their lives. It is discovering God's reconciliation through Jesus Christ. It is allowing the Holy Spirit to bring forgiveness and reconciliation among people who are hurting, both victims and perpetrators. The following section turns to the issues of reconciliation and healing.

4.   **Mission as Reconciliation**

One of the leading theologians in the area of reconciliation as a new paradigm for mission is Robert Schreiter. He acknowledges that there is no single understanding of reconciliation among people, but that every culture and language has concepts of who needs to be involved in reconciliation, how it should be accomplished, what constitutes justice in the new situation and what marks the end of the reconciliation process. Moreover, there is no single Christian understanding of reconciliation, as the concept has developed various nuances depending on the context and circumstances. Schreiter therefore contends that the best approach is to merely outline elements that must be considered in any process of reconciliation.[423]

In light of this, let me briefly highlight how the concept of reconciliation has been applied in the Namibian situation. For example, the meaning of reconciliation is expressed in some of the Namibian languages as follows: In *Oshiwambo* there are three words that deal with the *concept* of *reconciliation*, namely *ediminafanepo* (you forgive someone and he/she in turn forgives you), *ehanganifo* (someone takes the hand of one person, and then takes the hand of another person, thus bringing them together in friendship); and *etambulafano* (two people

---

[423] Robert J. Schreiter, *Reconciliation: Mission and Ministry in a Changing Social Order* (Maryknoll: Orbis Books, 1992), 13. See also Diane Stinton, "Prophetic Ministry Amid Conflict in Africa" in Stephen R Goodwin, ed. *World Christianity in Local Context: Essays in Memory of David A Kerr,* Vol. 1 (New York: Continuum, 2009), 103.

accept one another following a quarrel; acceptance takes place on an equal footing).

In **Khoekhoegowab** it is interesting to note that the root words for peace and reconciliation are the same, namely ≠*khîb* (peace) and //*kawa-≠khîbagus* (to re-establish peace). All the Khoekhoegowab words convey the sense that something that has been destroyed should be rebuilt. In other words, peace that has been destroyed should be re-established, or a relationship should be renewed. Here the focus falls on the prefix *re (or //kawa)-*, which means "again." For example, two of these words are //*kawa-/haos* (to be reunified) or //*kawa-/hû* (to be one again). The underlying notion is that of beginning anew, unconditionally.

In **Afrikaans**, the word for *reconciliation* is *versoening*. The verb is *versoen*, from which one draws both the verb and the noun *soen* ("to kiss" and "kiss"). Those who have a relationship close enough for them to be kissing are assumed to have been reconciled.

Thus, in most of the Namibian languages, there is the idea of living together in peace, of coming together, of joining hands and having peace, whatever the case may be. The final concept conveyed is that something new should have been established, so as to live together in peace and harmony. In short, the core issue involved is grounded in a reality that people were oppressed, that racism was practised, that there was a sense of being lost, displaced and homeless. The yearning to belong somewhere, to be somebody, to have a home and to be safe, is a deep and moving pursuit. Having lost one's place and yearning to find it are haunting images.

From a biblical perspective, reconciliation is, primarily and fundamentally, the work of the triune God bringing fulfilment to God's eternal purposes of creation and salvation through Jesus Christ. "For in him all the fullness of God was pleased to dwell, and through him to reconcile to himself all things, whether on earth or in heaven, making peace by the blood of his cross … For in Him the whole fullness of deity dwells bodily." (Col. 1:19-20). In the person of Jesus Christ, the divine nature and the human nature were reconciled, united forever. This is the starting point for human reconciliation with God. Christians have to actualise, by God's grace and our efforts, what they already have in Christ, through the Holy Spirit.

The Bible is full of stories of reconciliation out of which Christians can draw their own healing and reconciliation stories. The Old

Testament addresses, again and again, the estrangement between God and God's people. God desires and urges healing, reconciliation and restoration of a relationship that was broken and fragmented through human pride and various forms of rebellion against the God of life and justice. Similarly, in the New Testament, though the actual term "reconciliation" does not appear very prominently, the matter itself is prevalent throughout. Throughout his letters, Paul is greatly concerned that those whom Christ has reconciled in his body should not be divided, and that community life should be the first expression of God's plan to reconcile all things. He envisages the unity of not only Jew and Gentile, but also of slave and free, male and female in Christ (Gal. 3.28).

Apart from Matthew 5.24, where it relates to the reconciliation of individuals, the terms "reconciliation" and "to reconcile" – the Greek words *katallage* and *katallassein* – are only found in the letters of the Apostle Paul (2 Cor. 5.17-20; Rom. 5.10-11; 11.15; 1 Cor. 7.11, and then Eph. 2.16 and Col. 1.20-22). However, the apostle expresses the theme so forcefully that it emerges as a key notion in the Christian identity as a whole. Paul uses the term reconciliation in exploring the nature of God, to illumine the content of the gospel as good news, and to explain the ministry and mission of the apostle and the church in the world. The term "reconciliation" thus becomes an almost all-embracing term to articulate what is at the heart of the Christian faith.[424]

Consequently, the ministry of unity is a ministry of conciliation (Latin *conciliare*, to bring together). This refers more generally to the process of bringing various different parties into relationships of mutual benefit and enrichment, in order to live in a model of unity in diversity. Reconciliation refers specifically to the healing of broken relationships, the resolving of conflicts and wrongs of the past, in order to re-establish restored relationships - in both cases promoting peace, justice and solidarity.[425] In other words, reconciliation is a spiritual affair that includes theological, moral or ethical, social, political and economic issues. These demand a transformation of the entire human situation in

---

[424] *You Are The Light Of The World: Statements on Mission by the World Council of Churches 1980-2005* (Geneva: World Council of Churches, 2005), 96-98.

[425] Raymond Pfister, "Does Europe Matter? Towards a European Agenda for the Church in the 21st Century," *Evangelical Review of Society and Politics* 3/1 (June 2009): 37-56.

all its aspects, to one in which the hungry are fed, the sick are healed, and justice is given to the poor.

In other words, reconciliation can be described as a divine and human action that embraces the whole world, changing our relationship to God and people, and making us new creatures. It also means understanding and implementing reconciliation as a programme where God is reconciled with people. Furthermore, reconciliation is understood as a social and economic project, where the ownership and use of God's creation is intended for the benefit and well-being of all, especially those who are currently most in need of empowerment.

Finally, in the last thirty years of existence, the CWM has doubled its efforts to enable its member churches to be places that "sow seeds of reconciliation"[426] within the spirit of "sharing the experiences of Christ across all boundaries." This contrasts with the colonial period's imperialistic and expansionist ideology of "to spread the knowledge of Christ among heathen and other unenlightened nations."[427] This is a project of reconciliation in which the Church is called to participate, in bold humility.

We now turn to the aspect of mission as healing, recognising healing as one of the main themes in Jesus' public ministry. It is this mission that the Church is called upon to continue among the broken-hearted.

5. The Healing Ministry of the Church

Where does the Church get its inspiration to respond to the call to become healing and reconciling communities? The answer is found in the healing ministry of Jesus as a model for the Church to be explored today. From the very beginning, the ministry of the Church has been understood as an extension of the healing ministry of Jesus. This is illustrated in the parable in Luke 8.43–48, which presents a woman with chronic bleeding who has been ill throughout her life. She has numerous physical problems – irregular bleeding for twelve years, anaemia,

---

[426] "CWM Assembly Statement" (26 July 2003). http://www.cwmission.org/features/cwm-assembly-statement/print.html (accessed 11 June 2009).
[427] Des van der Water, *Work in Progress or Mission Accomplished? An Appraisal of 30 Years of CWM's Partnership in Mission* (London: CWM, June 2007), 22.

weakness, and infertility. Her social problems were even worse, because she was considered as unclean (Leviticus 15.19–30). She was probably divorced, abandoned by her family, and without friends. Grief, depression, and anger at society – and probably at God – filled her mind. Spiritually, she was cut off from God because no unclean person could go to the temple to worship or ask for healing.[428]

When she heard about Jesus, she was determined to go to him – even though she would make him unclean. But Jesus said to her, "Daughter, your faith has made you well; go in peace" (Luke 8.48). With her ears, the woman heard Jesus call her his *daughter*. With her heart, she heard him say, "Come into my family. You are clean and whole." It should be mentioned that when she is healed, she takes the good news to her home. According to the CWM, the theme of the "home" should be stressed in our mission activities. By focusing "on the importance of the home, family and the local context for the Gospel message we are declaring that, amongst other things, it is as important to engage in mission within our homes, on our doorsteps and within our own communities as it is to cross countries, continents and cultures with the Gospel message."[429] That is the model of healing: being touched by human suffering and extending this healing in word and deed.

To put it differently, this is an example where healing includes transformation of life locally and contextually, as well as in crossing cultural and religious boundaries.[430] In this connection, it becomes important for the Church to realise that its calling is a response to the charismatic gifts of healing. These equip the Church and enable it to fulfill that healing role.[431] As the past millennium came to an end, some promising signs of healing were cited, such as efforts to heal diseases, improve the health of communities, liberate those who were oppressed under colonialism and apartheid, and reconcile those of different ideologies, races and nationalities, particularly after the world events of

---

[428] Paul John Isaak, "The Gospel of Luke" in *African Bible Commentary*, general ed. Tokunboh Adeyemo (Nairobi: WorldAlive Publishers, 2006), 1220-1221.
[429] Van der Water, *From Ayr to Ocho Rios*, 18.
[430] T. R. Seim, *The Double Message: Patterns of Gender in Luke - Acts* (Edinburgh: T & T Clark, 1994), 57.
[431] *You Are The Light Of The World*, 149-150.

the Fall of Berlin Wall in 1989. Many looked ahead with hope to a new millennium of peace.

However, as old divisions were healed, new ones arose – especially with regard to what is known today as the "war on terrorism."[432] Furthermore, in North America, one of the most dramatic events in recent times was the way in which well-known symbols of human know-how, achievement and strength, were destroyed by speeding aeroplanes. These suddenly became weapons of mass destruction, as they crashed into fortresses of human might and security. This became a potent mixture of technological triumph, financial strength, military might, resentment, anger, hatred, mourning, and fear. This example reinforces the need for the missional Church to be engaged in missionary praxis for peacemaking and healing.

In summary, Jesus' healing is a model for the Church today. Jesus entrusts the apostles with preaching to, and healing, the sick. In other words, according to Jesus' instructions, the Gospel cannot stand without the concrete salvation illustrated by healing. Healing loses its meaning if it is not seen within the framework of the Gospel of God's reign. But we have thus far left out one key issue that relates to the ministry of healing, namely HIV and AIDS. I therefore focus briefly on this aspect because it is one of the mission priorities of the CWM.[433]

Today, the nightmare of HIV and AIDS is real. The disease affects not only the physical body but also the social body and millions of families within it. Hardly a family remains untouched by HIV and

---

[432] According to a statement by the Central Intelligence Agency (CIA) "counterterrorism is CIA's primary mission. Al-Qaeda remains the most serious security threat that we face, most serious security threat to America and to U.S. interests and our allies overseas. ... The goal must be to pursue al-Qaeda to every hiding place, to continue to disrupt their operations, and continue ultimately to work towards their destruction so that they do not represent a threat to this country or to our troops in the future. That's why CIA continues to work with partners across the world in intelligence, in law enforcement, and in the military to understand and counter the constantly evolving threat, both tactically and strategically." Statement made by the Director of the CIA, Leon Panetta, May 18, 2009 at the Pacific Council on International Policy. See *https://www.cia.gov/news-information/speeches-testimony/directors-remarks-at-pacific-council.html* (accessed 1 December 2009).

[433] Van der Water, *From Ayr to Ocho Rios,* 7-8.

AIDS. It is in families that death from HIV and AIDS has its greatest impact. The future of families is bleak in the midst of this pandemic. A loss of a parent, a sibling, a friend, colleague, child or spouse disrupts established family patterns and requires a caring community and ministry. The religious and social stigma is such that family members are subjected to great emotional distress, and carry a large burden of care for those affected. Family life is disrupted and children are orphaned. Families can no longer be sustained under its devastating power.

Furthermore, many mothers unwittingly infect babies, or even more alarming today, are raped by males who are HIV-positive. Two-thirds of the babies of HIV-positive mothers are born infected. In light of these tragic realities, will there even be a future generation? In a Darwinian perversion, society's fittest, not its frailest, are the ones who die, leaving the old and the children behind. Grandparents and grandchildren are wailing; like Rachel, they refuse to be consoled until life has been genuinely restored (Matt 2. 18).

The Church, as the household of God, needs to acknowledge that the body of Christ is HIV-positive. It is not just a problem "out there," but *our church has AIDS*. Healing is desperately needed so that those affected can be restored to relationships within their families, congregations, and communities. We need to become instruments of God's redeeming love so as to confront and transform the stigmas and practices associated with HIV and AIDS.

Although both women and men are affected, increasingly it is women - especially those, who are young - who are at far greater risk of being infected through sexual intercourse. Social norms and gender inequality do make it difficult for women and girls to negotiate for safer sex, since they do not have control over their partner's fidelity. In this connection it is absolutely right that the CWM addresses the issues of the ABC (Abstinence, Be faithful and Condom use) and SAVE, where S means safer practices; A means access and availability to treatment and nutrition; V means voluntary testing and counselling; and E refers to empowerment. Unfortunately, in some of the statements of CWM, these two positions are played against each other.[434] Furthermore, in the CWM HIV/AIDS policy and Strategic Guidelines, the option for SAVE is not

---

[434] "Why the ABC of HIV Doesn't Work for Women" (02 August 2007). http://www.cwmission.org/features/why-the-abc-of-hiv-doesnt-work-for-women/print.html (accessed 12/06/2009).

even mentioned. Instead, the policy document makes the pronouncement on ABC as follows:

> Because CWM does not subscribe to the viewpoint that HIV/AIDS is a punishment from God, instead of condemning those who are living with the virus, we commit ourselves to accompanying them on their journeys of hardship and suffering, care for them and engage them in guiding us, under God, to a meaningful and helpful ministry that, until a cure is found, will help the infected to manage their health, raise their quality of life and prolong their time of living. In the belief that 'prevention is better than cure' we encourage the promotion of abstinence before marriage and faithfulness within marriage, in accordance with the Biblical standards for Christian sexual behaviour. We recognize that the strategy which advocates the use of condoms by those who are not able to maintain either abstinence or faithfulness is controversial. However, instead of avoiding the issue, we encourage open and honest debate on this point.[435]

However, one should not play the positions of ABC and SAVE against each other. Rather, both should be recommended, while stressing that SAVE is a more a holistic strategy, particularly for women. There is no point in religious leaders talking about gender issues, if they have little regard for the women's position on women's rights and sexual matters.

This includes more open discussion on those practices that spread HIV and AIDS, especially unprotected sexual intercourse under conditions of gender inequality, whether within and outside of marriage. Here the primary ethical mandate is to refrain from doing what will harm the neighbour and to take appropriate measures to protect and enhance the life of the neighbour. In the face of HIV and AIDS, other moral rules or cultural considerations may need to be over-ruled for the sake of this central mandate.

---

[435] *CWM : HIV/AIDS Policy and Strategic Guidelines* (London: CWM, June 2005), 5.

From theological and ecclesiological perspectives, the Christian faith is a faith in a God who loves life. God became human so that human beings may have life in its fullness. There is little doubt that in the AIDS situation today, God would be on the side of life. God would not necessarily demand immediate moral perfection from people, who, for various reasons, cannot yet measure up to that ideal. Therefore the use of the strategies of ABC and SAVE should be strongly recommended by the Church. The challenge is for Christians to look critically at Christian teachings and theologies. To paraphrase Dietrich Bonhoeffer, in such a ministry of healing, the Church is only the Church when it exists for others.

When the Church exists for the other it means that such a church has a unique opportunity to enable women and men to explore ethical, theological, legal and biological issues related to human sexuality. The more access to correct information and supportive, non-judgemental counselling that people have, the better they will be able to protect themselves and others from contracting HIV. Further, the better care and support they will be able to give to those infected and affected by HIV and AIDS.

From such a position - to be the Church that exists for others – the CWM recommended the following guidelines to member churches for action on HIV/AIDS:

1. The formulation of HIV/AIDS policy statements affirming that the disease is not a punishment from God, and that the pandemic needs to be seen within the greater context of a sinful world and a fallen humanity to which God has sent his Son, not to condemn, but to save the world.

2. The adoption of theological/missiological positions and practical approaches in relation to those infected and affected by HIV/AIDS, that are premised on the purpose of God's redeeming love for all, and on biblically-based principles of inclusion, compassion, justice, accountability and responsiveness.

3. Re-examining policies and attitudes on sexuality within the churches in the light of contemporary concerns, contextual implications, biblical teachings, theological teachings and missiological trends.

4. Encouraging local churches/parishes/congregations and, in particular, parents, to assume responsibility to ensure that proper sex education is given to their young people/children.

5. Making every effort to enable local churches/parishes/congregations to be safe, welcoming places for church and community members who are infected and affected, and draw on the special insights and experiences of PLWA within their churches and communities in formulating local strategies and activities in combating the disease.

6. Empowering local church/parish/congregational leadership to focus on HIV/AIDS through its preaching, teaching, counselling and prayer ministries, and render moral and material support to local churches who have embarked on home-based care to PLWA.

7. Encouraging local congregations promote home based care through special training programmes.

8. Guiding local congregations on ways of integrating HIV/AIDS programmes with programmes on gender and poverty, and helping the churches to address youth health issues, with special consideration of the rate of infection amongst young girls.[436]

Finally, this is said in the knowledge that a loving God is in control of the situation and is the source of hope in the midst of hopelessness and desperation. God is the God of life. Death and destruction cannot have the last word. That is where Christian hope comes into the picture. All Christians become involved in this struggle, for their heritage and future.

6. Conclusion

Throughout this paper, I maintain that the historical evolution and paradigm shift that saw the London Missionary Society (LMS) reconstituted as the Council for World Mission (CWM) is marked by the addition of the new dimension of a local and contextual praxeological approach to mission. I describe this as the Church's understanding of

---

[436] *CWM : HIV/AIDS Policy and Strategic Guidelines*, 5.

Mission as Praxis for Peace-Building

itself as a missional Church that participates in God's mission and praxis, with special reference to peace-building, reconciliation, and healing.

However, the CWM has some shortcomings that need to be addressed. There has been a lack of major theological, missiological, ecclesiological and ethical studies undertaken during the ensuing three decades, especially from postcolonial perspectives. Publications are primarily the works of individual General Secretaries of the CWM. There are few substantial studies by groups of theologians, missiologists and missionaries from member churches, or various church and spiritual affiliations. Hopefully CWM will be more committed to such missiological, ecclesiological, theological, and ethical studies.

Such studies are necessary, and will enable the local Churches to re-discover a fundamental truth. That is, if Christians think they are required to remain sin-free and unstained at all times, they will never speak a word, never risk any action in this complex world – they will certainly fail to believe and act in bold humility. The nature and purpose of Christian mission requires prophetic proclamation and dialogue that is done in the spirit of annunciation of the Gospel, and the denunciation of injustice. Christians must say it in the context of dialogue, but they must say it, for they indeed have something to say. They are not ashamed of the Gospel, because "it is the power of God for salvation to everyone who has faith…" (Rom 1.16).[437]

Therefore, as Christians learn from one another as partners together in God's mission, they reaffirm the following wisdom from Pauline theology. For St. Paul, reconciliation is ultimately God's work. Certainly it involves the Church, other stakeholders and strategies, yet it cannot be programmed from the outset nor presumed in its outcome. To put it differently, the issues of peace, healing and reconciliation are enormous and complex, and will ultimately be fulfilled by God in Christ. Thus Schreiter concludes that since "it is the work of God, it is more spirituality than strategy, it is a new creation, it is encompassed in the mystery of the cross - it ultimately can only be grasped cosmically and perhaps eschatologically."[438]

St. Paul speaks of the new creation heralded by Jesus Christ and enabled by the Holy Spirit. "In Christ" he says, "God was reconciling the

---

[437] Bevans and Schroeder, 348-395.
[438] Schreiter, *Reconciliation: Mission and Ministry*, 381.

world to himself, not counting their trespasses against them, and entrusting the message of reconciliation to Christians. So, Christians are ambassadors for Christ, since God is making his appeal through us; 'we entreat you on behalf of Christ, be reconciled to God'" (2 Cor 5. 19-20). It is this "new creation" where the mission as peacemaking, reconciliation, and healing is the goal of Christian missionary endeavour - ultimately for justice and salvation. With Paul, Christians believe that peacemaking, healing and reconciliation are pivotal to the process by which that goal is to be reached. Reconciliation - as the restoration of right relations with God - is the source of reconciliation with oneself, with other people, with other religions, and with the whole of creation. Therefore in the words of the World Council of Churches ninth Assembly theme, Christians globally pray "Come, Holy Spirit, Heal and Reconcile" and transform Christians into reconciled and healing communities. It is the prayer of all Christians that the Holy Spirit will breathe healing power into their lives, and that together they may move forward into the blessed peace of the new creation.

CONCLUSION

Unfinished Agenda for Postcolonial Mission

Des van der Water

> We believe that we become participants in mission not because we hold all the answers and all the truth…All of us are still searchers…there are varieties of Christian experience…we have not entered. Therefore, we seek to form a missionary organization in which we may learn from each other.[439]

The aim of this book was not to present "all the answers" nor "all the truth" about partnership in postcolonial mission. What we have endeavored to do through the ten chapters of this book is to learn from the experience of the CWM—to collect and to critically evaluate the shared experiences of what it means to do mission in postcolonial contexts. In this book we have used postcolonial both chronologically and as a tool of analysis. In other words, postcolonial was used to designate a particular historical period where those who have been colonized achieve political and social independence. At the same time, postcolonial was also used as a tool of analysis, because we have recognized that while historically we may be living in postcolonial contexts, in reality given the socio-political, economic and other

---

[439] *Sharing in One World Mission* (1977).

disparities between the global North and the global South, colonialism takes on new forms such as globalization.

In the ten chapters of this book we focused on specific themes that formed the proposed agenda for mission in partnership in a postcolonial context. The selection of the themes was informed by the transversal themes for the Edinburgh 2010 Ecumenical Mission Conference. Several issues were raised in the chapters, but due to space constraints could not be probed further. These are the issues which form part of the unfinished agenda, or perhaps even matters arising that need to be taken up in future studies on partnership in postcolonial contexts. We discuss each of these matters in turn.

Theological Education

What becomes clear in this book is that theological education can never be seen as separate from mission. Indeed, the mission identity of the CWM owes a great deal to the theological and missiological insights that have emerged from the theological education of its leaders. Roderick Hewitt noted in his essay that the early development of the CWM (1985-1995) saw intentional emphasis on critiquing the role of theological education in facilitating the ministry and mission of the churches. Conferences with theological educators were held and new initiatives were undertaken to facilitate churches that wanted to develop relevant contextual models of ministerial formation for mission. Regional theological institutions of excellence were identified and significant financial resources were made available to develop chairs or departments of mission. The chair of Mission Studies established at Birmingham University, United Kingdom and the departments of Mission and Evangelism at United Theological College in Kingston, Jamaica and in Bangalore, India, bear testimony to the commitment of the CWM to theological education in mission. Unfortunately this commitment and vision has not been realized in other regions, such as Africa.

Further, a Network of Theological Enquiry (NOTE) that involved a select group of regional theologians was established by the CWM in November 1999. The purpose of NOTE was to reflect on various themes ranging from religious plurality to community and mission. to This book constitutes, among other things, another contribution in the commitment of the CWM to promoting

Conclusion

transformative theological education. It should also be noted that in the CWM sharing of financial resources, a significant amount is spent on scholarships for theological education in mission.

However, the current assessment of the CWM journey seems to suggest that the fast changing global context of mission necessitates an urgent review of its theological education in mission agenda. The Edinburgh 2010 Mission Conference raised urgent questions about the role and relevance of theological education and formation in postcolonial mission. Among the various issues that were raised during the Edinburgh process, we wish to draw attention to the following three issues. First, we are concerned about the continuing unequal allocation of resources and movement of theological scholars from South to North. Secondly, the continued use of imperial models of theological education in the global South, does not facilitate contextual formation of leaders who promote fullness of life for all. Thirdly, it is important to recognize that ecumenical theological education in mission must take seriously the presence and impact of students from Neo-Pentecostal traditions seeking higher theological education..[440] These global theological education in mission concerns cannot be neglected by the CWM in the next phase of its journey.

Ecumenical Engagement

The CWM has been consistent in its advocacy for ecumenical engagement by churches. Being an ecumenical mission community of Churches one would expect CWM to be more daring and radical in pushing the boundaries of ecumenical engagement. The CWM grew from a 22 member church organization in 1975 to 31 by 1989.[441] It decided that it would rather demonstrate its ecumenical commitment through qualitative engagement rather than quantitative growth. Therefore no new applications for membership in the CWM is being accepted. However, the CWM's commitment to global ecumenical organizations is expressed, among other things, through a sharing of substantial financial resources. In addition a designated Ecumenical

---

[440] For the full range of issues on ecumenical theological education in mission see Daryl Balia and Kirsteen Kim, eds., *Edinburgh 2010, Volume 2, Witnessing to Christ Today* (Oxford: Regnum Books International, 2010), 148-174.

[441] The Presbyterian Church of Korea was not part of the common mission history of the CWM member Churches.

Involvement Fund was launched to encourage its member churches to move out beyond themselves and act ecumenically to respond to life threatening realities within the regions. As mentioned above, investing in theological education was also another important area where the CWM demonstrated its commitment to ecumenical engagement.

However, in spite of these positive steps, one should still question whether the reasons given then for not accepting new member churches within the organization are still valid in this postcolonial environment. Ecumenical learning that is radical necessitates in-depth engagement with different experiences of mission in Christ's way. The CWM is still relatively a reformed "birds of a feather" ecumenical family. In line with the "body of Christ" identity advocated by St Paul in 1Cor.12 that highlights the unity-in-diversity of the church and the CWM's own missiological statements that invite churches to grow beyond themselves, as is evident in the number of United Churches within its membership, is this not an appropriate time to revisit the issue of welcoming new churches from other traditions?

Pentecostalism

One of the issues which appeared in several chapters, but which we think requires further debate and analysis, particularly within the context of mission studies, is the consideration of the growth of neo-Pentecostal movements in the South. While the shift of Christianity from the global North to the global South has been noted in several articles, what needs to be acknowledged is that this Christianity is of a different type and hue, and therefore its implications for the ways in which mission is conceived is crucial. Several studies have argued that, the global Pentecostal movement is growing at a phenomenal rate, with Pentecostal churches growing at the rate of up to 20 million new members a year.[442] Some countries like Ghana are reporting growth rates of 30 – 80%.[443]

What is interesting, however, is that the growth of these types of Christianity occur most in the developing world where poverty and other

---

[442] Harvey Cox, *Fire From Heaven: The Rise of Pentecostalism and the Reshaping of Religion in the 21st Century* (Cambridge MA: Da Capo Press, 1995), xv.

[443] Paul Gifford, *Ghana's New Christianity: Pentecostalism in a Globalising African Economy* (London: Hurst & Co, 2004), 38.

social injustices thrive. What is the relationship between poverty and injustice and the need for this type of spirituality? We also note that this brand of Christianity is also manifesting itself within economically wealthy nations of East Asia. However, its expression is fused with a conservative political discourse. What kind of mission is needed in these contexts, given that the missions currently in place focus on "deliverance" from evil spirits rather than deliverance from evil structures? Within other contexts there is emphasis on a "prosperity gospel" that markets the gospel as a product that delivers prosperity to those who invest well in their brand of Christianity. What is the missiological significance of a movement which tends to "spiritualise" social problems? Further an understanding of the growth of Pentecostalism beyond the sociological analysis is needed. What are the theological and spiritual benefits of such a movement? It should be noted that many of the CWM member churches demonstrate a charismatic and Pentecostal spirituality within their Reformed tradition. Therefore the CWM cannot afford to ignore this urgent missiological issue. What is the gap that these movements are filling and why is that offering so attractive to the global South, despite the fact that our social conditions are not improving. Most importantly for a postcolonial analysis is, what is the impact of foreign (particularly American) influences as expressed in tele-evangelism and other such media? These are certainly issues that need to be put on the agenda for a postcolonial understanding of mission.

Gender

What was evident in several of the chapters was the ways in which gender justice remains a challenge for mission. Nowhere was this clearer than in the Edinburgh 2010 Mission conference. The participants had directives to mainstream the issue of "women and mission" in all nine themes of the conference. Unfortunately, only two themes had this issue on their agenda. Why has gender justice come off the agenda in postcolonial times when one of the chapters in this book has shown that partnership in the area of gender has been the hardest for most of the CWM member churches from the global South? Is it because we think that because we are in a postcolonial period (historically) that we are also in a post-patriarchal period? If this is so, then we may need to revisit the items that we have on our agenda, or more appropriately the items that are not on our agenda. Again, the Edinburgh conference is telling in its disregard for the issue of HIV and AIDS. One ignores HIV and AIDS as a missiological issue at one's own peril in a postcolonial discourse. However, it is even more dangerous to ignore the link between HIV and gender injustice in a postcolonial context.

Postcolonial Positioning

The CWM's Strategic Review process examined, amongst other things, the location of its secretariat office, which is currently located in London. Its antecedent organization, the LMS, embraced the name of a place, London, rather than the name of a church to symbolize the non-denominational and non-sectarian character of its missional identity. However noble those intentions were during the era of colonialism, the location of London was not neutral. The reflections in the various chapters in this book indicate that it was and remains to this day a symbol of imperial, social, political, economic, and military power. The transformation of the LMS into the CWM in 1977 also included an intention to review the appropriateness of London as a base for the organisation's secretariat. In 2010, this review was completed and a decision was taken to retain London as the secretariat base of the CWM. This decision raises serious concerns about the purported postcolonial intent of the CWM. Could it be that the decision was motivated by unresolved issues from both the global North and the global South? Could it be that the real fears which motivated the choice was socio-economic and political perceptions of the South, rather than missiological ones?

Furthermore, Roderick Hewitt has argued that the CWM has depended on a "Northern bias" ecumenical theology to shape its own theological emphasis that is no longer sustainable. For the CWM to grow deeper in its ecumenical engagement in mission, it should seriously consider taking the lead in making a break with the mould of the Northern strangle-hold and immerse itself more into the soil of the theological and missiological soil of the wider world.

As can be seen from the foregoing discussion, there are many unfinished items on the agenda of postcolonial mission. The objective of this book was to add a distinctive voice to the understanding of what should be on the mission agenda in a postcolonial era, using the rich and diverse experiences of CWM as a case study. The chapters in this book confirm that the intention to become a more authentic postcolonial organization and movement has been only partially realized, and the challenges in an ever-changing world require greater missional risk-taking if the CWM is going to make a difference in our globalised world.

Selected Bibliography

Abraham, K.C. "Mission as Celebration of Life." *CTC Bulletin* 24/1-2 (2008).

Adam, Ian and Helen Tiffin, eds. *Past the Last Post: Theorizing Postcolonialism and Post-Modernism*. Calgary, Canada: University of Calgary Press, 1990.

Akitunde, D.O. "Partnership and Exercise of Power in the Christ Apostolic Church – Nigeria." In *On Being Church: African Women's Voices and Visions*, edited by Isabel A. Phiri and Sarojini Nadar, 80-95. Geneva: World Council of Churches Publications, 2005.

Ariarajah, S.W. "Wider Ecumenism: A Threat or a Promise." *Ecumenical Review* 50 (1998).

Ashcroft, Bill, Gareth Griffiths, and Helen Tiffin, eds. *The Empire Writes Back: Theory and Practice in Postcolonial Literature*. London: Routledge, 1989.

_____, eds. *The Postcolonial Studies Reader*. London: Routledge, 1995.

_____, eds. *Key Concepts in Postcolonial Studies*. London and New York: Routledge, 1998.

Balia, Daryl and Kirsteen Kim, eds. *Edinburgh 2010, Volume 2, Witnessing to Christ Today*. Oxford: Regnum Books International, 2010.

Best, T.F. and G. Gassmann, eds. *On the Way to Fuller Koinonia: Official Report of the Fifth World Conference on Faith and Order, Santiago de Compostela, 1993*. Geneva: WCC, 1994.

Bhabha, Homi. *Nation and Narration*. London: Routledge, 1990.

Bosch, David. *Transforming Mission: Paradigm Shifts in Theology of Mission*. Maryknoll: Orbis Books, 1991.

Brock, Rita Nakashima. "Feminist Theories." In *Dictionary of Feminist Theologies*, edited by Letty M. Russell and J Shannon Clarkson, 116-120. Louisville: Westminster John Knox Press, 1996.

Brown, J. "International Relationships in Mission: A Study Project." *International Review of Mission* 136/342 (July 1997).

Commission on World Mission and Evangelism. *Mission and Evangelism in Unity Today*. Geneva: World Council of Churches, 2000.

Commission on World Mission and Evangelism, World Council of Churches. "Towards Common Witness to Christ Today: Mission and Visible Unity of the Church." *International Review of Mission* 99/390 (April 2010): 86-106.

Cox, Harvey. *Fire From Heaven: The Rise of Pentecostalism and the Reshaping of Religion in the 21st Century*. Cambridge, MA: Da Capo Press, 1995.

Dube, Musa W. "Rahab Says Hello to Judith: A Decolonizing Feminist Reading." In *Toward a New Heaven and a New Earth: Essays in Honour of Elisabeth Schüssler Fiorenza*, edited by Fernando F. Segovia. 142-158. Maryknoll: Orbis Books, 2003.

Dussel, Enrique. *History and the Theology of Liberation: A Latin American Perspective*. New York: Orbis Books, 1976.

Fanon, Frantz. *The Wretched of the Earth*. New York: Grove Press, 1963.

_____. *Black Skin, White Masks*. New York: Grove Press, 1967.

Forrester, D. B. *Christian Justice and Public Policy*. Cambridge: Cambridge University Press, 1997.

Foucault, Michel. *Language, Counter-Memory, Practice: Selected Essays and Interviews*. Ithaca, NY: Cornell University Press, 1980.

_____. *Power/Knowledge: Selected Interviews and Other Writings 1972-1977*. Edited by Colin Gordon. Translated by Colin Gordon, Leo Marshall, John Mepham and Kate Soper. New York: Pantheon Books, 1980.

Gandhi, Leela. *Postcolonial Theory: A Critical Introduction.* New York: Columbia University Press, 1998.

Gifford, Paul. *Ghana's New Christianity: Pentecostalism in a Globalising African Economy.* London: Hurst & Co, 2004.

Guha, Rinajit and Gayatri C. Spivak, eds. *Selected Subaltern Studies.* New York: Oxford University Press, 1988.

Hayek, F. A. *Law, Legislation and Liberty, Vol. II: The Mirage of Social Justice,* 2nd ed. London: Routledge, 1982.

Heim, S. M. *Salvations: Truth and Difference in Religion.* New York: Orbis, 1995.

International Review of Mission 97/386-387 (2008).

Kang, Namsoon. "*Whose/Which* World in *World Christianity*? Toward *World Christianity* as Christianity of *Worldly-Responsibility.*" In *A New Day: Essays on World Christianity in Honor of Lamin Sanneh,* edited by Akintunde E. Akinade. New York: Peter Lang Publishing, 2010.

Kanyoro, Musimbi. *Introducing Feminist Cultural Hermeneutics: An African Perspective.* Cleveland: Pilgrim, 2002.

Kirk, Andrew, J. *What is Mission? Theological Explorations.* Minneapolis: Fortress Press, 1989.

Kobia, S. Keynote Speech, General Assembly of the National Council of Churches in Korea, 17 January 2009, Seoul.

_____. "Cooperation and the Promotion of Unity: A World Council of Churches Perspective." Lectures Reflecting on Edinburgh 1910 Commission 8, 27-28 April 2007, New College, Edinburgh.

Koh, Moo-song. "Robert J. Thomas: A Historical Study of East-West Encounter through His Mission," PhD Thesis, University of Birmingham, 1995.

Kwok Pui-lan. *Postcolonial Imagination and Feminist Theology.* London: SCM Press, 2005.

LaCugna, Catherine Mowry. "God in Communion with Us: The Trinity." In *Freeing Theology: The Essentials of Theology in Feminist*

Perspective, edited by Catherine Mowry LaCugna. 83-104. New York: Harper San Francisco, 1993.

Lebacqz, Karen. *Justice in an Unjust World: Foundations for a Christian Approach to Justice.* Minneapolis: Augsburg Publishing House, 1987.

Lossky, N. et al. eds, *Dictionary of the Ecumenical Movement.* Geneva: WCC Publications, 1991.

Lovett, Richard. *The History of the London Missionary Society, 1795-1895,* Vol. I. London: Oxford University Press, 1899.

_____. *The History of the London Missionary Society, 1795-1895,* Vol.2. London: Henry Frowde, 1899.

Mackenzie, Clayton G. "Demythologizing the Missionaries: A Reassessment of the Functions and Relationships of Christian Missionary Education under Colonialism." *Comparative Education* 29/1 (1993): 45-66.

Memmi, Albert. *The Colonizer and the Colonized.* Boston: Beacon Press, 1965.

Mignolo, Walter. *Local Histories/Global Designs: Coloniality, Subaltern Knowledge and Border Thinking.* Princeton: Princeton University Press, 2000.

Mission and Evangelism: An Ecumenical Affirmation. Geneva: World Council of Churches, 1982.

Moltmann, J. *The Passion for Life.* Philadelphia: Fortress, 1978.

Moore-Gilbert, Bart. *Postcolonial Theory: Contexts, Practices, Politics.* 1997; London and New York: Verso, 1998.

Nandy, Ashis. *The Intimate Enemy: Loss and Recovery of Self under Colonialism.* Delhi: Oxford University Press, 1988.

Neill, S. *Creative Tension: The Duff Lectures, 1959.* London: Edinburgh House Press, 1959.

Njoroge, Nyambura J. and Páraic Réamonn, eds. *Partnership in God's Mission in Africa Today.* Geneva: WARC, 1994.

Parvey, Constance F., ed. *The Community of Women and Men in the Church: The Sheffield Report*. Geneva: World Council of Churches, 1983.

Porter, Andrew. *Religion versus Empire? British Protestant Missionaries and Overseas Expansion, 1700-1914*. Manchester: Manchester University Press, 2004.

_____, ed. *The Imperial Horizons of British Protestant Missions, 1880-1914*. Grand Rapids, MI: Wm. B. Eerdmans Publishing Company, 2003.

Quayson, Ato. *Postcolonialism: Theory, Practice or Process?* Cambridge, UK: Polity Press, 2000.

Russell, Letty M. *The Future of Partnership*. Philadelphia: The Westminster Press, 1979.

Said, W. Edward. *Orientalism*. New York: Vantage Books, 1979.

Sharing in One World Mission: Proposals for the Council for World Mission. CWM, December 1975.

Shenk, Wilbert R. *Changing Frontiers of Mission*. Maryknoll, NY: Orbis Books, 1999.

Sonrono, J. "The Epiphany of the God of Life in Jesus Nazareth." In *Idols of Death and the God of Life*, edited by Richard Pablo. New York: Orbis, 1983.

Spivak, Gayatri Chakravorty. *The Postcolonial Critic: Interview, Strategies, Dialogues*. Edited by Sarah Harasym. New York: Routledge, 1990.

_____. *The Spivak Reader*, Edited by Donna Landry and Gerald Maclean. New York and London: Routledge, 1996.

Stanley, Brian. *The Bible and the Flag: Protestant Mission and the British Imperialism in the Nineteenth and Twentieth Centuries*. Leicester, UK: Apollos, 1990.

_____, ed. *Mission, Nationalism, and the End of Empire*. Grand Rapids, MI: Wm. B. Eerdmans Publishing Company, 2003.

Thiong'O, Ngugi Wa. *Decolonizing the Mind: Jan Carew, Fulcrums of Change*. Trenton, NJ: Africa World Press, 1988.

Thorogood, Bernard, ed. *Gales of Change*. Geneva: WCC Publications, 1994.

Vitorio, A. *God of the Poor*. New York: Orbis, 1987.

Werner, D. "Ecumenical Evangelism: Some Perspective for Panel Discussion." CWME and F&O Joint Consultation on Mission and Ecclesiology, Manuscript, 3-7 March 2009, Berekfürdö, Hungary.

West, Cornel. "The New Cultural Politics of Difference." In *Out There: Marginalization and Contemporary Culture*, edited by Russell Ferguson, Martha Gever, Trinh T. Minh-ha, and Cornel West. New York and Cambridge: The New Museum of Contemporary Art and MIT Press, 1990.

Wickeri, L. Philip, ed. *The People of God Among All God's Peoples: Frontiers in Christian Mission*. Hong Kong: Christian Conference of Asia; London: Council for World Mission, 2000.

_____, ed. *Scripture, Community and Mission* (Hong Kong: Christian Conference of Asia; London: Council for World Mission, 2003.

Wickeri, L. Philip, K. Wickeri, D. Preman Niles, M.A. Damayanthi, eds. *Plurality, Power and Mission* (Intercontextual Theological Explorations on the Role of Religion in the New Millennium). London: Council for World Mission, 2000.

Williams, Lewin. *Caribbean Theology*. New York: Peter Lang Publishing, 1993.

World Missionary Conference 1910 – Report of Commission VIII: Co-operation and the Promotion of Unity, Edinburgh/London: Oliphant, Anderson and Ferrier; New York/Chicago/Toronto: Fleming H. Revell Company, 1910.

Young, Robert. *White Mythologies: Writing History and the West*. London: Routledge, 1990.

www.ingramcontent.com/pod-product-compliance
Lightning Source LLC
Chambersburg PA
CBHW030135170426
43199CB00008B/79